M000306961

In Search of a Salve

In Search of a Salve
Memoir of a Sex Addict

K E Garland

NEW Reads Publications | Jacksonville

In Search of a Salve is a work of memoir. It is a true story as told by the author based on her memory and best recollections of the events of her life. Names and identifying details have been changed.

ISBN 978-1-7357219-8-9 (hardback)
ISBN 978-1-7357219-9-6 (ebook)

Published in the United States by NEW Reads Publications LLC. NEW Reads Publications is a registered trademark of NEW Reads Publications LLC

Printed in the United States of America

newreadspub.com

First Edition: September 2023

Cover Design by Gisette Gomez

Contents

Part I: ROOTED

Part II: ADDICTED

Part III: TRAPPED

Part IV: SELF-REGULATED

ROOTED

TRINA

1982

I was nine years old when I figured out that if I squeezed my legs together hard enough, it would create the most electrifying pulsation, in the general area my mother, her mother, and her mother called our "killa cricket." It was at the top part, which I now know is a woman's clitoris. This discovery wasn't happenstance. It was preceded by a chance encounter.

My mother, father, and I lived on the first floor of a Chicago two-flat. My great-aunt Lillian and Uncle James lived on the second floor with Aunt Lillian's parents: my great-grandparents. Aunt Lillian and Uncle James owned the building, which sat on the West Side of Chicago, right in the middle of Central Park Avenue. Directly across the street, women in ripped stockings and tight short skirts meandered in and out of a screened porch door, while men of all ages sat in folding chairs, sipping from the necks of bottles peeking from brown paper bags. When they finished, they'd leave the bags and their contents on the ground; eventually becoming one crumpled amalgamation, adding to several reasons why my family said, "It's too dangerous for you to go outside."

Next door lived a woman and her grandchild, India, who was about my age. She was my only friend on the block. While I'd spend summers playing board games with my Grandma Hunny in Covert, Michigan, India would visit her mother in Kankakee: a small city south of Chicago. During the school year, she'd join me to play inside my gate because I could never play at her house. A brown Doberman Pinscher lived in their backyard. It mirrored my steps whether I walked toward the street or the alley. The only thing that separated us was five feet of chain-link fence.

Seedy surroundings meant I had to remain in front of, or on the side of the building where I could be seen from any window. Most of the time, I played by myself. It was here where I learned to create a world apart from reality; to live in my own space of make-believe. I ran up and down the front stairs, pretended to cook food with leaves, dirt, and water, and then served it to whoever sat on the porch watching me, while the cadence of a Double-Dutch rope click-clacked on the concrete a few feet away. On this day, I played on the side of the house, within the confines of the carport, while Aunt Lillian peered out of the window every now and then. She didn't see a girl from the salacious home, walk across the street to talk to me. Her dirty white shirt covered her oversized jeans and dingy white tennis shoes. Two braids faced the sun and one stuck straight out behind her head. I met her on the street side of our home. Her name was Trina.

2

"Can you come out and play?" she asked.

"I'm not allowed."

"Can I come in there?"

"Let me ask." I ran to the back of the house, went inside, and skipped the stairs two at a time.

"Can I let Trina in the backyard to play?" I panted.

"Who's Trina?" Aunt Lillian asked.

"Just a girl who wants to play."

"Okay. But make sure I can see you when I look out of the window."

I ran down the stairs and out of the door, where Trina stood waiting. I lifted the latch that held both gates together and let her in through the carport.

We bounced a ball back and forth until Trina had a better idea.

"Let's play daddy and mama," she suggested.

Trina must've seen the wonderment in my eyes. *How would we do that? We're both girls.*

"I'll be the daddy," she clarified.

Still confused, I agreed.

Trina spouted orders—"Go to the store. Make dinner. Wash the clothes."

I was getting the idea. In this game, the mama did whatever the daddy said.

"Now, it's time to have sex."

My eyes widened. I wasn't sure what sex was, but I was confident it was something only boys and girls did.

"Lay down."

I lay on the grass, nearest our building. Trina climbed on top of me, her body flushed with mine—her belt buckle piercing my pelvis. Her gnawed-off fingernails rubbed against the edges of my hair and caressed my side ponytail. Then, she began pushing against my vagina in a circular motion, her two braids scraping my forehead. She breathed heavily. A sweet sensation sifted through the lower half of my body while her dirt-like scent wafted past my nose.

"Kaaathy?" Aunt Lillian called from the open window.

Trina jumped off of me as if we were caught in a sinful act. "Yeees?"

"Where are you?" she asked.

"Right here," I replied, as I took several steps back from the building.

"Oh, . . . I couldn't see you. Stay where I can see you."

I never told anyone about Trina, for fear that my family wouldn't let her be my friend anymore. But it didn't matter. Trina disappeared, and I never saw her again.

That night, when I was supposed to be sleeping soundly, in preparation for the next day's third-grade lesson, I squeezed my legs together and imagined Trina's body on top of mine. Shortly after, soft spasms rose from my clitoris to the top of my head, lulling me into a deep sleep. I learned to call on this ritual after spankings or other times of unease—like if my father yelled at me. It was an easy secret to keep, because I slept alone, until one night when I'd fallen ill with chicken pox. I lay on the right side of my twin-sized bed, and my mother lay on the left, pressed against the wall. My feverish body was uncomfortable and contorted, so as not to make physical contact and cause more awkwardness for me or my mother. But I was hot with sickness and needed comfort, so I shifted closer to the edge of the bed and squeezed my legs tight.

"Kathy. Stop shaking the bed," she said, unaware of the cause.

I thought she was asleep.

That night, I stopped my bedtime ritual for fear that I'd be found out, but my habit of self-soothing would continue throughout my life.

∞

The following year, my mother bought me a diary. It was pink, with white pages, and came with a small pencil. She said it was a place where I could keep my private thoughts. In it, I'd begun writing about boys I liked and superstars I wished I could meet. The diary provided a concrete place for me to play out my fantasies—which up until this point, only lived in my head. I daydreamed about Michael Jackson. He looked as if he was staring right at me on the cover of the *Thriller* album, and I frequently imagined him singing "PYT" to only me and then having sex.

The same year, shortly after my tenth birthday, I began my period. My mother showed me how to open the plastic wrapper, which held a pad, pull the strip of paper off, and apply the sticky side to my too-small panties. It would take years of walking around with a bright red spot on the back of my pants in elementary school, to understand the frequency and expectations of this routine.

Next, my father and I sat on the loveseat, where he explained how menstruation worked, with a banana balanced on his thigh. My father explained bleeding meant I could now get pregnant if I ever had sex, and that it was my responsibility to avoid such circumstances. A condom would do the trick. He pulled one out of his pocket, opened the small package, and showed me how to put it on the banana —a mock penis. But at ten years old, I couldn't comprehend what fake penises and condoms had to do with the pain in my lower abdomen or the blood that soaked the miniature pillow between my legs.

I squirmed as my father neared the end of the conversation.

"It's okay to be thinking about sex," he said. "Especially with famous people."

He said this was okay because, he too, used to think a lot about sex with someone named Nancy Wilson. Oh, how he wanted to be with Nancy Wilson. He went on and on about it, giving me enough time to understand this conversation wasn't just about safe sex or periods, it was about my "private thoughts."

I listened as intently as I could at ten years old and resolved to never write in my diary again. I shelved it on my bookcase and kept my private thoughts where they were safe—in my mind.

DADDY

1985

My mother spent much of her life on dialysis at Northwestern Memorial Hospital. For the first ten years of my childhood, I sat by her side, watching her crochet colorful scarves and oven mitts, as blood filtered through tubes, three times a week. When I grew too old to accompany her in the unit, I'd sit on a small chair in the hallway, or take the elevator to the cafeteria, where I'd devour turkey sandwiches and plain Lays to pass the four-hour procedure. Her dialysis visits were such a pervasive part of my life that I thought it was something all mothers did; something I'd one day do too. It would be a long time before I learned other mothers worked at jobs, while mine spent half a day trying to save her life.

In 1983, she received a kidney transplant, which required her to live in Madison, Wisconsin for months. Her mother, my Grandma Hunny, and Papa

Henry rented an apartment nearby and cared for her. During my mother's recovery, I spent some weekends with them, and other times, Grandma Hunny stayed in Chicago to look after me, while my father worked. For Halloween, I wanted to be a Witch Queen, so while my mother recuperated, my grandmother dyed an old dress black, stitched sequins from the bodice down, and made me a crown and scepter to create the costume I conceptualized and wore to school the next day.

But two years later, by the time I turned twelve, my mother's kidney transplant had failed—and in retrospect, our lives began to resemble a bucket list.

First, with the financial assistance of my family, my parents purchased their own two-flat. It was located further west on Monitor Street, a short distance from a prominent suburb and Ernest Hemmingway's hometown, Oak Park. The neighborhood was uniform; two-flats were set apart by varied brick colors. Our second floor was divided into two apartments. Grandma Betty, my father's mother, lived on the right. Days with her consisted of eating hot dogs and salad, with vinegar and oil dressing, and enough Mrs. Dash to create the illusion of salt. Her Catholicism seemed to require that she read *The Living Word* booklets every day in the silence of her bedroom by a dim nightlight. For a brief time, Diamond, my cousin, and Grandma Betty's oldest grandchild, lived on the left. She had moved from North Carolina years before to attend college.

Our new home on Monitor always appears in technicolor in my imagination. My mother allowed me to choose how my bedroom would be painted. I vacillated between magenta, violet, and lavender, and finally settled on a lilac, the same color as my glasses. My dresser and desk were white. I hadn't grown much taller, so my twin bed remained, but this time with sheets that accented the new lilac walls. A poster of a puppy was strategically placed over the closet and across from my bed—a reminder of what I'd own when "I got grown." After they'd purchased a dual-cassette stereo for the living room, my parents passed down their old system to me. I'd moved on from MJ to the much more local and popular sounds of house music mixes, which I danced to and recorded from the radio throughout the night.

The next change my mother made for us was attending church. St. Mathews United Methodist sat right in front of what used to be the infamous Cabrini Green housing project. It was a family tradition to worship there. I was christened at this church. On Grandma Hunny's mantel sits a picture of me in a frilly white baptismal gown, looking underneath bunches of lace as if to figure out the meaning of tulle. My grandmother also started a Pre-K program there, which I attended as a four-year-old. Whenever there was a church tea or funeral, Grandma Hunny, Aunt Lillian, their two older sisters and their children arrived. We weren't strangers to religion, just not regulars.

But by the time I turned twelve, the church became a major part of my week. My mother was the Sunday school teacher, and my father was the youth pastor. I'm not sure what my mother's motivation was for teaching Sunday school or for adding religious practices, in general, but we were fully committed. In addition to mandatory church attendance, she commanded me to memorize the books of the Bible. Matthew, Mark, Luke, and John were as much as I would retain. Saturday nights were reserved for Sunday school preparation, with me as the catechism class stand-in.

"Kathy, what do you think this means?" she asked.

I'd read Philippians 4: 6–7 Do not be anxious about anything, but in every situation, by prayer and petition, with thanksgiving, present your requests to God. And the peace of God, which transcends all understanding, will guard your hearts and your minds in Christ Jesus.

"So, it sounds like you're not supposed to worry about anything. Just pray," I answered.

"Good. That's good," she affirmed.

"Maybe it means we don't have to worry because God knows everything." I'd drone on and on, each interpretation more elaborate than the last, until my answer was sufficient to end the lesson.

Sunday morning, five teenagers and I would file into a small, dank classroom. Its gray brick, prison-like walls and "the power of Jesus" protected us from the Project's violence. Our group consisted of adolescents raised by single mothers or devoted grandmothers. Shaquita was a girl six months older than I, who spit quick words through a full set of metal braces. Her mother styled celebrities' hair on the West Coast, leaving her to be reared by her grandmother. We grew closer with each Sunday school lesson, and eventually spent weekends at one another's homes. Instead of Mr. and Mrs., she referred to my parents as "auntie" and "uncle," and we deemed each other "cousins."

For Sunday school, we gathered around a rectangular table, shoulder-to-shoulder, my mother at the helm. She made each of us read a passage aloud from a thin pamphlet; the same passages she'd had me read the previous night. Jay, a boy with a short, dry Jheri curl stumbled over words. Shaquita snickered.

"Shut up, Chiquita Banana!" Jay shouted.

More laughter.

"Hey!" My mother said firmly enough for everyone to believe she was angry.

Silence. Then, "Go ahead, Jay."

Jay would finally finish, and then my mother's practiced question arose, "What do you all think that means?"

Seconds lingered as we sat in the discomfort of quiet. Luckily, I didn't have the pressure of answering, like when I was in school. That is until my mother looked at me.

"Kathy, what do you think this means?" she asked.

Of course, I knew the answer, but this time we weren't sitting on the couch pontificating about the Word in our jammies. I had to decide. *Do I help my mother? Or conceal my intelligence?*

"I don't know," I whispered.

My mother's body tightened.

"What do you think, Tee?"

Tee's answer sufficed. I exhaled in relief. It was almost time for service. After church, my mother and father talked on the way home, but not directly to me. It wasn't until bedtime that she stood in my room's doorway and asked, "Why did you pretend you didn't know the answer to that question?"

"I don't know. I just didn't want to say it."

"You should never be ashamed to be smart."

Next, my mother planned a family trip for just the three of us. Although we were together daily, we'd never taken a family vacation to any place other than my grandparents' Michigan home. While my grandparents had introduced me to several states on road trips when Papa Henry would attend school board conferences, my parents were never there.

My mother spent weeks preparing for the trip. She prearranged dialysis appointments; and because it was scheduled during the school year, she micromanaged preplanned assignments from teachers. With our bags packed, dialysis treatments set up for various days and my worksheets in tow, we were off to Orlando.

The air felt eerily familiar as we deplaned. My lime-green pants and neon orange socks reflected perfectly off the Florida sun. I couldn't wait to wear my red cotton pants and rainbow-striped shirt; they would fit right in with the culture. We visited all the staples: Disney World, Epcot, and SeaWorld, and we drove to Busch Gardens in Tampa. We watched theater knights fight during a dinner show at Medieval Times and we swam in the resort's pool. But what I remember the most about this trip is not the tourist attractions. Those memories fade the more I age. The most fun I had in the Sunshine State was when my father and I rented bikes, while my mother completed her dialysis treatment. The day was simple. We rode down International Drive. It was sunny, but not unbearably hot. The sky was clear. The humidity was low. We stopped at McDonald's to eat and have ice cream—two things that had never occurred at the same time. Then we got on our bikes and headed back to the resort. I wouldn't know it for decades, but that memory stood out in my father's mind, too.

The year my mother's transplant failed, she sometimes returned to Wisconsin for treatment, but Grandma Hunny didn't stay with me. Maybe it was because I was older. Maybe it was because Grandma Betty and Diamond were upstairs. Either way, during one of my mother's return visits, I stayed home with my father to attend a funeral in South Bend, Indiana. Our new two-flat was more compact than the previous one. The shared bathroom between our bedrooms was only steps away in either direction.

One day, I heard the shower water streaming as my father freshened up for the drive to Indiana. I heard him turn off the water, from my bedroom. The only time my door could be closed was if I was getting dressed. Although I was already clothed, I remained in my room with the door shut, listening to a DJ's mix. My father knocked. I answered. He stood in the doorway with only a towel wrapped around his torso—something I'd never seen. My father always walked around the house fully dressed. Even if it was bedtime, he wore a set of matching pajamas, a robe, and slippers. His partial nudity shocked me.

He entered my room and leaned on my white desk. "Can I have a hug?" he asked, his erection noticeable in the middle of the towel.

Though I didn't want to, I wrapped my arms around him, as I normally would—but this time, with my head bowed. He lifted my chin and kissed me, first on the lips, then with his tongue forced into my mouth. I wanted to vomit. Suddenly, he stopped and left to get dressed. We drove to South Bend.

I could hardly wait for my mother to return, so I could recount the events that had made my skin crawl. I knew I couldn't blurt out details in my father's presence; he couldn't be there to defend his actions. So, I held the details in my belly, where each memory jumped with anticipation at the opportunity to confide in my mother. It wouldn't be long before my father needed to run to the gas station to buy a pack of Newports, leaving me with just enough time to reveal what happened.

My mother lay on her bed, drained from her dialysis treatment, watching their thirteen-inch black-and-white TV.

I sat beside her. "I have something to tell you," I said. Then, I whispered quick details for fear that my father would walk in at any moment.

"I'll talk to him," she said in the same tone that she'd warned of not being ashamed of showing intelligence.

The following day, I waited for my father to leave, went to their room, and sat on the bed next to my mother.

"Did you ask him?" I whispered.

"Yes." She wrapped brown yarn around a silver crochet hook.

"What did he say?"

"He said he was testing you," her eyes steadied on the hook and yarn. "To see if you'd say something if anyone ever did anything."

My father's answer was illogical. Why didn't he and I sit on the couch and discuss predatory behavior and how I should respond to it, the same way we'd talked about sex and condoms two years prior? I didn't know it then, but his "test" was a form of sexual grooming, and common behavior for fathers who look to their daughters for sexual gratification, especially if their needs aren't being met by their wives—a plausible scenario given my mother's constant hospitalization. It *was* a test—a test of my boundaries to see if any sexual abuse could continue.

My mother's muted response didn't match my father's infraction. I wanted her to yell and scream—to acknowledge his reply as nonsense. I wanted her to confront him in my presence as a show of protection.

At the very least a heated family discussion, where her anger could grow out of control; where she could roll her neck and shout ultimatums should he ever arrive in my room half naked looking to touch my body or worse—to have sex. *If this ever happens again, we're leaving* my fantasy version of her said. But she wasn't the neck-rolling type. She never even cursed. My mother's eyes remained focused on her crocheted chains; small brown loops of yarn created neat repetitive patterns. She couldn't even face me to report my father's ridiculous lie, much less threaten him in front of me.

After two more crochet chains, she added, "He said it won't happen again."

I stared at her and hoped she'd look into my eyes. She never did. Instead, we sat in silence, while she stitched more chains that formed a long link.

My father's "test" was a one-off, but I didn't need a lifetime of molestation to be considered sexually abused. A lone act defines abuse, and the sliminess of that singular evening remains etched in my mind, alongside riding bikes in Orlando. The kiss and my mother's reaction to it are wedged between the folds of my frontal lobe, reminding me of when I learned that adults could not always be trusted. At nine, I didn't have the language to describe Trina's acts as molestation or child-on-child sexual abuse, but I intuitively knew it was "wrong." Had I revealed what happened to any adult, I assumed there would have been consequences that exceeded a verbal reprimand and averted eyes. Adults in my family would've asked follow-up questions. There would have been more supervision to ensure my safety. However, there was no follow-up about my well-being when my father molested me, leaving me to independently deal with the remnants of his attempted grooming.

From that day forward, I feared my father's touch. He changed what were once natural interactions: full-frontal hugs turned to side hugs and pats on the back to ensure I never accidentally grazed his genitals. I received forehead kisses, but never returned his affection for fear his tongue would somehow find its way inside my mouth. The thought of touching my father repulsed me, and apprehension about hugging him remained well into adulthood. My lilac room, the only space where I could be alone, was deflowered. Headphones and house music helped me drown out the staccato of shower water. I no longer trusted my mother—who seemed adept at side-stepping her emotions and mine—to help me process my feelings. This was the second time she'd managed to avoid discussing a major event centered on sex. The vacancy provided a space for curiosity to breed; I grew more interested in this thing called sex that continued to interrupt my childhood.

TRÉ

1987 - 1988

What my mother lacked in emotional maturity, she made up for in intelligence. Before I was born, she earned a bachelor's in English from the University of Illinois Chicago. Her degree was a guidepost. When I was three, she taught me to memorize *Twas the Night Before Christmas* in time to recite it in front of Grandma Hunny, Papa Henry, and other family members. I learned to read when I was four. She organized and mapped out my K-12 education and is the person responsible for my early educational trajectory. My intellectual ascendancy began with being tested and then accepted into Skinner Elementary: a classical academic magnet school for gifted students intended to introduce and educate children in liberal arts.

When we lived on Central Park, I'd watch groups of children walk to their schools, which were somewhere nearby, as I rode a bus an hour away to the near West Side to study about Haile Selassie and create elaborate science projects. Our field trips consisted of CTA bus trips headed downtown, to giggle and sleep through Chicago Symphony Orchestra music. Sometimes we'd travel as a class to support other students in Academic Bowl competitions. We also learned Christmas carols in American Sign Language for the holiday season. Once mastered, we'd dress up and travel to City Hall to sing and sign songs like "White Christmas." It was common for the *Chicago Sun-Times* to take photos and report on our activities. As a newspaper subscriber, my mother would clip articles and discuss them with my grandmothers, aunts, and uncle. Whenever our school was reported on, a family member would display a wide grin and mention seeing me in the paper as if I were a featured soloist.

A few Skinner classmates continued seventh grade near their homes. But a majority, including me, attended Whitney Young's Academic Center; a program that specifically fed into its magnet high school for academically gifted students. At the time, it was one of the best schools in the nation and is the high school First Lady Michelle Obama attended.

In elementary school, I had little understanding of what it meant to be "gifted" and based my interpretations on others' responses. *Oh, you must be smart* was a common reaction when cousins or my father's co-worker found out where I attended school. However, by seventh grade, I fully understood what gifted meant. While most of our classes were in a building just for seventh and eighth graders, others, such as foreign language or physical education, required us to cross a bridge that connected the Academic Center with the high school to attend classes with high-school students. As I sat in Spanish with ninth graders who couldn't count to ten or reply when the teacher said *Buenos Días*, I became aware of the education Skinner afforded me.

I walked among thousands of intelligent students, smarter than me and not as smart as me, quite unaffected. I rarely took school seriously. Making friends in my neighborhood was a challenge, even on Monitor where I wasn't confined to a gate. Therefore, the school served as my playground. I looked forward to socializing, not solving quadratic equations.

Like most middle schools, seventh grade in the Academic Center was cliquey. Because it wasn't a neighborhood school, students hailed from all over the city. My circle included girls from a range of socioeconomic statuses. Friends came from single-parent homes; some were raised by their grandparents; others had working-class jobs and lived on the West Side like me. My circle was comfortable. I never had to pretend to be someone else or have things I couldn't afford around them.

We had most of the freedoms of a high school, such as ringing bells to signify a class change. Each bell offered me an opportunity to talk to my friends between periods. But that wasn't enough. Oftentimes, I whispered and passed notes during class, and was frequently in trouble, which led to the occasional "D." When this occurred, my parents would place me on punishment: no telephone or TV until the next report card was issued nine weeks later. These restrictions caused me to socialize more in school since I couldn't talk to anyone once I returned home.

I not only acquired more friends who were girls, but boys, too, who were friends and boyfriends. My sexual emotions increased exponentially and at thirteen, I devised a plan to see a penis attached to a boy's body.

"Is there anyone who wants to show me their penis?" I asked every seventh-grade boy. There were no takers. The whole class, and everyone in my circle, thought I was crazy.

"I don't want to have sex or anything. I just want to see one," I explained.

Once the eighth-grade boys heard about my request, CJ agreed. Together, we planned an adventure. We would cross the bridge, walk down to the other end of the second-floor hallway, and through the double doors that lead to the gym's stairwell. He and I would walk to the bottom, and there is where it would happen.

On the day of the reveal, a trail of seventh and eighth graders followed CJ and me to the doors. Crazy idea or not, people wanted to bear witness.

"I'm not showing everyone," he announced.

Of course not, I thought. I followed him down the stairs to the designated spot, where he pulled his penis from behind his underwear. I'm not sure what I expected. But the real thing was disgusting. CJ pushed his brown floppiness back inside and zipped his pants. We returned across the bridge, my disappointment apparent.

A week later, the counselor called me to the office. When I arrived, my parents sat in the tiny space waiting for me. Two sets of bulging eyeballs stared behind wired frames—one with anger and the other with sadness. Someone in the entourage had told a teacher what happened.

"I suggest you put her in an all-girls Catholic school," the counselor said.

Girls were alright, and I enjoyed Mass at Grandma Betty's church, but attending school with all girls, every day, all the way until twelfth grade, seemed excessive.

That evening, I sat at our dining room table, stared at our peach paisley wallpaper, and zoned in and out of a lecture.

What were you thinking? Why would you ask that? That wasn't safe. Maybe you don't need to go to that school. Maybe it's too mature for you. That boy could've raped you!

Our discussion was rhetorical. My parents didn't want an answer. They never did. Plus, I didn't have a reason, other than I was curious about what penises were and what they could do. What was so special about this part of the body that I needed to stay clear of them? Why wasn't it okay for CJ to show me his penis, but seemingly fine for my father to enter my room with his almost on display? What about this action would cause my mother to rethink her carefully planned academic trajectory for my life? This situation didn't shift my curiosity; it only provided an additional reason to maintain secrecy about sex and boys. Peers couldn't be trusted, and adults couldn't handle the truth.

∞

I didn't change schools then, so I was able to maintain relationships with the few boyfriends I'd amassed since the beginning of seventh grade. All of them were like me, though, thirteen or fourteen. My parents said I couldn't go on a date until I was sixteen, so "going together" meant passing notes during the day and having thirty-minute phone conversations at night. These interactions bored me. I wanted to be touched, to feel like I did that day with Trina, to feel as I did when I was alone in my bedroom, squeezing my legs together.

At the end of my eighth-grade year, I met a boy named Tré in Spanish II. He was sixteen and in the eleventh grade. Initially, we talked on the phone about school and what side of town we lived on. Then, the conversation changed.

"You ever had sex?" he asked.

"No, but I want to."

"Are you for real? 'Cause if you're for real, then I know how we can do it."

"I'm for real," I assured him.

"If you're serious, meet me behind the bleachers during gym tomorrow," he said. "Wear a skirt."

I did what Tré said. The long, flowered, pencil skirt I'd worn for Easter outlined my shape. White shoes matched my white short-sleeved shirt. I learned my lesson this time and told only two friends where I'd be. I waited in the locker room, while they dressed for gym class. Afterward, the three of us walked down the back stairs. They walked to the left. I walked forward and peeked behind the bleachers. He stood there, waiting for me in the shadows.

"You ready?" he asked.

"Yep."

I *thought* I was ready. Even though it was lackluster, sex and what it could be, had kept me up every night since CJ showed me what was in a boy's pants. I had no idea what was about to happen. I just knew two bodies, a girl's and a boy's, were involved.

I pulled my skirt up and pulled my underwear down.

"Lay down," Tré said.

I flinched when my butt touched the cold, wooden floor. Tré pulled his pants and underwear down with one motion. He tore open a condom and rolled it over his penis, which looked different than what CJ showed me, and much different than the banana my father fumbled around with years ago. It stood stiff and straight, facing me. His body lay on my five-foot frame, heavy and awkward. My heart beat so fast I thought it would burst through and run out of my chest. He pumped over and over. I froze. *Should I do something?* Even if I was supposed to do something, it wouldn't matter; I couldn't move.

Basketballs bounced against the maple wood floor.

"You okay?" he asked, still pumping.

What am I doing here? Maybe I should leave. I can't leave now. "Yeah," I said.

Suddenly, his body went limp. I don't know where the condom went, but he stood and pulled his pants up.

A gym coach blew his whistle on the other side of the wall.

"Aww . . . you had that one," an invisible student said.

Tré pulled me back into the moment with him. "You sure you're all right?" he asked.

"Yeah." I pulled up my panties and pulled down my skirt, making sure to smooth the crinkled, purple flowers as much as possible. "Yeah."

"When the bell rings, walk out and join the crowd," he instructed. "Look normal."

"Okay," I whispered.

I tried to avoid eye contact with other students changing classes, lest they could intuit what had just happened. When someone did catch my eye, I forced a smile. Somehow, I made it up the stairs and headed over the bridge back to the Academic Center. One of my friends walked with me.

"Did you do it?" she asked.

"Yep."

Our backpacks bounced up and down.

"How was it?" she asked.

I didn't answer. I didn't want her to know how sad I was.

"You have blood on your shoes," she said.

"What?"

"Your shoes," she pointed.

I looked down. Smeared red stains were on the sides. "Shit. I'll be there in a minute."

I stopped in the bathroom, wet a paper towel, sat on the toilet, cleaned the streaks off my white Easter shoes, and cried. Before I left, I stuffed a wad of toilet paper in my panties just in case. I wiped my face and walked to class to discuss Dickinson with the rest of the eighth graders.

I lost my virginity in the middle of a school day, on a cold wooden floor, when I should've been participating in sports. I wanted to want to go to gym class like everyone else, but the urge to meet Tré overwhelmed me in inexplicable ways, and I didn't know why. Other girls didn't seem to have this problem. They had boyfriends, whom they kissed and held hands with, and that was enough for them. Only I seemed to be looking at a boy's penis or sneaking behind the bleachers to have sex. All I wanted was the ability to live life without obsessing over boys and my sexual urges, but it was an unattainable dream.

JÖELLE

1989

September 3rd was First Sunday. My mother had fallen ill and had been hospitalized over the weekend. My father was at the hospital with my mother. I stayed home.

Our church and Grandma Betty's were a block away so, on that day, I rode with her. She dressed in all white to usher her services, chewed Doublemint gum, and peered out the window, her wig barely clearing the steering wheel. In-depth conversations weren't a part of our relationship, so the ride was quiet. She dropped me off and continued toward St. Josephs.

Word about my mother's sickness had circulated at church. Before service began, people asked about her well-being.

"She's fine," I answered. "I'm going to see her after this."

There was little need for concern. There rarely was. My mother always returned home.

In the past two years, I had earned the freedom to ride the "L" train and bus—not only to and from school, but also to meet my mother at the hospital after dialysis. Therefore, after church, I was instructed to meet my father at Northwestern. The route was familiar. I walked down Orleans to Chicago Avenue. I trekked east past the check-cashing spot, under the train, and past Moody Bible Institute. Grandma Hunny had taught me to look straight ahead, like I knew where I was going, and to keep my purse close. She called it "walking with purpose" and she assured me this would keep me from getting robbed. I walked past Water Tower and crossed Michigan Avenue. I walked down to Huron and headed to Northwestern Memorial where my father stood outside, waiting.

"How is she?"

"Not good," he replied.

We sat there for hours. My mother lay under white sheets weak, while slow, recurrent beeps signaled how much life was left in her body. Past experiences shaded my expectations. I was certain she would bounce back. My mother always returned home. They would give her some meds, and she'd be back the next day hounding me about starting junior year and taking the SATs.

September 4th was Labor Day. When I awoke, my father had already left for the hospital. When he returned, I knew. He looked like he'd lost a fight. His shoulders sagged; his eyes crimsoned.

"She's gone," he whispered. His arms wrapped around me like a vice grip leaving me no time for a side hug, as he sobbed into my shoulders.

When my father and I arrived at the ICU, he gave me a handful of coins and told me to tell everyone important about my mother's death. My first call was to her mother.

"I knew something was different this time," Grandma Hunny said. "I felt it in my stomach. We're on our way."

Next was a long-distance call to Shaquita, who by then, lived in California with her mother. Her grandmother had died a year prior, making her move mandatory. She wailed so loud that I held the phone several inches from my face until she finished.

The first half of that day was a blur of sliding coins and ringing phones. My father hung around like a wet towel.

My grandparents arrived a couple of hours later. Papa Henry stood near the ICU's entrance. He pulled out his handkerchief and dabbed his nose. Spurts of sadness caught in his throat.

Grandma Hunny pointed to the room. "Have you been in there?"

"No."

"Do you want to go in there? Do you want to see your mama?"

"No."

"C'mon. Let's go in there. You need to see your mama."

No one argued with Grandma Hunny. Whether you were sixteen, like I was at the time, or a grown man, like my father or her husband, you agreed with her and did whatever she said. She towered over me in stature and demeanor. Her voice was sterner than anyone I'd ever known, including my mother's. So, even though I didn't want to, she and I walked into the room together.

My mother's body was stiff. Her eyes closed. I'd seen dead bodies before: my great-grandfather, my great-aunt, and plenty of people, but only in coffins, not fresh. Not hours in. Not my mother's. My eyes burned.

"She just couldn't fight no more. She'd had enough." Grandma Hunny touched my mother's chest. "Here, you wanna feel?"

"No."

To be standing in a small white room, staring at my mother's dead body was one thing. To touch her was another.

Grandma Hunny looked at me. "Don't be sad. Don't cry. You had your mama for a long time. Sixteen years is a loooong time."

In my youth, I was notorious for crying for all manner of things and for an excessive amount of time. Over the years, I'd learned to silence myself for fear of being *given something to cry about*. I did as I was instructed and dried my tears, but the pain lingered.

My mother had recently added mowing the lawn to my chore list, so when we arrived at our house, I complied. Adults talked over and around me. They made funeral arrangements, organized pies and fried chicken, while I made straight lines in the grass. Up and down, down and up, I mowed until the grass turned to mulch.

When I finished, my father handed me a wad of money. He told me it was my job to keep it safe. I went to my room and closed the door, something my mother would've never allowed. People had gifted us over two thousand dollars. I tucked the money into my pillowcase and prepared for bed. My father said I didn't have to go to school the next day, but I didn't see a reason to stay home.

Every first day of school is the same, and this one was no different—except each time I ran into a friend, they'd ask me how I was, and I repeated, "My mother died yesterday."

"Your mom died?" Camille asked. "Shouldn't you be home?"

"If my mom died, I'd be home," another friend cosigned.

They looked at me as if I'd landed from another planet.

"I'm fine," I said.

We held my mother's funeral on September 7th at eight o'clock at night. I peeked at Grandma Hunny throughout the service. Her back was as straight as our wooden pew. My father's best friend sang "How Gentle God's Commands." Reverend Willis praised my mother's strength through illness. He commended her past four years as the Sunday school teacher and a "faithful servant" to St. Matthews. Grandma Hunny didn't flinch. It was hard, but I blinked back tears, just like my grandmother had instructed, just like my grandmother seemed to be doing. Afterward, my grandmother's smile glistened every time someone extended their arms for a hug or offered condolences. My stomach twisted in knots.

People milled around outside the sanctuary after the service, including one of my mother's former employers. He stood a foot taller than me and held my hand between his. I remembered going with her to the part-time job in a dark, musky, downtown building. His pale skin reddened, and tears flowed as he assured me of how much my mother's presence meant.

My friends saved me from an abyss of emotions. We stood in a circle, and I made them laugh about exorbitant church hats and sparkly shoes too bright for a nighttime funeral. Just when I was about to tell another joke, my father came over.

"I want you to meet somebody," he said.

"Hi. I'm Joëlle," she extended her chubby hand and smiled too hard. We were the same height. "Your dad used to babysit me when we lived in the Projects. I'm sorry to hear about your mom."

I shook her hand and returned to my friends.

Two days after my mother's funeral, Grandma Hunny, Papa Henry, my mother's sister, Aunt Diane, and her husband, Terry, came over for a family meeting. The four of them sat lined up on our couch against the longest wall. My father and I sat on the loveseat, which was pushed against the shortest wall. The family meeting's topic: What do we do with Kathy?

"Tony, Kathy can live with us if you want," Grandma Hunny started.

"We can bring her back for visits," Papa Henry sweetened the pot.

"She only has two years left of school. I think she'll be fine here with me," my father retorted.

Visits to the small Michigan town where my grandparents lived were acceptable when I was younger, but those trips had grown dull with each teenage year. The thought of living among weeping willows and never-ending green spaces invoked boredom. When I was twelve, I sat on the toilet in my grandparents' Pepto Bismol-colored upstairs bathroom, bawling and repeating, "I just wanna go home," during a summer visit. When I opened the door, my grandparents greeted me, smiling.

"*I just want to go home*," Grandma Hunny had mocked in a sing-song tone.

There was no way I could *live* there.

I stared at our peach paisley wallpaper. My mother had hung it herself when we first moved to Monitor. She carefully lined up each section to assure no one would notice where it was misaligned in some places.

"Why don't we ask Kathy what she wants?" Terry interrupted, snatching my attention in the process.

Grandma Hunny wrinkled the skin between her brows, which had become a permanent furrow, even when she wasn't angry, "Ask Kathy? Why would we ask *Kathy*?"

"I just thought we're talking about her so . . ."

Grandma Hunny ignored him. "She doesn't know what she wants. She doesn't know what's best for her. She's sixteen. *We'll* decide what's best and she'll do what *we* say."

Foolish man. He had only been in the family for a few years. He hadn't figured out the chain of command. I had no say. I was my parent's only child, and subsequently, Grandma Hunny's only grandchild. My opinions were inconsequential. Grandma Hunny said all the time that "children should be seen and not heard, unless directly asked." I'd grown used to sitting among adults, fading into the background.

With my fate in others' hands, I returned to the peach paisley wallpaper. I reminisced about the time it took my mother to choose the color and hang it. I thought about how disappointed she was about a bump in the middle of the dining room wall. She figured out how to affix the wallpaper, so the bump wasn't noticeable. She had also reupholstered the chairs just a few years ago to match the paisley. They were a putrid green when we lived on Central Park Ave. Now that we had our flat, she wanted a fresh look to match our new space.

"We'll be fine," I heard my father say. "We've got each other. Right, Baby?"

"Right," I answered.

Seven days after my mother's funeral, Joëlle reappeared. Younger than my father, but close enough in age as adults, she was a divorcee who lived an hour away in a single-family home on the South Side. Her two children, a son, and a daughter, attended HBCUs in Louisiana and Mississippi. She came from a large Louisiana family of brothers, nieces, and nephews. Most of them lived in Chicago. I learned all of this when she drove the three of us to River Oaks Mall to help me find leotards for jazz class.

It took me a while to understand what was happening. At first, she simply came to the house a lot. My father was recovering from a spinal injury and his metal neck brace prevented him from driving. In my teenage brain, Joëlle was there because he couldn't drive. But when she started picking me up from school, clarity emerged: they were in a relationship. We'd spend afternoons traveling to Joëlle's family's homes. One time, I laughed and smiled as much as I could, as the two reminisced with a lady who hadn't seen either of them for years. The lady was smitten with the idea that they had found each other. Eventually, I grew uninterested and nodded off on the stranger's couch.

"I can't believe you fell asleep," Joëlle seethed after we left the woman's apartment. "You have to know that's rude."

I waited for my father to jump in, to say something, to defend me. When he didn't, I replied,

"I was in school all day. I didn't even want to be there."

"That doesn't mean you go to somebody's house and fall asleep," she hissed.

Driving back and forth from one side of town to the other grew costly and time-consuming for Joëlle. The solution was for my father and me to spend the night at her house, which consistently smelled like fried gizzards and smoked ham hocks. The first night we tested this experiment, I slept in her daughter's room. The next morning, she looked at my clothes thrown all over the place and proclaimed me rude for not keeping them neatly folded in the suitcase, while I visited her house. She reminded me that this wasn't *my* room. I was a guest, so I should act like it.

I muttered an "okay," while wishing she would go back to wherever she came from.

Four weeks after my mother died, my father stopped asking me if I wanted to accompany him. Instead, he'd pack a bag, kiss me on the forehead, and announce that he was "going to get laid."

KATHY

1989

The most shocking part of my mother's death was that she was physically present one day, and then ceased to exist the next. Up until her death, my primary world consisted of my mother, my father, and me. When it was time to grocery shop, the three of us picked through canned goods and frozen food together. From seven o'clock at night until ten, my parents sat interlocked on the couch, and I curled up on the loveseat, where we watched television together—*The Love Boat* and *Fantasy Island* on Saturday night, and *Alice* and *One Day at a Time* on Tuesdays. When my mother and father wanted to see the latest movie, the three of us packed up chips, bottles of Coke, and blankets, and went to the drive-in, where I sat in the backseat and watched Eddie Murphy's career blossom. Those moments dissipated in an instant.

My mother's death and my father's preoccupation with Joëlle created a depth of loneliness and a vacuum of silence I was ill-prepared for. When my mother wasn't dealing with her illness, she carried a lightness that manifested through Prince's lyrics. Whenever I heard *Dearly Beloved, we are gathered here today*, I knew the air would float with *Purple Rain* album refrains. She'd start with "Let's Go Crazy" and croon and move through each cut until she reached the title track, and then she'd watch the movie, mesmerized like a teenage girl. Prince's eccentric vibes filled every crevice of our home. If my father played DJ, then he'd pull out his Kool Moe Dee album and repeatedly play "Wild Wild West." I remember the day the three of us visited two record stores looking for the song he'd heard on the radio. The lyrics riled him up and brought back adolescent memories of living in Cabrini Green—a time he rarely talked about. But with my mother's death, the music stopped. Our home was empty, and the silence was loud. Too loud.

I was sixteen and my mother no longer held the reins of my life. That meant I could do what she had previously forbidden, like change my hair. When I was ten she decided she could no longer endure the fight associated with taming my big afro; many times, we both ended up in tears just so I could don two braids with bright barrettes. She scheduled an appointment at a hair salon, and a relaxer turned my hair into long, soft strands that hung well beyond my shoulders. I enjoyed this look, but I was approaching junior year. Girls at my school wore trendy hip-hop styles, like MC Lyte's layered look, not boring brown tresses like a child. Before her death, I had asked my mother if I could get a new hairstyle. Her answer was a firm "no." However, in my abundance of unsupervised free time, I was not only alone, but I also didn't have to ask anyone for permission. I made an appointment with my usual hairstylist and told her to cut it all off into a bob.

The first four weeks of life after my mother's death were a hodge-podge of figuring out what it meant to be by myself, learning how to fill the silence, and determining who was paying attention. Teenagers want independence, but adults are there to remind them to eat their veggies and drink water. I was doing neither. Some days, I'd turn on the radio as loud as I could and listen to the DJ's latest mix. Then, I'd blare a television show, while repetitive percussions played in the background, just to cut through the silence. Grandma Betty nor my father inquired about my new hair. Instead, they discussed it with one another. The only person who spoke directly to me about it was Diamond, who said, "Everyone needs to chill about your hair. All they did was lift it in the back."

This was my routine until my friend Mika walked home with me from the bus stop one day.

Mika and I had known each other since we were six-year-old first graders at Skinner. Our mothers knew each other before we were born. They'd worked at a local union together championing workers' rights. We saw each other at union meetings sometimes, which made her my first best friend.

Mika and her family were the only white people on their block in a sea of Black faces. Her parents had an office of books piled from the ceiling to the floor. Whereas our books were neatly lined with spines facing outward, theirs sat double-tiered and seemed to hang off the edge of bookshelves, begging to be read and reread. Others stacked up waist-high on the floor as if ready for a professional reference.

I reveled in the way Mika's family interacted. She and her brother stood inches apart and screamed at the top of their lungs to one another. Her mother told me to call her "Sarah," and her father, "Noah." I delighted in this privilege and used both as often as possible. When Sarah or Noah would ask Mika or her brother to do something, they'd ask, "Why?" The first time I witnessed this, I braced myself for the slap that was sure to follow. But there was none. Sarah or Noah would simply explain the reason for asking their children to complete a task.

When my father picked me up, I let out a big, "Bye, Sarah!"

"Mrs. Cohen," he quickly corrected.

"But she said to call her Sarah."

"I don't care what *she* said. *I* said to call her Mrs. Cohen."

When we moved to Monitor, Mika's house was a twenty-minute walk away from me on Mayfield Avenue. We were physically closer, but our friendship grew distant. By the time we transferred to Whitney Young, our relationship floundered. However, an empty house made space for her to reenter my life, and luckily so. When I began high school, I developed a habit of taking the long way home, because most of my friends lived on the South Side. When my mother died, I did this less, opting for a direct route; this led to meeting Mika and another friend, Tim, on the Austin bus. Some days I'd jump off several blocks early to walk with them. We'd drop Mika off on Mayfield, and then Tim and I would walk to his home. On other days, this combination shifted, and Mika and I would walk Tim home. And sometimes, I'd beg Mika to walk me home.

"Who's gonna walk me home?" Mika would ask.

We'd both look at Tim, who lived equidistance between us.

"Alright. I'll walk b-both of you home." He stuttered.

I introduced her to my new hobby: watching *Degrassi High*, with the radio playing in the background.

"How are you listening to the radio *and* watching TV?" Mika asked while turning the radio off.

I would just laugh, unaware that my hobby was a coping mechanism to drown out the quiet. We'd enjoy a couple of episodes, and then Mika would leave. One Friday I convinced her to spend the night. My father usually didn't return home until the following afternoon, so she had time to wake up and leave before he walked through the door. This particular Saturday, he came home earlier than usual.

"Go hide!" I whispered.

I sat on the loveseat and acted as if I was watching television.

Five minutes later, my father stood over me, "Kathy, why is Mika behind your bedroom door?"

"I thought you'd be mad if she was here."

He told me Mika was welcome at our home anytime. All I had to do was let him know. After that, she was there more often, and my body exhaled. The familiarity of our friendship created a semblance of stability. Her companionship made the lonely spaces in between more bearable; she filled the gap my mother had left. She was by my side as I reconstructed my identity sans a mother, like when I decided to get a second ear piercing. Mika agreed to go to the mall with me and hold my hand if need be. I smiled from our house to Claire's, excited that my new look was coming together.

"Are you eighteen?" the piercer asked.

"I'm sixteen."

She handed me consent forms. "If you're sixteen, you need your mother's permission."

"I don't have a mother," I said, voice raised. "My mother died four weeks ago. What the fuck am I supposed to do if I don't have a mother to sign this stupid-ass paper?" Tears formed in the corner of my eyes as I yelled. I looked at Mika. "Will you tell her I don't have a mother?"

Minutes later, we left. I had a second piercing and instructions on how to care for it. I wished I'd had instructions for the anger that brewed.

$$\infty$$

Adjusting to a new life was like holding my breath underwater. Opening my mouth risked drowning; keeping it closed did, too. Mid-October my father had his neck brace removed. Afterward, he resumed taking me to school in the mornings. One fall morning around six forty-five, a car ran into us two blocks from school. It was just like those buckle-your-seatbelt commercials that used to play nonstop during the late eighties. My body jerked forward, and my head slammed into the front windshield. Glass shattered everywhere. Blood dripped down my face. My stomach churned as I held back vomit.

"I'm sorry, Daddy. I should have had on my seatbelt. I'm really, sorry."

My father jumped out of the car and yelled at the driver. "You ran that stop sign! You were supposed to stop!"

The ambulance rushed me to Cook County Hospital. Every major city has a hospital that's known as the place where people with no insurance or no

money can go. Cook County was that facility. Joëlle
met us there. After running a battery of tests, and
because I had a head injury, the doctor recommended
I stay overnight. My father kissed me on the forehead
and Joëlle grabbed her purse.

"You guys are gonna leave me here?"

"Joëlle has to work in the morning," my father
explained.

"You'll be all right," she smirked. "You're not
afraid to stay here, are you?"

"No."

I wouldn't give her the satisfaction of knowing
that I *was* scared. I'd never stayed in a county hospital
ever—let alone by myself. The last time I was
hospitalized, I was fourteen years old and had gotten
hit by a car crossing the street to St. Matthews.
Shaquita watched from the front of the building. Her
favorite story seemed to be recounting how my body
flew into the air and landed on the driver's windshield.
It was the scariest thing she'd seen. My family said
that I lay unconscious in Northwestern Hospital's bed
for a day or two. As I came to, my swollen lips ached,
and my tongue scraped across my front teeth; part of
the second one was missing. A woman hovered over
me.

"Do you need anything?" she asked.

"Just my mommy," I replied.

I was relieved once I realized the woman *was* my
mother. My mother, on the other hand, worried about
brain functioning and years of lost gifted education.

Two years later presented a new truth. My
mother's death was real. The consequence was more
than not hearing her sing Prince songs anymore. Six
weeks after her burial, I had to reconcile the idea that
she wouldn't be coming to console me in the dark
corner of the hospital. She wouldn't be sitting in the

corner in the middle of the night, under a thin woven blanket praying for recovery. Neither would my father. In their place would be a nurse who only came when I slid out of bed and yelled out of the door into the vacant hallway.

Ever since we'd lived on Monitor, we'd begun buying and decorating live trees for Christmas. The fresh pine smell filled the house and signaled *it was Christmas time!* My father kept this tradition and dragged one in a couple of weeks before the holiday. However, there was a new tradition. My family didn't decorate the tree with me—Mika did.

The substitution of Mika for my father to decorate the tree ahead of the holiday didn't bother me. However, on Christmas morning I awoke to something I'd never seen. Emptiness. If my mother were alive, our house would've smelled like bacon, Swiss cheese, and tomatoes, in preparation for her famous holiday breakfast sandwiches. If she were there, the stereo would've blared Donny Hathaway's "This Christmas." I didn't know what to do. *Should I open gifts? Should I wait for my father to come home? Maybe I should go be with Grandma Betty and Diamond.*

I turned on the Christmas lights like my mother would have and sat in silence for a couple of hours.

"Merry Christmas!" my father said when he walked through the door.

"You should've been here this morning."

"What's the problem? I'm home now," he said.

"But you weren't here when I woke up. No one was here."

"THE WORLD . . . DOES NOT . . . REVOLVE . . . AROUND . . . YOU!" he hollered. I wondered if Grandma Betty heard her son yelling like a crazy person. Later, when Diamond and I were both good and grown, she confessed they both did. It is the one memory she vividly recalls from that era. Diamond told me that she headed downstairs to find out if everything was okay.

"No!" Grandma Betty stopped her. "Never get between a father and his child."

I walked to my room, closed the door, and sat on the bed. Tears fell, one by one. Those seven words clarified my reality, which had no resolution. I dressed and prepared to drive with my father to our traditional Christmas dinner with my mother's side of the family. I hoped the normalcy would provide temporary warmth, but inside I knew the truth. I was alone.

A few weeks prior, I had called my grandmother to explain our living conditions.

"Grandma, I can see the thing in the back of the refrigerator."

"Kathy, what are you talking about?"

"The thing in the very back. It looks like a dial. I've never seen it before. We don't have any food."

Grandma Hunny and Aunt Diane drove from out of state and the three of us grocery shopped. I was proud to show my father how I'd problem solved. But he was not only unimpressed, but also irritated, especially after finding out who bought the food.

"Don't you ever do that again! Keep our business in this house. You understand?"

I nodded.

Christmas afternoon, I remembered the dictum and practiced it well: *keep our business in this house.* At Aunt Lillian's, I donned the biggest, brightest smile as she hugged me close to her breasts, and Uncle James teased me. I told corny jokes that made my grandparents roll their eyes and shake their heads. My duality was flawless. I doubt Aunt Diane or Uncle Terry suspected a thing. No one knew my father had yelled at me hours prior for wanting him home the first Christmas after my mother's death. They also didn't know that how they interacted with me, as I suppressed grief for my mother's death was important for how I was learning to function.[1]

Three months after my mother's death, no one in my family mentioned it. I learned to compartmentalize who I was and what emotions I showed: be sad and angry inside, and bubbly elsewhere. There was no conversation about my mother or how I felt; it was almost as if she'd never existed.

"You're so strong," everyone said.

I wore my "strength" like a badge of honor, and in the end, everyone applauded me for it; everyone praised me for not grieving.

KENNY

1990

Kenny and I met at my first job in the summer of '89, White Castle. He was nineteen and at least six feet tall. I noticed him on my first day at work. His thick, gold herringbone chains and rings sparkled against his dark skin. His crooked white teeth set him apart from others. I watched him when he showed me how to cook the tiny burgers. It was hard to pay attention, but I didn't want Kenny to think I was slow. It was important for me to show I was smart, so I made sure to be attentive to the order: onions, burger, bun.

Two weeks later, Kenny said he liked me. But White Castle had rules, and this was a full-time job he couldn't lose. I was finally sixteen and permitted to go on dates, but my parents would have never approved of me seeing a nineteen-year-old, who, according to the law and them, was a man. So, we talked on the phone but never saw each other outside of the restaurant . . . until my mother died, and I quit working.

Kenny bought me a Christmas gift, a red Coach duffle bag. Nearly every girl at the high school had one, and even though my circle of friends didn't judge one another based on name-brand fashion, I coveted a three-hundred-dollar bag my parents could never afford. He brought it over during one of the days when my father was with Joëlle. He asked when I would be able to get out of the house to spend time with him. I bundled up the courage to ask my father if I could go on an actual date.

"Who is this Kenny? I need to meet him first," he said.

"Just a guy from White Castle. You and Mommy said I could date when I was sixteen," I reminded him.

He looked at Joëlle, who on this day, happened to be at our house. "Oh, Tony. She can go on a date. Can't she?"

"How old is he?"

"Eighteen."

"I still need to meet him," my father said.

Kenny picked me up in his Mustang. My father also had a Mustang, but it was gray and used. Kenny's was shiny and new, all black, with windows so dark no one could see inside. At the time, I didn't know anyone who drove a car like that and didn't understand the symbolism of what it meant for a nineteen-year-old to own one. He met my father and Joëlle as promised, and then we were off . . . to his first-floor apartment, which was ten minutes away.

The space was bare. His room had one full-size bed pushed against the wall. On it, was a gray fitted sheet, a matching, crumpled-up flat sheet, and one pillow. At the head of the bed was a small wooden TV tray, with a shade-less lamp. Kenny removed his shirt and sat on the bed.

"You ever done this before?"

The back of the bleachers flashed before me. "Once, but I don't know what I'm doing," I said.

"Don't worry. I'll show you."

He took off all my clothes. I stood there, uncomfortable as he stuck his chewed-up gum on a piece of paper on the TV tray. We kissed. He then took off the rest of his clothes and lay on the bed.

"You're so pretty," he said.

"Thank you," I beamed.

"Come here. Lay on top of me."

We kissed some more, while he rubbed my body. He grabbed a condom from the TV tray, ripped it open with his teeth, and put it on with one hand. He scooped me up and sat me on top of him.

"Now, move."

"Like this?" My hips made awkward jerky movements.

"No. Like you're dancing."

Kenny didn't know I only performed carefully choreographed jazz routines in expensive, multicolored tights—pas de bourrées and such.

"Like this?" I moved in circles.

He placed both hands on my hips and moved them. "Like this. Slower," he instructed. "Here. Let's do this." He lifted my hips off him, and I lay under him, waiting.

Kenny took control, thrusting and panting until he finished. This was another experience that solidified, for me, that sex was letting some guy you liked pump a couple of times until he decided for both of you that you were done. Even Trina had shown me that.

Kenny went to the bathroom. I heard the toilet flush, and then he returned with a wet washcloth. "Here. Wipe off so you don't smell like sex when you go home."

I cleaned myself and re-dressed. My muscles, tense and tight from the past few months, loosened. Afterward, Kenny and I lay on his bed and talked for two hours. I described how my father used to be home all the time—now, it was as if he couldn't keep still. On Saturday nights when my father would stay home, his favorite cousin, a woman my mother disliked, would travel from South Bend with her eleven-year-old daughter. My father would pack ground-up marijuana leaves in his pipe; while his cousin would carefully place the weed in short, white rolling papers. Then, she'd lick the paper to glue it together. They'd sit on the same couch where my mother used to be, entangled in my father's arms, self-medicating, while my young cousin roller-skated on my mother's hardwood floors.

I told Kenny about how I'd yelled that day. "If Mommy was here, you wouldn't be doing this!"

My father and his cousin exhaled small clouds of smoke, looked at me, and laughed as if my pain was a joke. Watching him bred hatred.

Each confession I uttered, while wrapped in Kenny's arms removed resentment. He didn't say much, but strokes of my hair sent calm ripples throughout my body. Whatever pain I had drifted away at that moment with him. Despite the lackluster pumping, the afterglow of sex became a vehicle for relaxation.

We timed leaving his house to coincide with the end of a movie we never saw. He pulled into a parking space across from my home, leaned over, and kissed me on the lips.

"Stay sweet," he said.

"I will."

When I entered, my father and Joëlle sat on the couch.

"How was the movie?" my father asked.

"It was all right."

I called Kenny every day for a week after Saturday, but he never called back. I even paged him 911 but received no response, so I called White Castle.

"Is Kenny there?"

"Kathy?" The unasked question was loud in the manager's voice. She replied, "Yeah. He's here."

"Can you tell his ass to call me back? Otherwise, I'm coming up there!" I threatened.

"Kathy, you can't call here cussing and acting crazy. You gone make him lose his job. You want him to lose his job . . . 'cause of you?"

"No," I said quietly.

"Well, don't call up here no more looking for him," she reprimanded.

I hung up the phone, confused. I thought we had a good time. I thought Kenny liked me. He said I was pretty. We had sex. What did I do wrong? The sadness that had disappeared when I was with him, reappeared. The emotion seemed to always be there, just beneath the surface, impossible to shake.

∞

My father and I learned to exist without my mother in parallel worlds. He clung to Joëlle as if his life depended on it. I hung out with Mika at home and other friends at school—but mostly, I kept to myself. Our worlds didn't intersect, unless my father forced them to, like when he announced we'd be going to church one Sunday. We hadn't attended since my mother's funeral, so I was surprised when he said he wanted to go. I was even more surprised when Joëlle picked us up and drove in the opposite direction toward her side of town. The church looked like it should've been a strip mall candy store. The sanctuary was no bigger than our living room, and instead of pews, there were folding chairs.

I sat quietly through service wondering why we didn't go to St. Matthews. As an adult, I realized the absurdity of the idea. My father would've been met with judgment and criticism had we shown up to my family's church where my great-grandmother was held in high esteem, with his new girlfriend, less than a year after his wife's death. When service ended, Joëlle introduced me to the preacher. I stuck out my hand, as I knew to do, but instead of shaking it, she held it tight between her warm palms.

"You know God loves you, right?" she asked, holding her clasp.

"Yes," I replied.

"You know Jesus loves you, right?"

"Yes."

And then suddenly, as if on cue, she and the tiny congregation encircled me, while Joëlle and my father slid back. The congregation spoke in tongues and shouted for God to save me *in the name of Jesus*. A single tear crept out and sat on my right cheek, and I closed my eyes and prayed my prayer. I wished that this nightmare I'd been thrust into would end. I imagined I was at St. Matthews giggling with Shaquita. A woman noticed that one tear had turned into a stream. *Yes, God. Speak to her, God.* I continued to pray for an escape that never came until my mind drifted off to Sunday school with Jay calling Shaquita 'Chiquita Banana' and my mother reprimanding them. If my mother had been there, none of this would've been happening. I prayed that when I opened my eyes, I would return to the predictability that had existed just eight months ago when Daddy loved Mommy and Mommy loved me. But when I raised my eyelids, strangers still surrounded me, shouting, *yes, Jesus! Heal her, Jesus!*

My father and Joëlle stood hand-in-hand, grinning as if they'd solved a puzzle. They had the wherewithal to suspect that something was wrong with me but seemed bewildered about what the *something* could be. When I look at photos from that period, I appear sad. One photo, in particular, is of the entire junior class. Mika and I are sitting in the front row, with all of the other short people. Everyone around me is smiling. It was two months before the end of junior year; we were about to be seniors. The day was sunny and warm enough for us to be taking a photo outside in the Midwest. But I'm stale-faced with empty eyes. I looked as if I should be giving the photographer the middle finger. Concrete proof of my grief is documented in the school's artifacts. Is that what my father and Joëlle saw? Is that what landed me in the middle of an intercession?

No, this wasn't my father's idea. As a child, he was an altar boy in Grandma Betty's church; when he married my mother, he converted to Methodist and was the "youth minister." Now that he was enamored with Joëlle, I was stuck standing in the middle of a Pentecostal church surrounded by elders shouting for healing, salvation, and deliverance. I suffered the consequence of his romantic whim. They recognized my pain but didn't know what to do with it, so they turned it over to Jesus. Jesus could heal anything. That was the consensus, no matter any family member's denomination. I had expressed my concerns with my father's behavior to Grandma Betty: smoking weed in the house, announcing his sexual activity, all of it.

"Pray about it," she said, her *Living Words* scattered across the living room table. "I'll pray, too."

She gave this advice with the tone of a single mother who knew details about her youngest son to which I wasn't privy, something she had seen in him and prayed about before. Catholicism had safely gotten her this far; Jesus had protected her and her children, and He would also help me. There were no other words, no consolation or guidance, not even *how* to pray, just that I should.

My mother's Sunday school lessons from previous years confirmed the idea. Philippians taught me that I should neither worry nor be anxious. Jesus could heal anything. But it was hard to reconcile. Even though an omnipotent God knew what occurred, anxiety and concern continued to fill my body and soul. Perhaps I wasn't praying hard enough. "Saving" me showed me that I was the source of my problem. No one else was to blame. My father's and Joëlle's Christian principles were shrouded in fornication, which according to the Bible is a sin. Even though they never found out about the night at Kenny's apartment, somehow, I was the one chosen to stand among strangers, who prayed for me without understanding what or for whom they were interceding. To this day, I'm bewildered about the surprise intercession. The only conclusion I've determined is that my father and Joëlle believed Jesus could heal anything, even my grief, which they witnessed, but didn't want to attend to.

∞

Everything my mother introduced me to, was an activity that relied on independence: reading, studying, writing, and swimming. I learned to swim when I was three. My mother had taken me to classes at the YMCA. I don't mean I learned the basics, such as holding one's breath and floating around, though that was a part of the instruction. I mean that by the time I entered kindergarten, I knew how to accurately position my body and arms so that I could freestyle to the center of the pool. I don't remember specific lessons, but when it came time to prove I knew how to swim in gym class years later, muscle memory supported me. The gym teacher had to separate us into two groups: those who could swim and those who could not. To prove our skill, we had to float and tread water. Both had been ingrained in me since I was a child and reinforced over the years on vacations with my grandparents. Whether treading or floating, the body must be calm. However, while treading water, you must also move your arms and legs while remaining calm; not in a state of fear or panic. If you are successful, onlookers will see your head slightly tilted back, none the wiser of your limbs moving below the water. Near the end of my junior year and after the intercession, that's what life had become for me—treading water.

I sought peace, mostly finding it at school, because life there hadn't changed. My friends and I would grab a personal pizza from the food truck, or we'd take the bus downtown, get a quick bite to eat, and make it back just in time for class. But on one spring day, our usual plan failed. Not only were we tardy, but we also didn't have a pass. Mr. Korner, our English teacher, wouldn't let us in until we could present one. Camille had an old tardy slip that a teacher had filled out in pencil. We erased the names, dates, and times, and filled in the new information. Voila. We returned to Mr. Korner's class with our "pass." He stared at the small gold paper and shifted his eyes behind his circular frames from the pass to us, and back to the pass.

"Have a seat," he said.

The next day, I was called to the office.

"We checked with Ms. Wilson. She said she didn't write this pass for you three. You're being suspended for forgery. Five days. Is this the number where I can reach your parents?"

My father picked me up from school. He didn't yell. He didn't lecture. He didn't say a word.

"I'm sorry, Daddy," I said to break the silence.

"How are we supposed to make it if you don't listen? You just can't follow the crowd."

"Follow the crowd?"

"Doing whatever your friends tell you to do. Cutting class."

"I didn't cut class. I was late. And it was all our idea to go downtown," I corrected.

"Whatever it is. Forging notes? Now, you're suspended? Don't you want to *be* somebody? Don't you want to *do* better?"

"It won't happen again."

"I know," he said. "You're going to live with Grandma Hunny in Covert."

Living with Grandma Hunny couldn't happen. I asked for another chance to prove my goodness. I'd tread harder this time.

He looked over at me. "You can't get in more trouble."

His comment confused me. Aside from the time Grandma Betty's car broke down on the South Side and left me and Mika stranded, even though my father told us not to drive that far, I didn't know what "trouble" he referred to. I'd done everything he'd asked, even being nice to Joëlle.

"I'm not. I just have one more year, remember? I won't. I promise." And then I asked, "Does this mean I can't have my birthday party? It's Saturday."

My father quieted for a few minutes. "Only because I said yes before."

My seventeenth birthday party was the first day since we'd buried my mother that my family had visited our home. Four of my favorite cousins came over and played games in my cramped room. Music played throughout the house. Grandma Hunny, Aunt Diane, Grandma Betty . . . everyone was there and seemingly happy. My family sang the birthday song, sliced cake, and showered me with hugs and kisses. It was the first time life felt normal, like when my mother was alive. With my head tilted back, my arms and legs moved fluidly underwater.

The next morning, four overstuffed garbage bags sat in the middle of my bedroom floor. A brown bear flopped out of one; my toothbrush and lotion fell out of the other. My father had crammed my entire existence into black trash bags while I slept. I'm certain that if he could've stuffed me in one of those bags without waking me, he would have.

"You're going to live with your grandmother," he said.

I could feel my arms and legs moving faster, hindering my ability to tread. "Daddy, no! I can *do* better. I can *be* better," I cried.

"You walked around here frontin' in front of everybody yesterday like everything is all right. You're suspended!" he shouted. "Get your stuff. Let's go."

All my life I had been adept at reading what adults wanted and doing that thing, but it had been challenging to determine what my father wanted. I was strong when I wanted to cry. And I was silent when I wanted to protest. I'd accepted his new relationship with Joëlle the best I could, and the idea that she "loved him," as she confided to me one day. I'd even learned to be alone. In the midst of it all, I'd managed to successfully be promoted to the twelfth grade at one of the top high schools in the nation, something many bereaved teens do not accomplish.[1]

But none of those things mattered. I failed an exam no one had prepared me for: what do you do when your mother suddenly dies, and your father abandons you? I stopped treading and allowed the water to cover my neck, ears, and mouth, and drowned in my grief.

EDDIE

1990

Grandma Hunny and Papa Henry arrived the day after school ended to take me to Covert. My grandfather remained in the driver's seat; my grandmother stood near the car door; my father was on the side of the house. Mika and Tim had walked over to see me off. We hugged each other individually, and then Tim held Mika as her eyes turned red and a stream of tears flowed down her face. When we could delay no longer, I watched their bodies dwindle from the backseat window.

"This was like a real production, huh?" Grandma Hunny joked.

Yep. Real movie-like.

Grandma Hunny demonstrated no explicit understanding of friendship. She didn't know Mika and Tim were the reason I didn't curl up into a ball of sadness. Their sendoff was appropriate. Their presence proved someone cared for me. I thought friends were supposed to cry when they were sad. For some reason, tears were never appropriate for Grandma Hunny, not when my mother died and not when my father sent me away, so I internalized, sinking further in my grief, as we drove two hours east of Chicago. I also strategized. Living with my grandparents was temporary. I had one mission: to graduate from high school. This time next year, I'd be eighteen. No one would tell me what I could or could not do, ever again, and I would live where I wanted and do what I wanted; I would be in control of myself.

The 130-mile drive to my grandparents' white two-story Michigan house was familiar, yet different.

"You're not visiting this time." Grandma Hunny said while Papa Henry drove. "This is not a vacation. You'll have responsibilities."

I'd ridden on the M-140 many times for summer visits.

"You'll have to wash the dishes," Grandma Hunny continued.

Nothing had changed in the years I'd been coming here. We turned left and passed Watervliet, a small town with a gas station, a burger restaurant, and a few other shops on the road.

"You hear me?" Grandma Hunny asked.

"Yes," I replied.

After a long winding path of countless trees, we passed Covert Public Schools: the building where all the town's children, kindergarten through twelfth grade, were educated.

"You'll have to wash your clothes," Grandma Hunny said.

We passed a fire station and library on the left and a small, dilapidated gas station, resting on the right. All these things had been there for as long as I'd been visiting. We approached Thirty-Second Avenue, my grandparents' road. There was a corner store on the right and a field to the left. We continued a half a mile until we reached my new, temporary, home—the white house with the pink door.

Finally, there was silence.

∞

Attending Covert High School was the first time I'd gone to a school that wasn't for gifted students. Technically, there was only one class to complete for graduation: English IV. The school's counselor had never seen anything like it, and he didn't know what to do. There was little the school could offer.

"We can fill her day with a few other things, but otherwise, maybe she can do work study?"

Senior year should have included AP Language and Composition. I should have been enrolled in AP Spanish Language and Culture; however, in the year that I was supposed to complete college preparatory courses for an assumed freshman year of college, my schedule included English IV, typing, basic computer programming, auto mechanics, and work-study. Aunt Diane arranged for my work-study job to be with one of her former employers, Citizens Bank. The first day of school I experienced bouts of diarrhea at the thought of riding the school bus with strangers, as opposed to taking the bus and train to a school with friends I'd amassed from the time I was six. When I wasn't on the toilet, my stomach churned with nervousness.

I attended school until Papa Henry picked me up at noon (because Grandma Hunny said I couldn't be away the whole day without her seeing me). Then, I drove their spare '84 Mercury Marquis to work twenty minutes away in South Haven, where I sat at a large calculator-looking machine for up to seven hours and processed checks. I received two hundred dollars a week and reminded myself of the plan: finish high school.

Shortly after school began, several boys visited my grandparents' home, in hopes of courting me. Though I was flattered, my sights were on finishing high school and leaving Covert. One week into senior year, I met a boy in computer class named Eddie. I was minding my own business, ignoring students and my new surroundings like I'd promised myself, when I heard a deep voice.

"You have a booger hanging from your nose."

"Huh?"

"Right there," he tapped the side of his nostril.

"Oh, God!"

"It's all right, Shorty. Just thought you should know."

Eddie and I talked every night after that. He lived in a yellow and brown, two-story house on the M-140 curve, directly en route to my work-study job.

The first time I visited his house, I was amazed. A forty-eight-inch floor-model TV filled one corner of his living room. We sat on his mother's leather sectional and watched a movie. He had a natural comedic sense. I laughed even when he made fun of me and how "cool" I tried to be with a booger hanging from my nose. We kissed, and then we had sex on the floor hard enough to leave a rug burn on my lower back.

Sex with Eddie wasn't like losing my virginity behind the bleachers or "dancing" in the bed with

Kenny. Sex with Eddie felt like floating in the pool, arms outstretched, body in stasis. With him, I was safe, and I wanted to drape myself around him. With Eddie, I mattered. We had sex two more times that day, and our bond cemented. I was never letting him go.

It was late September when I noticed I hadn't had my period since August. It had been seven years since my father showed me how to put a condom on a banana, so I wasn't entirely sure what was happening.

"What does it mean if my period is late?" I asked Eddie's mother.

She took a drag of her cigarette, blew out a puff of smoke, and said, "You either skipped a month or you pregnant. And if you pregnant, you need to talk to Eddie."

Eddie said I should get an abortion.

I knew nothing of abortions or how to go about getting one, so I spoke with the only woman who looked trustworthy, my senior English teacher. She was a brown, petite, no-nonsense lady. Her church dresses and high heels felt like home. Instead of eating in the cafeteria, I'd sit on the floor in her office and talk about the week's assignment.

Her jaw dropped.

"What? Who's the father? Eddie?"

Even though I'd just met her a month prior, somehow, I'd disappointed her. "Yes," I replied.

"I thought you were different," she started, then stopped. "Have you told your grandmother?"

Grandma Hunny had been the director of a community center for as long as I could remember.

She'd overseen adolescent workers during a summer youth program and served meals to senior citizens. She provided retired residents with information, like how to attain their social security checks. Papa Henry was still an active member of the school board and had been for years. They knew everyone in the township in some capacity. Supporting their newly arrived granddaughter through an unexpected pregnancy was not on the agenda, nor was it socially appropriate.

"She'd kill me," I said.

My English teacher neatly wrote the name Planned Parenthood on a sheet of paper and underneath it, a phone number.

Naivete led me to believe I could walk into a clinic and receive an abortion on the same day. Instead, the first visit was to confirm the pregnancy, schedule a day for the procedure, and commit to a form of birth control. I was, indeed, pregnant. Eddie and I would be back in two weeks. I chose the pill.

"I heard you threw up at school today," Grandma Hunny said. Her principal friend had replayed events I thought only I knew, by the time she picked me up.

"Yeah. Probably something from last night."

My answer was plausible. Grandma Hunny never cooked. She brought under-seasoned, leftover lunches in sectioned, Styrofoam plates from the Center. When mold appeared, she directed me to cut it off and eat the good part. On a good day, the food was tolerable. While pregnant, it sat in my mouth like mush.

"I also heard you don't eat lunch with the other kids."

"Nope. For what?"

"Listen. I know your mama died. I know you're adopted," her voice drifted. My stomach churned. I wanted to open the car door and throw up on the grass. Grandma Hunny wanted to discuss something no one in my family ever had—me being an adoptee.

When I was ten years old, I found a book in our home that stood out among the others lined on the shelves. It was called *Why Was I Adopted?* Intrigued, I plopped down to the floor, crossed my legs, and began reading. It was written as if the person was talking directly to me. The book described how one's mother and father gave them the "gift of life," but then it changed to explain how ". . . sometimes something may happen so that the family you began with is not the same as the family you have now."[1]

I kept reading.

The book described how the reader had two sets of parents: birth and adoptive.

A few minutes later, I looked over at my mother, who had been watching me. She stood in the opposite corner of the dining room.

"Why are you crying?" she asked.

"I feel sorry for these people."

"Why?"

"These babies don't know who their parents are, and someone else takes care of them?"

"You shouldn't be sad," she replied matter-of-factly. "Because *you're* adopted."

The pit of my belly dropped to my feet as I tried to determine how this new information fit into my former reality. I held back tears and swallowed hard. I had many questions. The book sounded as if being adopted was a wonderful event. But, not knowing where I came from didn't feel wondrous. It was confusing. Imagining I was born to a mother and father, who for some unknown reason didn't want to raise me, didn't sound extraordinary—unusual maybe —but not special. My new revelation felt deceptive. My mother, father, Grandma Hunny, Aunt Lillian—all of them—instantly seemed like strangers, not family. Who were they? Who was I? Where were my *real* mother and father? What was this ten-year lie? Why hadn't anyone told me? Though I was surrounded by family that shared love for me, I felt rejected by a biological family that, up until a few minutes prior, I had no idea existed.

The last few pages included a series of questions that adoptees may have, like "What if I want to know more about my birth parents?" According to the book, this is "natural," and I should "talk about it with my Mom and Dad."[2] But I didn't. Just like everything else that required depth and feeling, my mother didn't seem interested in talking about it, just in me not having a negative emotion or reaction. I walked to my room and placed a pillow over my head to muffle my distress, which instead of being sympathy for strangers, was now reserved for me. There was no more conversation about adoption or what it meant in that or any future moment.

But here I was, awaiting my Planned Parenthood appointment, pretending not to be pregnant, while my grandmother offered compassion for my unique situation for the first time in seventeen years.

"If you ever want to talk about it, just say something," Grandma Hunny finished.

I closed my eyes, and held back tears, while vomit simmered in the recesses of my throat as I wished this part of my life would end. Living in Covert. Going to school in Covert. Being pregnant. Having to get an abortion.

I swallowed. "No . . . I'm okay. I don't even think about it."

Eddie and I, sixteen and seventeen years old, drove to the clinic in his mother's blue Chevy. We sat in the waiting room and watched daytime television with other women of different ages until they called my name. I knew it was the right thing to do. I had been raised in an older family that prided itself on being classy. Grandma Hunny and her sisters dressed up in flowy dresses, flesh-tone stockings, fur stoles, and costume jewelry to attend church and fashion shows; sometimes they were one and the same. They told stories of how, when they were growing up, wearing red shoes signaled that a woman was a prostitute. When they saw a woman with red shoes, they'd point and whisper to one another, *red shoes, red shoes,* with childlike delight. These lessons of what it meant to be a woman filtered down to my mother and then to me. One time, she reprimanded me for the way I interacted with boys. Diamond's male friends had stopped their car in front of our home and rolled down the windows. Diamond stood on the driver's side; her butt wagging from the window as if she was headless. I did the same, just on the passenger's side. My mother drove up and beeped the horn, beckoning me for a lecture.

"Women don't talk to boys out of car windows, with their tails hanging out; that's not ladylike," she'd said.

My mother would've been mortified to know I'd had unprotected sex and gotten pregnant. Her voice was clear: *that's not ladylike.*

At the time, the only other person I knew who'd had a baby as a teenager, without a husband was my grandmother's nephew's daughter. The elders in my family spoke about my cousin in hushed tones, almost pointing like children who'd spotted another pair of red shoes. I could tell they were shocked, but not surprised. My grandmother's oldest sister and her children were the type to drink, smoke, and party. It was almost expected for her to *have gotten herself pregnant and had a baby.* But not me. Grandma Hunny's children were different. Aunt Diane and my mother went to college, then wed, then had children—not the other way around. So, with an abortion, I not only escaped shame for myself but also for my family. An abortion kept our side of the family's name intact. No matter the rationale, I am grateful I was able to make my own decision about my body, even if it was to further a façade.

When we returned, Eddie's mother had made meatloaf and mashed potatoes. The meal at Eddie's house tasted like a holiday compared to the leftovers I'd been eating. I savored each bite of fresh ground beef and creamy potatoes. I lay on the sofa for several hours, fading in and out of sleep, lulled by their big-screen TV. Before I left, I hid the paper bag full of antibiotics and pain meds in my backpack and arrived at my grandparents' house around eight at night, as if I'd been working all evening.

I revised my objectives: Keep Eddie, graduate high school, then move on.

∞

Grandma Hunny's friend convinced her that I couldn't *just live with her.*

"If something happens, Hunny, then you can't even take her to the hospital because you're not her legal guardian," she said.

Two months later, in November, Grandma Hunny, Papa Henry and I drove to the Van Buren County Courthouse. My father met us there to give up his parental rights.

The judge was confused by the idea. "You know she'll be eighteen in a few months, right?"

"Not in my house," Grandma Hunny said. "Eighteen means nothing in my house!"

The judge asked when my mother died. My grandparents and father searched one another's eyes for an exact date.

"September fourth," I said.

Right before the judge granted Grandma Hunny temporary custody, my father wanted to speak. He looked right at me, but as soon as he started talking, I stared through him. The words *love, always be there,* and *temporarily* floated through the air and intermingled with the wind blowing in an opposite direction.

When he finished, Grandma Hunny looked at me and asked, "What was that all about?"

"I don't know," I replied. And had I been grown, I would've added—*and I don't give a shit.* My father chose to philander with Joëlle, instead of raising me. I chose to suppress the pain of that reality and Eddie would help me do that.

COVERT

1991

Papa Henry poured cornmeal, sugar, and boiling water into a little bowl and blended the yellow mixture. The oil he'd put in a black cast iron skillet popped and skittered, ready for him to pour tiny round cakes into it. I sat at the kitchen table and stared out of the bay window.

"What are you going to do once you graduate?" he asked.

College was a given, but unlike elementary and high school, no clear path was laid out. My mother hadn't organized that far into my life's future. I perceived living in Covert as a sort of impromptu prison sentence and had intended to pack up upon time served.

"I'm going back to Chicago," I replied.

Papa Henry flipped the hot water cornbread over.

Grandma Hunny laughed. "What are you gonna do there?"

"Go to school."

Grandma Hunny's smile remained. "Who do you think is gonna *help* you there? There's no one there to *help* you."

"You're better off staying here and going to school," Papa Henry confirmed, pouring coffee from a metal contraption.

Facing my father's abandonment was exhausting. My grandparents were right. My father had no obligation to me. He had sold the two-flat off Monitor, eloped with Joëlle, and moved in with her. Grandma Betty had moved to an independent living community on the near-North Side. She had one bedroom, one bathroom the size of a closet, a living area with space for one couch, a table, two chairs, and a kitchen with only enough room for one person. Living with either of them was not an option. I wanted to go home, but I didn't have a "home" to go to. I didn't know what type of help Grandma Hunny thought I'd need, but seeking a degree at a Michigan University made sense just in case, especially if my grandparents were going to pay for it. My new plan was to apply to Western Michigan, a university forty-five minutes away from my grandparents' house. Full liberation would have to wait.

I had the highest GPA of the seniors; however, there were rules for valedictorian status. One of them was that you could not be head of the class if you'd attended the school for only one year. I was unfazed. Being number one at Whitney Young was never in my future, so not being on top at Covert High School seemed reasonable. I wasn't supposed to be there in the first place; my enrollment was a fluke, and whoever had worked hard to be valedictorian at this school deserved it. Because of this, the president of the senior class asked me to speak at a different senior celebration.

The baccalaureate ceremony was new to me, and so was speaking in front of a crowded auditorium. But I was up for the challenge. I was honored that even though I'd declined an invitation to join the cheerleading team, I'd refused to attend sporting events, and I'd spent one hundred percent of my free time with Eddie the past eight months, for some reason they believed I should deliver a few words on their behalf.

My grandparents, aunt, and uncle attended. My father opted out. At the podium, tremors seized my hands. They had been a constant part of my life. I can't remember a day when my hands didn't tremble. It was the reason why I refused to paint my nails; red and pink polish covered more of my finger than the nail, so I stopped doing them altogether. In elementary school, the shaking worsened when faced with a teacher's question. Any paper I held would flutter and reveal a visible demonstration of my uncontrollable nervous system. The tremors returned when my mother died but had mostly subsided since I'd met Eddie.

I placed my typed remarks on the podium and prayed the audience wouldn't notice my shaky hands. I began with an analogy.

When a baby is born, it cannot walk. It crawls. Even though it has legs, they are wobbly. It seeks help from those around it, usually its parents.

I extended the metaphor.

. . . kind of like life. First, you need help finding your way, so you look around and seek assistance from those who can, usually your parents. They guide and support you.

I ended with the same comparison.

. . . though we appreciate all your help, now it's time for us to stand on our own two feet. We've learned to stand and walk, with your assistance. Now, it's time to trust that we can journey on our own.

The audience applauded. Afterward, students hugged me, and passersby congratulated me on a speech well done. The message was well-received by all, except one.

When we returned home, Grandma Hunny untied her headscarf and put her purse on the table. "I know everyone's saying how great that speech was, but I didn't like it. No. I didn't like it at all. It seemed like you were saying once you're grown, you don't need help."

That's exactly what I was saying.

"And that's just not true," she continued.

Aunt Diane never contradicted her mother when she spoke, and by now, Terry had also learned to simply smile and look preoccupied. Grandpa Henry sat in an armchair with newspaper pages spread out. I followed suit and kept quiet. However, I consciously knew I wouldn't be tied to my grandparents forever. They couldn't foresee the future I desired, which was nowhere near them. Earlier that school year, I'd told Grandma Hunny and my Aunt Diane that I had no intention of living in Michigan after college.

After my proclamation, they exchanged glances. Then, my grandmother said, "You don't know where you're gonna live."

"You might live in Detroit," Aunt Diane added.

When she was younger, my grandmother had given up an opportunity to apply for nursing school in the state of Washington. When I inquired why, she yelled, "Washington? Washington! Do you know how far away Washington is . . . away from my mama and papa?!?" Fear kept her grounded. Grandma Hunny's two older sisters lived upstairs from one another in a two-flat, until their deaths; her oldest sister's daughter and son lived across the street in their own building. My grandmother was the first of her sisters to leave Chicago and live with her husband, but it wasn't across the country. It was across the lake.

Aunt Diane earned two degrees and fell in love along the way. Her boyfriend, who she'd met in college, lived in California. She followed him there, but for some reason, returned to Michigan and never remained more than two hours away from her mother. Living close was the prototype. Depending on each other was the model. The family needed one another, and one had to be in proximity to provide support. But by seventeen, Grandma Betty and my father had shown me differently. In some ways, my mother had, too. I'd learned that family could be physically close, but emotionally distant. A family could be close enough to bring a loaf of bread, but never near enough to touch one's suffering. And so, I had decided early on that I wouldn't adopt my family's example. My baccalaureate speech conveyed this, and perhaps, the thought of me living farther than two hours away scared Grandma Hunny.

Prom had been an event in which I'd planned to participate no matter where I graduated high school. The day of, I drove to a department store's salon in a nearby town to touch up my relaxer and freshen up my haircut, which was now an asymmetrical bob. The right side was layered, and the left hung past my ears, like Pepa from Salt-N-Pepa. Next, I went to the store's makeup counter, where a cosmetologist applied foundation and lipstick for free. Months prior, Joëlle gave me the number to her seamstress friend. After a couple of trips to her friend's house in Chicago and a few hundred dollars later, the dress was completed. It was white, satin, and sleeveless, and like my hair, asymmetrical. The left side stopped right above the knee, while the right side went a little past. A big, black bow was connected at the waist. Except for a broken zipper, which Grandma Hunny fixed minutes before I left, the dress was perfect.

Eddie wore a black tuxedo. We indulged my grandmother with traditional prom pictures in the living room. One together, one with my grandparents, and one with the four of us. At the venue we participated in obligatory prom behavior: dinner and official pictures in front of a fake backdrop. An hour later, we left with another couple.

For the majority of my senior year, if I wasn't at work or school, I was with Eddie. I was rarely interested in what the township or the school offered and created a chimera of companionship where only he and I existed. One night I told my grandmother I was driving to Walmart. Instead, I drove to Eddie's. Time stood still while we watched TV. But it kept moving at Grandma Hunny's house. I arrived home an hour and a half later for what should've been a twenty-four-minute trip.

"Where have you been?"

"Walmart."

She snatched my glasses off with one hand while simultaneously slapping me, an art she'd perfected while raising my mother and aunt.

"Don't lie to me ever again. I saw your car at Eddie's house."

The left side of my face stung. I never told her another verbal fabrication. Instead, I began sneaking out. There was no waking my grandparents once they closed their eyes for the evening. I would slowly re-dress and wait for Eddie to pull his mother's Chevy to the front of the house. He would sit with the headlights out. One time we drove to a house party somewhere deep in the woods in somebody's trailer.

"Kathy?" my cousin, Bobby squinted.

"Oh shit! Please don't tell Grandma," I begged.

He laughed. "Don't worry, girl. Your secret's safe with me."

Another time we drove to Chicago in the middle of the night with Eddie's older brother. Sneaking home for a few hours of partying was pacifying. Then, there was the time we simply drove back to his house. His brother had a party. He and Eddie cut open a watermelon and poured liquor inside. Eddie and I nestled into a corner of their pool and lost ourselves in gin and one another. The euphoria of our relationship was tangible. Life was tolerable with Eddie. Every time our bodies wrapped around one another, I felt like the most important person in his universe, so we had as much sex as humanly possible. But I was a teenage girl who hadn't mastered a birth control pill regimen. I was pregnant again by April. I had my second abortion before May—right before baccalaureate, prom, and graduation. This time there was no meatloaf or mashed potatoes, just judgment and disregard.

Our destination prom night was Eddie's friend's house. But that didn't work, so his friend led us to a vacant home. The four of us bought and drank bottles on bottles of gin. Eddie and I had sex on a dusty round bed. The other couple spent time in an adjacent room. Gin filled my belly and revealed an erratic array of emotions. First one tear, then another. The next thing I knew, I was sobbing hysterically.

"I don't love you, Eddie. You were just something to do while I was here in this fucked up town."

There was truth in the statement. Our relationship shouldn't have lasted as long as it did. Had we been in Chicago, we would've had options and separated. We had what is now called a toxic relationship. There was the time I contracted crabs, and when I asked him how these tiny bugs could have possibly infiltrated my pubic area, he said it was because I was fond of petting stray dogs. There was the time I saw him driving his mother's blue Chevy with another girl in the passenger seat. We drove fast and furious through the streets of South Haven as if we were in a car chase scene from a movie franchise. Liquid courage allowed me to reveal what my adolescent mind knew, and body sensed. What actually happened is that I was in the early stages of using sex to regulate my emotions, to calm my tremors. While the effects of sex: easing anxiety and depression are normal biological functions,[1] using sex as a coping mechanism, whether consciously or unconsciously, to ease stress and anxiety is unhealthy.[2] But what did either of us know? I was seventeen and had learned to use sex like cigarettes; he was sixteen and thrilled that I was the one to help him lose his virginity.

He moved away from me. "Fuck you then!" he shouted.

"I didn't mean to say that. It's the liquor. I swear," I apologized my words away, and said sorry for telling the truth.

Afterward, I vomited on the bed.

He forgave me.

We stayed in that empty house drinking, having sex, arguing, crying, laughing, and sleeping, until Eddie's friend's sister knocked on the door. It was five in the morning.

"What are you doing in here? And Kathy? Your grandmother is looking for you. Put your clothes on and get out of here!"

My head rang as Eddie pulled into Grandma Hunny's driveway. She met me at the screen door. "You're not grown. Who do you think you are? You were supposed to go to prom and come home, not spend the night out." Her rhetorical questions were reminiscent of my mother's. The familiarity silenced me.

I *was* grown. The judge said it. The court documented it: Temporary custody until May 23, 1991. And I was scheduled to graduate in less than two weeks. Covert and Eddie were about to be memories, as planned.

∞

My father visited twice after he gave up his parental rights. The first time was two days before Thanksgiving. He, Joëlle, and I were scheduled to spend the holiday in New Orleans with her daughter, who attended Xavier. Plans changed because they didn't have the funds for the three of us to vacation together. They drove me to Chicago, where I independently flew standby. I enjoyed partying with college upperclassmen, but the idea incensed my grandmother. Upon my return, I overheard Grandma Hunny tell my father the two of them couldn't operate like this. Rumor has it that she also told him to leave me alone. The next time my father came to Covert was six months later for graduation.

In addition to my father, Grandma Betty, Diamond, and other North Carolina cousins surprised me. Mika and another friend from high school drove over. Having familiar faces surround me provided the regularity I craved. Sitting on the auditorium's stage with twenty-four other seniors was less lonely and embarrassing with family and friends there. They reminded me that I hadn't been forgotten.

In preparation for company, my grandmother had asked me if I wanted to have an open house after the ceremony. Parties were a huge part of my childhood. I'd watched my mother create instant celebrations for the most trivial of achievements, proclaiming, "Punch, is just punch; punch in a punchbowl is a party!" I agreed to an open house, thinking Grandma Hunny would assume this responsibility. I was surprised when she agreed, but said I'd have to pay for and organize it myself. Times like these were when I missed my mother the most. She would've delighted in the idea of preparing an open house for my high school graduation, all while I survived several interrelated traumas.

I wanted to celebrate, so I accepted the task. Blue balloons and matching plastic flatware filled the dank basement. *Congratulations Kathy!* was written in blue icing on the sheet cake I'd ordered. After graduation, family and friends caught up and I soaked up what I perceived as love—attention.

Joëlle hadn't come, but she'd sent a gift with my father. I began to open the large rectangular object.

"Be careful," my father beamed with pride.

The wrapping held a golden frame. Inside was a collage of pictures from the time I was a baby through the age of sixteen. It was a tradition she'd begun with her children. One hung in each of their bedrooms and now I'd have my own.

"Don't forget the card," my father said.

I read it silently.

Congratulations on your graduation! Remember to be as nice as you look in these pictures. No one likes a nasty little girl.

Swallowing emotions was second nature. Ignoring the stress that was stacked in my stomach was commonplace. "Tell Joëlle I said, 'Thank you.'" I wondered if that was nice enough, or if I should add a fake smile to cover-up the hurt of being denigrated by my father's current wife.

Once everyone left, I showed my grandmother.

"It's such a thoughtful gift, but the card is like wrapping it with trash. You just have to focus on the gift," she said.

I tried, but I'd also acquired a knack for internalizing events and ruminating. Had my father read and co-signed Joëlle's words? Was I a 'nasty little girl?' Is that why I was sent away, so they could live happily ever after, without my *nasty* interference?

My grandparents were right, and my baccalaureate speech was premature. Obviously, I was going to need help; and when I did, it would come from my grandparents. My new goal was to attend Western for four years and never look back.

ADDICTED

WILL

1991 - 1993

Addiction is rooted in trauma.[1] However, there is a difference between Trauma and trauma.[2] Trauma is perceived as a singular event that changes a person and her life, such as fleeing a country due to war or being raped by a family friend. Society implicitly agrees that events like these are disturbing and can cause PTSD.

Conversely, trauma refers to a series of smaller events experienced over a period of time; how one responds to trauma differs and depends on each individual's capacity to deal with stress, which varies for everyone.[3]

Death of a parent, car accidents, and sudden relocation are types of traumas, but are perceived as common: Death occurs. Accidents happen. Teenagers move. However, experiencing a series of trauma in a short time frame,[4] in addition to how the traumatized person and those around her react to the trauma, affects how the person learns to deal with life.[5] When caretakers treat traumas as ordinary events, the person affected does not receive the support or comfort needed to heal. Likewise, if traumas are avoided or downplayed by the person who experiences them, this can lead to "a disruption in emotional function"[6] or what is now commonly referred to as emotional dysregulation.[7] Psychological trauma can ensue.[8] As a result, addiction forms as an attempt to regulate emotions; it's an effort to assuage discomfort.[9]

This is how life culminated for me in the fall of 1991. I unconsciously packed my trauma and dysregulated emotions alongside crates of clothing and notebooks and pursued a bachelor's degree. My family seemed to breathe a collective sigh of relief at the idea. *She made it. All is well.* Their unspoken words were expressed in every exhale. The thoughts were mutual. Attending college was proof of wellness. However, my actual well-being was never investigated.

Western was a university of hills. Classes were atop a hill. The dorm where I lived was down a hill in an area called The Valley. My roommate, Shamika, was a Covert graduate who had befriended me. I had settled into the room a couple of days before her arrival where I snuggled in my bed satisfied with beginning a new phase of my life.

When Shamika arrived, so did several roaches. Brown insects of varied sizes crawled out of staplers and milled about her bedposts. By the second week of the first semester, my grandmother paid extra for me to room alone. A single room provided excess freedom and allowed Eddie, who was finishing high school, to frequently spend the night. Semester one of college was similar to my senior year. I made few friends, studied, partied occasionally, and awaited Eddie's visits.

The second semester of undergrad, I was pregnant a third time.

I was no longer ignorant about how babies were conceived, or what I was supposed to do to prevent such an occurrence. What my father hadn't shared, Planned Parenthood had explained several times over. The error rested in taking birth control seriously and consistently. But this is hindsight. At eighteen, internalizing thoughts grew increasingly self-deprecating, a common occurrence in traumatized people. I was convinced I must have either been the dumbest teenager to ever live or fated to have Eddie's baby.

I'd independently paid for the first two abortions; however, this time, I was penniless. I was stuck and needed help; my baccalaureate speech taunted me. Eddie's mother convinced him that he didn't know whose baby this was. After all, I had been in college for months, and who knows what or who I was doing? Eddie knew. He'd spent several weekends in my dorm bed and was the father, yet he refused to help.

I called Grandma Hunny.

"I'm having a baby," I whispered.

"What?"

"I'm pregnant."

"We're going to Planned Parenthood. I'll call you tomorrow and let you know when," she decided.

My voice raised, "No. I'm having a baby."

"Do you *want* to have a baby? You have to finish school. You know, it's not murder or anything like that. What you have now is a *mass*. It's not even a *baby* yet. How are you going to have a baby? Who's going to watch the baby?"

"Shamika."

"The girl with roaches?" Grandma Hunny laughed. "I'll be there tomorrow," she said and hung up the phone.

Revealing to her that I'd already endured this procedure would also require telling her they'd bookended my senior year under her care. I lacked the courage and didn't want to add further disappointment, so I called my father.

"Daddy, I'm pregnant," I said when he answered the phone. "Grandma Hunny wants me to have an abortion."

"You have to make that decision. Whatever decision you make, you're the one who has to live with it. Just know I'll be there for you whatever you decide," he said.

I'd waited for the day to control my life, but not like this. My baccalaureate speech reverberated in the back of my brain: *Now, it's time to trust that we can journey on our own.* I wanted my father to simply tell me what to do. I wished I could will my mother back to life. She would have assumed control and an abortion would not be the answer. I remembered how concerned she was when Tee, one of my Sunday school friends, was pregnant, and how disappointed she was when Tee chose abortion. One thing was clear. I couldn't trust my father's words. He hadn't "been there for me" the past few years, so I was doubtful that he'd suddenly "be there" for a grandchild. My grandmother arranged and paid for my third abortion.

She filled the car with conversation on the way to the clinic, and on the way back. I wanted to dissolve into the landscape that whizzed outside the window.

"Don't you feel better? Like a weight has been lifted?" she asked.

Avoidance.

"Umm-hmmm," I answered.

Except, I didn't. Having one abortion due to making a mistake as a clueless teenager was one thing, but having a third one, as a result of not taking a birth control pill on a schedule was embarrassing. This abortion carried three times the shame. Who gets pregnant consecutive times? Only losers, I'd decided. Who has had three abortions in less than two years? Just me, I figured. In my adolescent mind, having a baby was less disgraceful than having a third abortion, so I encased myself in a layer of self-loathing, not realizing that having the baby and becoming a teenage mother could have carried with it countless unknowns, stigmas, and its own kind of shame.

Eddie and I should have separated after the third pregnancy. For some reason, I couldn't, and I leaned into the opposite action—I told him when he graduated, we could get an apartment. I fantasized with him about marrying and having kids. It was a grand narrative, with which I conspired and filled with bold lies. Grandma Hunny would never allow me to move into an apartment with a boy while pursuing a degree she and my grandfather paid for. Furthermore, if I wanted to have his children, I could have by now. I didn't want to—and I really didn't want him.

In year two, Eddie graduated and began to fulfill the first part of our pledge: he attended a business college in the same town where I was. He'd rented an apartment less than fifteen minutes away. But I'd met a new boy. His name was Will. He was from Detroit. It was his first year. He was an education major, like me.

His birthday was in May, like mine. He was an only child, like me. His glasses were as thick as the bottom of a throwback Coke bottle, but that was okay. Our meeting was destined. Will and I had sex within the week. Like Kenny and Tré, he pumped and panted on top of me, while I lay there, daydreaming. My relationship with Eddie lingered in the background.

Our commonalities meant Will and I were supposed to be together. However, other parts of our connection proved otherwise. The first incident was when Will's favorite cousin, Tammy Junior came to campus. I'd never heard of a girl being a junior, but Will said she was named after her mother. Tammy Junior had protected him throughout childhood, which explained how he made it unscathed with his glasses in a Detroit public school.

"She's meeting us at the football game," he said. "Don't be nervous. As long as you don't do anything to hurt me, she's cool."

Tammy Junior and Will sat next to each other behind me. I stared at the field in silence.

"What you tell her? She looks scared to death!" she laughed.

"Just told her not to do anything to piss you off."

Clarity is oftentimes presented in spurts; flashes of intuition beg to be heard. Sitting at that football game in front of Tammy Junior, I suspected Will wasn't my forever love, but like my continued relationship with Eddie, I feared a break-up. I didn't want to be alone.

Will and I took a semi-independent road trip to Chicago. He and I drove the Marquis my grandparents had given me, while my grandparents trailed behind. We popped a cassette tape in and sang Shai's "If I Ever Fall in Love" in perfect harmony.

"Rewind that. Let's sing it again," he urged.

"And if I e…," I began.

"Noooo. Like it was last time," he whined.

"I did sing it like last time."

"No, you didn't," he said and pressed stop. We drove in silence for the remaining hour.

The road trip confirmed my feelings, but we remained in a relationship.

For another getaway, Will took me to his home in Rosedale Park. He'd spoken about his military retired father and beautiful mother with such fondness that I couldn't wait to meet them.

"So, you're from Chicago?" his mother asked as she handed me a bathrobe to cover up my pajama shorts.

"Yes," I said, tying the sash.

"So, tell me. Do you prefer Neiman Marcus or Lord & Taylor?"

What a strange question. In general, my mother shopped at a store called Venture, a place that sold stale pizza and clothes. It's where I received my first relaxer. If she was fancy, then we'd go to JCPenney; we went to Marshall Fields to splurge, and Neiman Marcus when red tags signaled there was something she could afford.

"Neiman Marcus," I answered, "'Cause they have more sales." I sensed the answer was inadequate for her monogrammed bath towels and petite hand soap.

The four of us stared at the television. Will and I sat on the couch, backs aligned with their taut sofa, chins tucked. His parents sat in Victorian-style armchairs. The next day we saw a movie and then his parents drove us back to campus.

Will and I argued constantly. One day, he was so infuriated that he hurled an apple onto my dorm wall, scaring the shit out of me. Most of the apple fell, but a lot of chunks hung onto the white stucco for the remainder of the semester, symbolic of our union. His friends thought I was being abused, so they told a professor, who happened to be friends with my grandmother.

"Are you okay?" she asked.

I assured my grandmother I wasn't being abused, and I grew less fond of Will as the semester wore on. I began to strategize. I'd wait until Christmas break and slowly cease communication when we returned for classes after the new year.

Of the three months of the Fall semester, I spent the night at Eddie's apartment once, where we argued about my leaving the bathroom wrapped in a towel, while his friends sat in plain view. It was something he'd brought up senior year when we went swimming at Covert's pool.

"You like the attention," he said.

"What are you talking about?"

"You saw all those dudes looking at you in your swimsuit. You liked it," he accused.

I denied it, the same way I denied trying to show myself to his friends, who sat around his kitchen table, making eye contact with me when I left the shower. I couldn't help where their eyes landed. It seemed delusional that we considered ourselves still together. Eddie lived in the background of my new life, one where I spent more time on campus and was sexually active with Will. There was nothing secret about my relationship with Will, but I consciously kept it from Eddie. I knew having two boyfriends was wrong but holding on to both of them felt secure.

One night, I returned to the dorm after studying at the library. As soon as I walked through the door, the front desk receptionist looked as if he'd seen a ghost. He said someone had left a package for me. It was a portrait a New Orleans street artist had drawn.

Each side of the plastic frame was crumpled in several sections. The picture was scratched and torn as if someone had punched the middle. Smudged and smeared charcoal replaced what were once beautiful lines, illustrating the contours of my face.

I'd given the portrait to Eddie a year prior when I returned from Thanksgiving with my new stepsiblings. A voicemail from him confirmed he'd returned it to the front desk. He was looking for me. He was pissed. My heart raced as I dialed his number. He'd run into a man I'd briefly dated named, Jamal at a fast-food restaurant. I met Jamal when I initially moved from Chicago. That summer, I stayed with Aunt Diane and Terry for a few weeks. Somehow, Jamal and Eddie realized they not only both knew me, but that I had also agreed to the same grandiose lie: moving into an apartment, marrying them, and having kids.

Eddie was on his way back to the dorm to "talk about it in person." I told him I had a new boyfriend, who would be happy to engage in dialogue. Will rounded up his two friends. Eddie came with two friends. Six men stood in the hall and glared at one another. No fight ensued, but Eddie and I officially broke up. Surface-level descriptions dubbed me a cheating girlfriend, not a traumatized little girl addicted to men and sex. Onlookers judged this event as a drama-filled mess created by an inconsiderate young woman. At the time, I agreed. I felt as if someone was pointing at me, whispering, "Red shoes, red shoes." I didn't know how to be in a relationship with men. I just knew how to enact unhealthy coping mechanisms to deal with the trauma I'd ignored.

∞

"Alphas are having a house party. Let's go," Keisha said.

She and I met during our first year of undergrad. Partying with her and our friends, Kenya and Ami was commonplace. We poured cup after cup of pink Boone's Farm in between choosing outfits, doing hair, and applying makeup.

"You wearing those black Girbaud's again?" Kenya asked.

"You know she is," Keisha answered for me.

I was. They were my favorite. A colorful rayon blouse and a pair of black suede booties made it look like I'd tried, but not too hard.

As usual, we piled into Ami's Saturn and bounced along with "Hot Sex's" hard baseline. We arrived to find people lounging on couches and sipping from red cups, while rap music blared.

Within ten minutes, a guy approached me. We swooned over being from the same hometown. Instead of shouting over lyrics, we agreed to go where we could hear one another. A quiet place was the apartment owner's bedroom. Our conversation was immemorable. One of us turned off the lights. As we sat on the bed and continued talking, I reached to unbutton his pants, confident we were ready for the same thing. He pushed my hands away.

Drunkenness and ego formed my confusion. "What's wrong?" I asked.

"Nothing. Let's just talk."

"You don't wanna fuck?"

"No. Let's just talk," he insisted.

We talked. We drank. We kissed. I undressed. Surely, my naked body would shift his stance. It always did. This time, it didn't. He sat on the bed fully clothed, telling me how beautiful I was, while I begged for intercourse.

"Why won't you fuck me?"

A commotion on the other side of the door disrupted my childlike pleas. "In here?" Keisha said as she flung the door open and flipped on the lights. Five people trailed behind her. "Kathy! You, okay?"

"Yes," I answered, the room's brightness spotlighting my nudity.

"You wanna be here?" she confirmed.

"Yes. Can you turn off the lights and leave?"

"I just wanna make sure you *wanna* be here."

"Yes," I assured. "I want to be here."

She and everyone else pivoted. The room darkened, and I re-dressed. I took a deep breath and stared straight ahead in preparation to walk down the hall, which seemed longer than I remembered.

"Are we leaving soon?" I asked Ami as I held the doorknob.

"In a minute."

I sat at the top of the stairs outside of the apartment door. Five minutes passed. Then, fifteen. Thirty minutes later, I assumed we weren't leaving, so I began to walk.

My toes tingled in the Michigan snow. A white outline of salt damage formed on the edges of my booties. It would be the last time I'd wear them.

I contemplated the previous four years. What was I doing wrong?

The next morning, I listened through the wall as Keisha recounted the night's events to Riki, my suitemate.

"Hey, girl!" Keisha hollered when I opened the bathroom door connecting our rooms. "Where'd you go?"

"I walked back."

"From the apartment to the Valley?" she asked, then she shrugged. "Kenya and I are going to a party on campus tonight. You going?"

"Yep," I replied with confidence.

"I didn't think you'd wanna go…after last night."

I'd already suppressed the previous night's events and was ready to follow our weekend ritual and walk to the next party.

House music vibrated throughout the empty gymnasium's walls. A group of people danced in a small circle. I found a random guy to sway in rhythm with and watched Keisha out of the corner of my eye, laughing and talking with the DJ. The music lowered, and I heard her voice over the microphone.

"I'd like to dedicate this song to my girl!" she shouted. "You know who you are!"

Then, one of the most popular house songs at the time played.

There're some whores in this house.

There're some whores in this house.

My insides burned as the refrain repeated. But I refused for her or anyone else to bear witness to my raw emotion. I'd been through worse. I raised my arms high and flailed them about, signaling that her attempt at humiliating me was a failure.

"Heeeey!" I shouted as naturally as I could, hoping my words were loud enough to hear. "Thanks, girl!"

Avoidance.

My dance partner cocked his head at my overreaction. "Oh. That's my girl," I explained. "She just dedicated this song to me."

That night, I returned to the dorm with a new moniker—ho. I was wearing red shoes and people were pointing. But I refused to call myself that. It seemed crass. Instead, I began proclaiming *I liked sex.* Doesn't everyone?

The winter semester wore on. Ami faded into the background of campus life. Keisha, Kenya, and I didn't speak much, except when I asked if they knew who put dog shit on my doorknob. They assured me they did not.

∞

After I was christened a ho, I spent fewer weekends on campus and more time returning to the city that offered indescribable solace. Chicago cradled me. Its busyness, tall buildings, and bright lights slowed my heart rate. My reputation preceded me on campus, so I snuck home as often as possible. One of the seven credit cards I'd attained guaranteed a Greyhound or Amtrak ride. The blue line took me straight to Grandma Betty's house, where I knew my secret was safe; she never told her son where I was. We both knew my whereabouts were irrelevant to him, anyway.

When I was home, I met up with friends with whom I should've graduated high school. We'd sweat for hours at the Warehouse, lost in the deep bass of tribal beats. That's where I met a fraternity boy from Western Illinois. Long-distance phone calls meant we were a couple; sometimes, we'd meet up in the city. He wore a crimson red jacket everywhere we went and blurted out *"Bum stiggedy, bum stiggedy, bum hon,"* the beginning of a Das Effect song, every five minutes or so, out of the blue. Attention from this new beau overshadowed his bizarre, Tourette-like outbursts. We'd walk on Lake Michigan, eat a deep dish at Giordano's, and spend hours in a hotel room having sex.

"I have AIDS," he announced one time.

I felt lightheaded. *What the hell?* I thought. "You have what?"

"AIDS," he repeated as if he was gesturing outside of the window, admiring the John Hancock Center.

"Why would you have sex *and then* tell me?"

"Just kidding, girl. I don't have AIDS," he laughed. Then, he turned serious. "But what if I did? You don't really know me. You have to be more careful."

Fraternity Boy had a point. Although I rarely saw Will, I'd had a threesome with the Director of Multicultural Affairs and one of his friends. Occasionally, I'd meet up with a married man I'd met at a Chicago club. But why would I stop? Every time a man told me I was pretty or undressed me with his eyes or hands, I felt my significance and value in the world increased and my stress level decreased. The admiration boosted my confidence and sex cemented my self-worth. How could I stop? I was deep into chasing waterfalls, the unimaginable depths of the springs dark, but I knew how to tread water. I knew how to swim.

BRENT

SUMMER 1993

U ndergrad was separated into two phases: before the Alpha incident and after it. Brent and I met in 1992 before the incident. Summer school provided a place for me to reside instead of my grandparents' house. There was no issue convincing my grandparents of the value of attending college during the summer months. They agreed to anything related to academics. But students were scarce from May through August, and activities were scarcer. My mother always said, "If you're bored, then you must be a boring person." Meaning, you should always know how to entertain yourself.

In May 1992, I was determined not to be a boring person. Though, walking around the mall, which took about fifteen minutes, was my only choice of entertainment. Before driving back to my aunt's apartment, I stopped across the street, ordered a burrito supreme and hard-shell taco, and settled into my seat.

His bronze complexion and reddish-brown hair caught my eye as soon as he entered the restaurant. He and his friend sat ten feet away in front of the restaurant's window. I looked everywhere, except in their direction. I bit into my food and stared into oblivion, pretending not to notice him as he walked toward me. He stood in my peripheral, just a few inches taller.

"Excuse me," he started. "Do you have the time?"

His hazel brown eyes were captivating. I glanced at his watch, then at mine. *Cute*, I thought. I gave him the time and he turned to walk away.

"Is that all you wanted?" I asked.

He clasped his hands in front of him. "Well, no. Actually, I wanted to know if I could have your number?" He flashed the brightest, whitest, straightest smile. I'd never seen anyone like him before, yet our meeting was familiar.

"Do I know you? Are you from Chicago?" I asked while writing my number on a napkin.

"No. No. I'm from Detroit," he said with pride. "I'll give you a call."

Brent visited me at Aunt Diane's apartment. We sat on the bedroom floor, leaned against the sofa bed, and pontificated about life.

"It's gonna take a long time to kiss you, huh?" I asked.

He scratched his head, confused by the statement. He didn't want to touch me. He didn't want to kiss. He wanted to get to know me. We planned a formal date for when the semester began, but it never occurred. During those months I was preoccupied with Will, Eddie, the fraternity guy, and whoever else gratified my sexual whims. But we did run into each other a few times on campus. Each time I saw him, I showed all thirty-two teeth, and yelled, *heeeey*! And each time, Brent offered a stoic glance, lifted his hand, and offered a quiet *hi*.

I had no reason to believe that when I saw him walking in, the summer of 1993, after the Alpha incident that he'd do more than glimpse my way and sheepishly raise his hand. But I slowed to a five-mile-per-hour roll anyway and hollered, "Heeeey! You need a ride?"

He shrugged and said, "Sure."

Brent exuded calm. He softly sang Swing Out Sister songs and moved his fingers melodically in the air to the rhythm of Boney James. Even his favorite A Tribe Called Quest songs were those that featured Q-Tip's smooth lyricism, as opposed to the party hits I bobbed my head to. Brent embodied positive energy, and as a result, became my sun. Just as the sun provides life for human beings, so did Brent for me. I bathed in his rays, and each moment we were together, my collection of traumas seemed to disappear.

Eddie and I had spent a lot of time together, but it was oriented toward sex. Brent and I interacted in ways new to me. Our first date was a movie. Afterward, we stood outside his apartment, and he bounced a ball.

"You want to play four square?" he asked.

"What's that?"

"You've never played four square?" he asked incredulously. "I'll show you. The ball can only hit the ground once. You have to hit the ball back to me before it hits the ground a second time."

We laughed and joked, while we bounced the ball back and forth. Playing with other children my age wasn't a significant part of my life unless I was at school, and even then, it was a structured lesson for gym class. Playing as a young adult with a man who was interested in me was foreign, yet inviting. Brent and I wandered hand-in-hand into the comic book store, a place I'd never been. While much of my childhood was filled with reading books in neighborhood libraries, Brent had delved into comic books and their characters. He shared his affection for Green Lantern and Black Bolt. He compared the difference between the movie and television Batman with versions he'd read. I absorbed his lessons and eventually watched *Batman* every afternoon, so I could relate.

Brent enjoyed drinking as much as I did, and his two-and-a-half-year age difference meant my friends and I didn't have to pay the local homeless guy to buy liquor. One night, after we'd had several drinks, I returned to my room to retrieve a pack of Newports, a habit I'd developed senior year. Smoking was strictly reserved for post-drinking to maintain a relaxed state. I pulled out a cigarette and placed it between my lips.

"What's that?" he asked. "What're you doing?"

"A cigarette," I replied.

"Ummm. I can't be with someone who smokes," he said.

I placed the tube back in the pack, threw it away, and never lit another for fear of losing him.

We double-dated with Riki, one of the last college relationships I'd maintained with a girl. Her boyfriend played Chanté Moore throughout the night. I'd heard Moore's lyrics before, but somehow, they held new meaning with Brent by my side. Our date began at Red Lobster, where even though Brent had little money, he dined on salad and cheddar biscuits, while I cracked crab legs and dipped the meat into a small ramekin of butter. Afterward, we went to a nearby park, where he pushed me on a swing. Riki and her boyfriend watched.

"Brini," the nickname Riki had given me—short for Cabrini Green, her sole knowledge of Chicago—"You're in love!" she exclaimed.

My insides softened, and we frequently gazed into each other's eyes, but the "L" word was excessive, especially when I'd used it before with people like Eddie and then discovered it was the other "L" word —lust. So, I avoided saying it and focused on the time Brent and I shared.

I thought the lack of honesty is what had kept me in so much drama the previous year and had secretly promised myself to be as truthful as possible with anyone new. I tested this newfound authenticity with Brent.

"I'm adopted," I shared.

"That's cool, so is my cousin."

"My mom died when I was sixteen."

"That must've been really hard for you."

"My dad gave up his parental rights and sent me to live with my grandparents when I was seventeen. I hate him." I braced myself. Surely, he'd think I was like the banged-up cereal box everyone avoids at the grocery store.

"A lot happened, huh?" He put his hand on my heart. "So much hate in there. You have to let it go."

I recounted the sex. The abortions. The Alpha incident—which had now grown into a campus rumor that I'd had sex with six men in one night. I'd been immortalized into a superwhore.

He'd already heard. "I don't care about any of that," he said. "I just like you, the way you are. None of those people have the right to judge you. Everybody's having sex." Then, he surprised me. "I love you."

Hearing him profess his love was intoxicating. I wanted him to say it repeatedly. So, he did. I was in disbelief, and although I felt similar, I couldn't return the phrase. Maybe I didn't know what love was. Maybe my feelings were betraying me again. It seemed love-like, but I wanted to be sure I wasn't saying it as a favor, and there was another thing to tell him.

Will hadn't been a part of my life, sexually or otherwise, since the middle of the previous semester, but we hadn't formally broken up. When classes ended, he left campus with an open invitation to visit him during the summer; instead, I was enmeshed with Brent.

"I have a boyfriend," I revealed. "But we can be friends."

"I don't need any more friends," he said. "You have to choose. Either me or him. You can't be with both of us."

Brent had given me an ultimatum for something I'd never done before—end a relationship before fully committing to a new one. The choice was clear. Will was expendable. Brent wasn't. Brent had unconsciously disentangled the bundle of stress my nervous system had become and served as a source of co-regulation.[1] His calm calmed me. In retrospect, I could have broken up with Will over the phone, but in my new sense of "authenticity," I chose to tell him to his face. Two weeks later, I caught a ride to Detroit with Riki.

I'd intended to tell Will when I arrived, but he nearly jumped up and down with excitement describing the evening's events, depleting my courage. Our date began at a greasy shack, where we ate frog legs and fries. Next, we saw a movie. I flinched when Will grabbed my hand and wished it were Brent's. I'd talked myself into telling him once the credits rolled; however, I grew physically ill and blamed it on eating oily amphibian appendages. As soon as the movie ended, I passed out in the lobby.

"Her blood pressure is really low. Is she pregnant?" I heard the paramedic ask as I faded in and out of consciousness.

My eyes rolled around out of focus. Will's thick lenses magnified his bulging pupils; he stared two inches away from my face. "*Are* you pregnant?"

"What? No. Of course not."

I broke up with him before I returned to campus.

Riki rocked me back-and-forth, while I cried. *How could I be so fucking stupid?*

Brent scratched his head. "We're not ready for a baby."

"But I can't have another abortion. You're about to graduate. We would make great parents," I reasoned.

"I love you. But we're not ready for a baby."

I didn't want Brent to leave, so at twenty years old, I scheduled my fourth abortion in three years. I returned to Chicago so as not to use Kalamazoo's Planned Parenthood. Mika traveled with me to the facility nearest to Grandma Betty's apartment.

"You know you can't keep using abortions as birth control," Mika warned.

I knew.

"And you've been sneaking home, partying?" she scolded.

I knew. It had mostly stopped, but the city, with its house-music scene and my high school friends, called to me. I exhaled whenever I arrived.

The Chicago clinic was larger, whiter, and resembled a hospital. White blankets were neatly folded over the arms of leather recliners. Next to each was a table with water and medication. I sank deep into the overstuffed chair, while the nurse covered my shivering body.

"Take these," she showed me the pills. "It's for the pain."

I knew.

The familiarity was shameful, the process lonely. Riki was in Detroit. I thought of Brent; passing one class determined he'd graduate. He'd paid for the procedure, so his absence was forgivable.

The nurse checked my general well-being and returned with a brown paper bag. "Your pills, condoms, and pamphlets are in here. Who's driving you home?"

"We took the bus."

"You couldn't get someone to drive?"

"No." Her eyes shifted from judgment to concern and then sorrow. "I'll be fine," I replied.

Hiding most of the pain and walking towards Mika, I vowed to be more diligent with protecting myself, but not out of concern for my health. In four weeks, Brent had introduced me to a new way of being in the world; he'd provided a safe space, and I feared what would happen should he leave.

The remaining eight weeks held a steady stream of love, liquor, conversation, and sex. Brent and I held hands and walked in the rain. When the sun shone, we stopped and lie on the campus grass, staring at the sky. We maximized our limited time. Fourth of July weekend, I trekked home for a festival, called the Taste. My friends and I visited our favorite booths, and I met another man. It was the first time I lacked interest in being chosen. Experiences without Brent lacked luster. Late that night, I called him as I prepared to sleep on Grandma Betty's couch.

"I love you," I confessed. "I realized it today."

With proclamations of love floating around, Brent and I began planning for the future. Before our meeting, he had planned to move to D.C. or work on a cruise ship after graduation. Neither of these goals included living in Kalamazoo for two years, while I finished my degree.

"Don't go," I begged.

Brent agreed, and upon graduating chose to move back to his parents' Detroit home because it was the best place for him to attain a job. Our relationship continued long-distance.

Before he left, I revealed a final truth, "I've cheated on everyone I've been with."

"How do I know you're not going to cheat on me?" he asked.

I looked at him and replied, "I just won't."

This wasn't a lie. I believed my words. I thought cheating was tied to willpower and a sense of morality. I thought having sex outside of a committed relationship was about making conscious choices about the type of person I wanted to be at each moment. I thought cheating was about upbringing. Cheaters came from "bad" homes, where they witnessed cheating. I thought connecting with a great guy, with whom I felt safe and secure would save me from wanting to have sex with other men. I thought wrong.

UNDERGRAD

1994

Change is inevitable, but it is not something I've ever known how to deal with. The next two semesters were filled with inescapable change. Fall brought a chill, but romance lingered. Love sustained me throughout the weeks and helped me to focus on studying. Riki and I had become best friends and lived as roommates in another dorm on the nicer side of campus with third- and fourth-year students, who dedicated their time to school or work. Brent began his first job after graduation as an accountant at The Detroit News. An adult salary equaled financial freedom. At twenty-three years old, he maintained the type of college life with which he'd grown accustomed, but this time with money, his childhood friends, and no rent payment. His job allowed him to make frequent Greyhound bus trips back to Western, a choice he made because he had no car, and because his parents had restricted me from spending the night at their house. A bus ticket was less expensive than two nights at a hotel.

Life was good. Easy. I no longer had to tread water. I could float.

But seasons change. In Winter 1994, I was hired as a resident assistant in a dorm. Room and board were benefits of the job, which placed me one step closer to being independent of my grandparents. I rolled huge white bins up and down the hill back to the Valley for the new position. Winter also afforded Brent transportation; he bought a burgundy Eagle Talon. His new car and my single room as an RA helped him to visit more and allowed us to establish the routine of our relationship. Every Friday, by eight at night, he picked me up in front of the dorm. Even if I worked, weekends were devoted to us. Brent left as late as possible Monday mornings, oftentimes making it back to Detroit just in time to begin his workday. Weekend after weekend, we repeated this pattern.

Monday through Friday, we talked on the phone for hours. We conversed into the night, answering each other's hypothetical situations. *What would you do if you had to suddenly take care of me? What if I needed a nurse? Would you care if the nurse was sexy?* Right around the time the snow began to thaw into small puddles and the leaves' greenness returned, our telephone ritual ended abruptly. In a time before cell phones, social media, or apps, this meant I couldn't find him.

"Hello, may I speak to Brent?" I asked.

"He's not here," his mother replied.

Later that day when I knew he should've gotten off work, I tried again. "Hello, may I speak to Brent?"

"Heeee's not heeeere, girl," his father replied in a sing-song voice.

This exchange continued for two days. Internalizing replaced calm: *Did I do something? What's happened?* In my rumination, I developed several scenarios: *Maybe he didn't know how to break up with me. I knew it was too good to be true.* The familiarity of abandonment replaced co-regulation. Once again, someone who'd said they loved me disappeared, unexpectedly leaving me alone. Within forty-eight hours, coping mechanisms kicked in. Step one: move on. College men always approached me, whether I was single or not. It didn't take long for me to slide underneath someone whose name or face I don't remember. Step two: *Avoidance.* None of this mattered. If Brent leaves, who cares?

Before I reached step three: accepting that I was alone and no one cared, Brent called. His mother had thrown him out of the house. She was tired of him making poor decisions with money, such as weekend visits to see me, tired of his hanging out with his friends during the week, instead of washing the dishes or mowing the lawn as she'd asked, and tired of seeing her adult, employed, and degreed son living in her house doing what he pleased. She'd told him that he had to leave…that day. He was homeless. While I used sex to get over an inexistent breakup, he cried at his desk because he didn't know where he would live. I didn't want my poor decision-making to ruin our relationship, so I kept my behavior a secret and justified my lie of omission by reasoning that he didn't need my faux pas on top of an already stressful situation.

In the summer of 1994, I was offered an assistant director position at one of the main campus dorms. It would help me practice being an AD when students returned in the fall. One day, I ran into Eddie. He invited me to his apartment, where we'd agreed to casually pick up our intimacy. Going to his place was a conscious decision I'd made in the middle of the day. I suppose that's why I lay there naked and crying moments before we were supposed to have sex. There was nothing on which to blame or justify my choices. I wasn't drunk. Brent hadn't ignored me. I thought love had cured me, but that's not how addiction works. One must resolve trauma to heal addiction, and at the time I didn't know I was traumatized or addicted. I just knew I had an uncontrollable urge to have sex with men but desired to be in a committed relationship.

"What's wrong?" Eddie asked.

"This is wrong," I said.

I told Eddie I couldn't be with him because I had a boyfriend I cared about. He understood and we agreed there was nothing else we could do for one another.

Weekends with Brent were hard after my cheating and near slip with Eddie. We'd established a relationship on honesty, so holding onto lies about sexual indiscretions was unbearable. He knew everything else about me, but I suspected disclosing I'd cheated and *almost* cheated would be too much. If he'd leave because I smoked a cigarette, then he'd certainly leave if he knew about this part of me, I hadn't figured out how to control. Eventually, the guilt overwhelmed me. I partially confessed during one of our phone conversations, leaving the near miss with Eddie out.

"You know how stupid I look?" he asked. "Coming up there to see you and you had sex with somebody else? People probably laughing at me."

"But I hadn't heard from you," I said, hoping he'd understand what even I didn't fully comprehend.

Love kept us together, and we believed our shared emotion was sufficient. Brent believed all I needed was love. I believed his love made me whole. But as the author and spiritual teacher, Don Miguel Ruiz once said, "Your love will not change anybody." It was naïve for either of us to ever think it would.

MJ

1996

My grandmother once told my father he was in a unique position. She couldn't have another daughter. I couldn't get another mother. But he could find another wife. Her words proved true. He and Joëlle divorced in 1994, and he met another woman named MJ.

MJ and my father met at his job as an O'Hare Airport limo service driver. Similar to Joëlle, MJ was born and raised in the South. Her home state was Arkansas. She spoke with a slow, long drawl that required patient listening. She'd independently raised three grown daughters and owned her home. She had also married three men prior. Her wish was for my father, her daughters, her grandchildren, and I to be one big happy blended family, so, unlike Joëlle, she went out of her way to include me in activities. However, she underestimated the unresolved issues wedged between my father and me.

Unlike Joëlle, she wanted a church wedding with ceremonial traditions consisting of her new and old family. Brent was a groomsman, and I was a bridesmaid. They married in February 1995. After the wedding, Brent and I returned to her south side home. My oldest stepsister and her husband joined us. We sat around MJ's kitchen table, drank brown liquor, and played Spades. Eventually, we agreed to take our post-reception party elsewhere and let my father and MJ enjoy their wedding night. At our new destination, one drunk conversation led to another. In Detroit, I'd practiced driving Brent's Talon, which had a manual transmission. After a lesson, he would do what most good teachers do; he'd say I was doing a *great job*!

My new brother-in-law commented on how nice Brent's car was, and then turned to me, "You know how to drive it?"

Relying on past "great jobs" I'd received, I replied with a confident, "Yes."

"No, she doesn't," Brent replied.

And that was the ignition to an inebriated argument. Intent to prove him wrong, I begged for the keys. When we left, he agreed, and after less than a minute, I landed right on the sidewalk in front of a White Castle. Our argument continued, which prompted me to jump out of the car. Brent sped off.

He'd planned to drive around the corner, apologize, and come back. By the time he returned, I'd hopped into a car full of men, who thought it odd for me to be standing outside in the wintertime at three in the morning in wedding attire. They drove me to MJ's. Brent pulled up minutes later, afraid he'd lost someone's daughter. When he walked into the house, he was both relieved and livid to find me there. The four of us stood in the lighted kitchen on my father and MJ's wedding night. Brent scratched his head and decided he was leaving me. Though it is common for bereaved women to experience bouts of neuroticism, my erratic behavior had become too much for him. Earlier in the year, after a New Year's Eve party and too much Old Grand-Dad, I'd jumped out of his car in the middle of a snowstorm. My father's wedding night was the proverbial last straw. He wanted to drive back to Detroit right then.

"Who's going to love me now?" I asked between sobs.

"I love you," my father answered, genuinely perplexed by my outburst.

My father didn't understand that the past six years had taught me what his love looked like. My father's love embodied abandonment. He'd visited me twice in Covert and once in undergrad.

He rarely called. I bore the brunt of our interactions. If we communicated, it was due to my efforts. My father's love was forgetful. I'd had five birthdays since he'd sent me to Michigan; he had overlooked four. My father's love was empty verbiage, accompanied by inactivity and inaction. He'd promised to send me money for school but never did. The love my father professed was a noun I'd learned to live without. Brent's love was an unconditional verb. He'd proven it repeatedly, so if I lost his love, then I'd lost *at* love and my suspicions of myself would be right. I was bad. I was unworthy of having what seemed to be the most basic emotional connection. If I lost Brent, then I'd lose everything.

Brent and I stayed together. He proposed Thanksgiving of 1995.

∞

I graduated from Western a month later. I'd counted enough graduation tickets for those who would attend. It was a given that my grandmother would be there; she and Papa Henry had funded the majority of my education. My grandfather's complications with heart failure meant he had to stay home. Although my father hadn't been involved, it was assumed that he and MJ would also come. I'd invited Brent and my soon-to-be mother-in-law. It was my grandmother's job to pass out the graduation tickets.

While I lined up on one side to enter the building, my family stood in conflict on the other side. My grandmother had brought Aunty Carlotta, her first husband's sister. She and Grandma Hunny had been the best of friends for decades. However, she and I were not close, and there was no reason for her to be there. There weren't enough tickets. Instead of my grandmother recognizing that her uninvited, plus one was the problem, she blamed my father for bringing MJ.

She told MJ that as the third wife, she needed to sit this one out. Brent's mother offered to remain in the hallway, but Grandma Hunny ignored her suggestion. She insisted it was MJ who needed to retreat. My grandmother also relayed information I'd told her in confidence. I explained that MJ wanted me to call her "mom," and it made me uncomfortable. MJ's adult daughters referred to my father as "dad," but the only person I'd ever used the term "mom" with was my mother. I'd chosen to call MJ by her first name. My grandmother felt it appropriate to present this as further proof of why MJ's seat would be in the hallway. She conceded and remained in the corridor, while Aunty Carlotta and others watched me receive my bachelor's degree.

Brent retold this story as soon as commencement ended. In two years, he hadn't met this aunt and was surprised by her appearance and the dispute. I apologized to his mother and ensured this wasn't a typical family interaction; I didn't want her to view my family as dysfunctional.

But we were. The dysfunction rested neatly between my father's and grandmother's unspoken grief. The way my grandmother sat with her back as straight as a board at my mother's funeral is an image that has been fixed in my brain for decades. That day, I sat in awe as I watched her not so much as flinch with emotion. We were burying her daughter, and she had no tears to bat back.

Over time, I viewed her differently. I began to see the fracture of her guise, slivers of emotion appeared as glints of light, like this graduation incident. Disallowing MJ to enter graduation illustrated my grandmother's true feelings: she was angry. She tolerated my father's attendance because he was my father, but how dare he bring his third wife to celebrate a degree for which he did not contribute? How dare he flaunt his privilege for all to see—the ability to do, what she had so eloquently described as that which neither of us could—find a replacement for my mother.

He only showed his face to commemorative events, where it would seem odd for a father not to be in attendance. He disappeared when times were hard, times when my grandmother had attempted to tie life together for me when no one else would. I'm not sure my grandmother ever saw him as a grieving person or as just a man her daughter had married, "who could get another wife," which he had done twice.

I didn't want MJ there any more than Grandma Hunny did. I'd rather my mother be accompanying my father; after all, she was the one who outlined an educational path for college graduation to occur. A bachelor's was the manifestation of my mother's foresight. But I didn't have a choice. I'd accepted my mother's permanent absence long ago when my father and Joëlle left me in the county hospital seven years prior. Though he never said a word about my mother's death, my father grieved out loud. His longing for love lay bare for all to see as if begging for any woman to coddle him and remove the pain of loss. Thus, whoever he chose for his wife would be by his side. She would be at my college graduation. He'd set this pattern when he dated and married Joëlle, and I accepted it. But my grandmother didn't have to agree to anything, and she made it clear the day I graduated. She said what none of us could. To my father: haven't you hurt this girl enough with your selfish actions? To MJ: we're still grieving; you're not welcome here.

The messiness of emotions always sat in the pit of my belly and rotted when it came to my grandmother. Although I was no longer a child, I continued to operate under the rules by which she raised me. It was my graduation, but my opinion of what occurred was irrelevant. My grandmother's chest swelled with pride every time she recalled the events of graduation as if she'd saved the day, and I know in her mind, she felt like she did. But I wished she would have admitted that she missed my mother; that she wished she would've been there to see me graduate college; that she would have been proud of me. That would've been more appropriate than sending MJ to the hallway like a toddler. Instead, she'd shown my father and his wife that their union and presence were irrelevant, especially when it came to any event regarding me including my wedding day.

∞

My mother married my father on Saturday, September 20, 1970. Aunt Diane married Terry on Saturday, September 20, 1986. And because I didn't want to wait a year, I married Brent on Saturday, September 21, 1996. Each of us wed at St. Matthews. Grandma Hunny delighted in having three different decades of identical aerial views, each wedding party standing at the same altar, backs of wedding dresses, bridesmaids' figures, and tuxedos forming a semicircle of custom. She was giddy with tradition. But I vacillated between emotions like a player racking up points on a pinball machine.

My grandparents paid for embossed invitations, elaborate photography, and the bridal party's horse-drawn carriage ride to the Water Tower. There was one other pre-ceremonial detail.

"Can Daddy walk me down the aisle?" I held my breath and asked. It was something for which he'd asked me to seek permission.

"As long as no one thinks he paid for it," Grandma Hunny replied.

My grandparents and other family members constantly reminded me that while my father was *still my dad* when it came to the financial aspects of being a father, he didn't contribute. And when it came to him participating in things that were father-like, my grandparents didn't want him involved. Even before the wedding, Papa Henry was surprised that Brent hadn't asked *him* for my hand in marriage. *How odd*, I thought. Not only was the practice antiquated, but I also had a father. If he were to ask anyone, wouldn't it be him? Was he my dad, or wasn't he? None of us knew how to navigate a father who cleaned up nicely and arrived just in time to smile for celebrations. Therefore, I remained in the middle of my father's requests and my grandparents' frustrations for his lack of contribution. Just the thought of mediating their interactions led to heart palpitations and stomach aches every time I had to mention my father to my grandparents or every time the three had to share space. I assured Grandma Hunny that no one would credit my father for any part of the wedding, and they allowed him to walk me down the aisle. A façade; as if he'd done more than just show up. I hoped everyone would behave.

Shaquita flew from California to be my maid of honor. By 1996, our lives had diverged into two distinct paths. Hers included two children by different fathers. She was pregnant with a third by the time she arrived. I struggled to understand how our lives seemed so different. My father once explained to me that we weren't equals, but anyone who would've examined the truth of our backgrounds would have seen similarities. I aborted fetuses, while she birthed children, and in between, we both longed for our parents' love. We weren't so different after all. Two other bridesmaids were friends from high school, who had always made time to party with me.

Amitra, another friend I'd known since seventh grade, had offered to do the bridal party's make-up for free. While she applied Mary Kay products, Mika walked in.

Her watery eyes spoke before she did. "I just want to say," she started.

"Nope. Not now. You are not about to make me cry." *Avoidance.*

She held her message—a bridge connecting nostalgia to the present.

Brent's father wondered why his brother wouldn't be his best man, so Brent agreed, and his brother fulfilled this duty. His cousin was a groomsman because one of his aunts, the groomsman's mother said a cousin needed to be in the wedding. To round things off, Brent's good friend from the neighborhood stood by his side.

Keeping a wedding dress wasn't important to me, so I followed my aunt Diane's example and rented one from a small dress shop in Detroit. No one had shopped for it with me, so it was a surprise for all.

"Where'd you get that hoochie-mama wedding dress? Off-the-shoulder? A split up the middle?" Aunt Diane smiled as she eviscerated what was left of my confidence.

Ten months prior when I'd announced our engagement, Grandma Hunny had judged my weight; I was 125 pounds.

"You're supposed to wait until you get married and have children to get fat," she'd said.

After our conversation, I ate 1200-calorie meals and bounced around with an aerobics video four times a week. On our wedding day, I was the smallest I'd ever been: one hundred pounds and a size one. I'd already succumbed to my grandmother's criticism; there was no space for ridicule about the type of dress I'd chosen, especially when no one had offered to help me find one. I never responded to my aunt's remarks. Only smiled. But not too hard.

That's what my grandmother had said in her role as temporary wedding coordinator. "Don't smile so hard." The photographer wanted a candid, pre-wedding picture. My natural smile had always been wide, but to appease Grandma Hunny, I shrank it. Clicks later, the photographer noticed.

"Tell her she needs to stop being mad. It'll show in the pictures," he advised.

Years later, I appear as a dazed and confused little girl in our wedding photos, as if someone dressed me up like a doll and forced me into marriage.

As it neared time for me to become Brent's wife, Aunt Diane, Grandma Hunny, and Terry whispered in a small circle.

"What's wrong?" I asked.

The three exchanged looks, then looked off, ignoring my question.

"Is something wrong?" I asked, again. "Why aren't we starting? I thought we were starting on time?"

The three elected Aunt Diane to break the news to me. "Brent isn't here," she said softly.

My eyes bulged.

"But . . . he's coming. Don't worry. His brother left the ring at the hotel, and they had to go back and get it."

This was the first time I noticed how my family handled me—with kid gloves. They were afraid of my response; they feared I'd turn into a raging, angry, crying mess if I knew this information, so they'd tried to hide it from me for as long as they could. I didn't spiral. It was a late wedding, not a jilted one.

Prince's, "The Most Beautiful Girl in the World" played, while our wedding party strolled in. This was Brent's idea. I imagined my mother smiling at his choice. If she had been there, they'd have communed over which Prince album was better. His favorite cousin served as an usher. After seating guests, she rolled out the white aisle runner, and the organist played Mendelssohn's customary wedding song. My father escorted me to my future husband, just as he'd desired. Brent and I stood amidst a perfect backdrop of burgundy and cream. Instead of a song, Brent's friend, Darryl recited a poem.

"Did you like it?" he asked afterward. "You had a strange look on your face."

The "look" he'd noticed was a combination of wrangling emotions and blinking back tears. The day's events were surreal. Seven years prior, my mother's body lay lifeless in a rose-pink casket in the same spot where Brent and I promised to be with each other forever. *I'll be married with two kids* was a fanciful teenage dream I'd written in my senior book as a five-year goal. But it wasn't something I thought would ever occur, especially not in five years. It wasn't something I'd thought through.

When Reverend Willis said *and obey*, I repeated the word.

"Obey?" I asked, out loud and in front of our guests. They laughed, but the connotation of the word struck me at that moment. Of course, I'd heard similar vows in movies and television shows, but I hadn't investigated these phrases or what they meant. All I knew was if you loved someone, then you planned a wedding and married as my mother and aunt had. Much of my pre-wedding time had been devoted to perusing bride's magazines, not analyzing traditional wedding vows. I loved Brent, and I was overjoyed that he'd chosen me, but even as I stood at the altar, I wondered why? Why would Brent love someone as broken as me? Why would he marry someone who got sloppy drunk and jumped out of cars? He constantly reassured me that he simply loved me; that was it. Brent and I were best friends. When we weren't working, we spent hours together. Neither of us had a group of friends for separate reasons, so *we* were each other's company. Marriage was the next logical step. His parents, aunts, and uncles had laid out a similar path for him as well. Like me, he followed what he was shown.

I was envious from the ceremony through the reception. Seeing Brent's youthful-looking, golden-brown parents, who'd been married for years spotlighted the nontraditional family to which I belonged. His parents *were* the parents I desired: healthy, financially secure, and loving, like the nuclear families I'd read about in psychology class, or the Black families depicted in sitcoms. I had yet to become accustomed to where I fit into my father's choices and life, or if I needed to at twenty-three years old. I also wasn't sure where my father and stepmother fit in mine.

Weeks before we wed, Brent's parents hosted a family dinner: my grandparents, aunt, and uncle were invited, but for some reason, my father and MJ weren't. I never questioned it. I didn't even miss them. Graduation, however, had taught MJ her place. She and my father milled about in the background, not excluded from the wedding party, but not included. The photographer documented the imbalance. Brent and I stood in the center, with his father and mother to his left, my father to my right, and a space where my mother should've been. MJ watched.

I was an illusion of perfection. I suppressed unresolved emotions about the past, bonded together growing emotions about the present, and said, *I do*. Our wedding served as a symbol for the previous years and the years to come. I was a dressed-up ball of pain, and no one seemed the wiser. After the ceremony and once the photographer had finished staging and taking hundreds of pictures, Papa Henry sat in his wheelchair, pulled out an off-white handkerchief, and wept.

"Oh, Henry," Grandma Hunny said, looking away. Aunt Diane's eyes turned glossy.

One of my mother's cousins joined in. "Uncle Henry got everybody all teared up, huh?"

Her question broke the emotion, and everyone laughed, but no one verbalized what had occurred, and I was on the outside of a shared understanding. Similar to when I'd graduated high school and then college, their tears felt like a collective sigh of relief, as if each achievement represented a signpost toward wellness. I was married. But I was not well. I was Mrs. Garland, but I still felt like the teenager who was thrust into figuring out life on her own in 1989. Instead of engaging with a family, who'd tiptoed around my grief and their own, now I had a husband to tiptoe around, too.

Brent's parents paid for our honeymoon to Puerto Vallarta. On our first night there, we went to a club. I hadn't had one drink on our wedding day, so I made up for it at the Mexican dancery. Scantily dressed bargirls walked around with plastic, flashing necklaces. They enticed me with a multitude of shots. I lost count of how many times each girl blew her whistle, tilted my neck back, and poured liquor down my throat. I left in a lucid haze, ready to have sex as a wife. On the cab drive home, I sat on Brent's lap, facing him, my dress pulled up just enough to lure him.

"Not now, Bae. The cab driver is watching."

I looked over my shoulder and exchanged glances with the driver in the rearview mirror.

"So. Let him watch," I taunted.

I couldn't convince Brent to do more than make out, so I sat back down and pouted. Every, now and then, the cab driver's eyes and mine met in the rearview mirror. He hoped to see a show, and I'd hoped to give him one.

The following day, Brent and I made it just in time for our snorkeling excursion. This was my first time seeing a body of water other than Lake Michigan. The Pacific Ocean invited me in ways the lake hadn't. The fine, white sand and crystal blue water were more magnificent than television portrayals. As we entered the boat, one of the shipmates recognized me.

"You the girl from the club last night. You had on a red dress, no?"

"I diiiid," I smiled. He was talking about a dress that covered and showed everything, simultaneously.

I recounted the brief chat to Brent, who'd already sat down. I'm not sure if it was confirmation of what he'd suspected all this time or an in-the-moment realization, but he looked me in the eye and said, "You like that don't you?"

"Like what?"

"Attention. You like attention from men."

The real answer was I didn't know. On the one hand, I'd grown accustomed to men's attention. It was a given. My short height and long, reddish-brown hair attracted men. My high cheekbones and wide eyes garnered looks. It had happened all my life. Attention wasn't something I had to seek. Men looked at my round booty and wide hips, not once, but several times as I passed, deciding whether they were going to approach me. I was used to it. But being recognized in a small, Mexican city, where men see thousands of tourists and beautiful women per day boosted my ego. However, Brent's accusations reminded me of Eddie's; what they'd both noticed is common and distinct for women who live with sex addiction—delighting in male attention.[1] For female sex addicts, garnering male attention is powerful; knowing that others want you, is considered a power move.[2]

But I didn't want to think about any of this. I wanted to enjoy the remainder of our honeymoon. I wanted to ride mopeds through cobblestoned Mexican side streets and forget about why my father had found two wives in six years. I wanted to lose myself in resort drinks with small hot pink umbrellas and forget about my grandparents and their apparent hatred of my father. The joy was where we were, in another country, far away from everything that caused me pain.

Had I realized I had a problem, instead of a personality flaw, I wouldn't have dated Brent, much less married him. When he said *he didn't need any more friends*, I would have politely declined the relationship; I wasn't ready. Had I known the desire for men to see me was a behavior that a psychologist should address, I would have asked Grandma Hunny to fund therapy sessions instead of reception dinners. But awareness would have required me to live in the real world; it would have demanded I be present with reality, and I had mastered the art of pretend, whether it was in my head or in Mexico.

"No," I answered, vehemently denying what he knew to be true. What would Brent or I do with the truth, anyway? Instead, I focused on learning how to use my snorkel to breathe underwater.

MRS. GARLAND

1999

"Take off your shirt," he said.

It was 1988 and we were in high school. I'd known him since seventh grade. I don't remember his name, just that he'd invited me to his house, which was within walking distance from mine. I unfastened the first button.

"No. No. Stop," he said. "Somebody told me you'd take your clothes off if I asked, but I didn't believe them. I just wanted to see if you would do it."

I don't remember who the *somebody* was, but like most of my sexual proclivities, after that day, I knew it was socially unacceptable, and if I didn't want to be the topic of discussion and rumor, then I shouldn't do it, or I should keep it private. The "*it*" is exhibitionism, a compulsion to show oneself in public, usually to strangers.[1]

I'd made it through high school and much of undergrad without having the desire to be nude in public spaces. It wasn't until the summer before I graduated college in 1995 that the urge resurfaced. Brent had gotten an apartment off Third Street in Detroit's New Center area. The 600-square-foot, one-bedroom held just enough space for our hopes and dreams. The small balcony faced a quaint neighborhood of brick homes and was chic and trendy. Brent and I were heavy weekend drinkers. As soon as Friday arrived, either he or I would ask, *what are we drinking?* We'd imbibe for a few hours, have sex, and do it all again Saturday. We weren't discriminative when it came to what we drank, just that we would. Before graduation and my fall internship, I had to take one summer class. When I found out I could mail completed assignments back and forth to a professor, I opted to live with Brent for four months. My temporary job at an insurance company and Brent's full-time accounting position kept us busy during the week. The liquor store, which was within walking distance, fulfilled our weekends.

For some reason, we decided to indulge on a weekday. We stopped at the liquor store and chose something neither of us had ever had before, Bacardi 151. We finished a fifth by ourselves. The apartment shrank and spun. Brent passed out.

Liquor has always energized me. The more I drink, the more alive I become, talking, playing, and engaging. That night was no different. I was drunker than I'd ever been and bored. The balcony looked inviting. *Maybe if I go out there, I can find someone to talk to*, I thought. So, I did. Half-naked.

Detroit is similar to most major cities; someone is always walking up and down the street, even in the middle of the night. I stood there for a few minutes before I saw a man walk toward our apartment.

"Pssst," I whispered.

He looked up and when he noticed my breast peeking through the railing, his eyes bulged. He told me I had nice titties, and a rush of pride swelled over me.

"Come down here," he said.

I threw on a T-shirt and shorts and walked down the few flights of stairs. By the time I reached the outer door, the man had disappeared. When I went back upstairs, I realized I didn't bring the key. I banged on the door, but to no avail; Brent was in a deep slumber. I couldn't sleep in the hallway and didn't know what to do. I remembered that Brent's friend's father lived a couple of blocks away. So, I left the apartment and walked to his house. The friend's father said very little. He drove me to Brent's parents' house.

The next morning, I awoke to a near-empty home, Brent's mother and father were gone; his brother, a man my age, sat watching TV.

"I woke up and didn't know where you were," Brent said when I called his job.

He'd gone to work and promised to get me as soon as possible. Until then, I sat in a sea of shame and stomach aches, while 151 coursed through my digestive system.

Brent attempted to make sense of the night on the way home. *How did I end up outside of the apartment?*

"You asked me to leave, so I did," I lied. Then, I told the truth. "I couldn't get back in, so I went to Gerald's dad's house because you were passed out."

Brent accepted the rendition as fact. He and his father had a conversation about what happened, and his father gave simple advice. "You gotta be careful with some of that stuff. You can't drink everything."

We agreed and never drank 151 again. I assumed high-proof alcohol must've been the reason I felt comfortable showing a stranger my breasts. I told myself exhibitionism wasn't something I would do in my regular life unable to understand that this was my regular life. I dismissed this incident and the one in high school as one-offs. Inebriation bore the blame. There was no other explanation.

A year after we'd married, Brent and I got drunk and stayed at Grandma Betty's place. At the time, I still preferred to sleep on her couch or floor in her teeny-tiny, assisted living apartment than stay with my father and MJ. That's when it happened again. Brent fell asleep, and like a light switch, something clicked, and a voice urged me to leave the apartment to show my body to someone...anyone. I quietly slipped my sandals on, grabbed Grandma Betty's keys, and slowly closed the door behind me. There was no destination. I just walked, seeking anyone who wanted to see a naked body. Streetlights and club lights blurred into one hazy blob. People entered Zanies' Comedy Club across the street. I veered right, behind a restaurant. There, I saw a man standing against the wall. His dirty gray jogging pants hung off his body, and his oversized white t-shirt stretched to cover his protruding belly.

"You want to see something?" I asked.

He motioned with his fat, white fingers for me to come closer.

I stood a foot away from him and lifted my shirt, showing my breasts.

He reached out to touch me.

"Unh-unh," I said.

He dug into the front of his stained jogging pants and told me to turn around, to pull my shorts down. He tried to touch me again.

"No!" I screamed.

He reached back into his jogging pants and masturbated.

Satisfied, I returned to Grandma Betty's apartment. As I approached the door, I saw Brent standing outside in his pajamas.

"Where have you been?" he asked.

My heart beat outside of my chest. "I just took a walk."

"A walk where? At this time?"

"Just up the street," I said. "I was just walking."

There's no way I could reveal the truth. Brent would want to know why, and I didn't have an explanation. I knew it was wrong and unsafe, but at that moment, there was no fear. The idea that a stranger could've kidnapped or raped me never crossed my mind. In a drunken exhibitionist mode, my priority was the reaction to being seen nude. The result was exhilaration, like an orgasmic release. And just like an orgasm with the wrong partner, once the exhibitionist compulsion was satisfied, the light switch flipped off, I came to my senses and snapped back to my regretful reality. I couldn't make sense of my actions. Exhibitionism wasn't something I'd ever do. If a friend told me this story, I'd think they were mentally ill, and I'd be right.

Unlike sex addiction, exhibitionism is consistently listed in the Diagnostic and Statistical Manual of Mental Disorders (DSM),[2] the definitive handbook that mental health professionals use as a reference. Likewise, it's listed as a characteristic of sex addiction,[3] but society has portrayed it as the illegal actions of dirty men in trench coats, who flash unsuspecting women and children. Research has primarily consisted of men who have been caught and imprisoned for unlawful sex acts.[4]

The prevailing narrative is that exhibitionism is an act of criminals. However, women can be exhibitionists, too. But women flashing their breasts in public spaces is oftentimes met with two opposite judgments: either it's seen as acceptable "party" behavior—who can forget the topless teens and young adults who flashed MTV cameras while on Spring Break—or it's viewed as whorish conduct[5] and rarely something women of color partake in. Thus, a Black woman, like me, would rarely be diagnosed as an exhibitionist. But it didn't matter what the media or studies showed. I knew something was wrong, and I didn't know how to remedy it. Instead, I kept my behavior a secret and steered clear of all dark liquor, deciding that was the issue.

∞

"We could do this anywhere," Brent has always said.

This referred to our relationship. Our love wasn't confined to a place in the world; we were the love, he and I, and our little bubble. It was September '96 and we had decided Detroit would be our home. He was from there, and his family folded me into long-established routines: his father worked until evening, stopped to buy lottery tickets, and crossed his fingers that he won more than he spent; his mother cooked greens and smoked turkey necks and invited us to weekly Sunday dinners. In between, his cousins gathered around solid oak dining room tables and celebrated birthdays.

We moved from Third Street to a bigger one-bedroom apartment: East Jefferson Avenue was on one side, and a view of the Detroit River was on the other. Freshly manicured lawns and polished parquet floors greeted us. Brent had a full-time job, and shortly after we married, I found a teaching position at a magnet high school near our apartment. Like the city, the ninth-grade classes I taught were full of brown faces; their curriculum was based on an African-American anthology. Countee Cullen and Claude McKay were mandatory, not supplemental. Teacher autonomy meant I could complement poems with relevant resources. One of my first lessons was an assignment centered on Tupac's murder, which had occurred two weeks before I began. Students and I read *Vibe* articles, and we discussed the importance of Black lives, the beef between rappers, and how Black people were perceived in the media.

A year before I began this job, I sat in my methodology prof's office, unsure teaching was the right path for me. I wondered what else I could do with an English education degree, other than teach. He had little advice. Now, I had my answer. I was in Black teacher heaven. Here is where I belonged—molding Black students' minds, helping them gain perspective on their place in the world. I awoke energized and with a clear purpose, and exhibitionism was a memory of a former life. Two weeks after my hire date, the principal called me to her office.

"We've done a ten-day count," she started. "We don't have enough students for you to teach. Instead of firing you, I've made you a building sub. You'll still receive your regular pay."

A ten-day count was a numbers game. A common occurrence across American schools that I'd never heard of. If enrollment was high, schools needed more teachers; too few students meant layoffs or moves to other schools. The principal had done me a favor by keeping me as a building sub with a first-year teacher's salary. But it didn't feel like it.

When I was a permanent hire, I woke up early and beat the students to the class. As a substitute, I arrived with the teenagers, just in time to clock in. I was frequently sent to the "standard education" side of the building, where students who lived in the surrounding neighborhood learned basic skills; they weren't introduced to the Harlem Renaissance or its authors. As a sub, I was bound to the lesson plans the real teacher left, which consisted of worksheets where one circles the noun and underlines the verb. One boy, six feet tall, would join me in the hall when the bell rang. "When you gon' let me fuck Mrs. Garland," he'd ask every day until I threatened him with police involvement for his harassment. Though my position was temporary, the department chair allowed me a permanent desk in the English department office, which contained rows of dark wooden desks facing one another, like a warehouse. Long, dim lights hung from the ceiling. With no classes to plan, I kept to myself and read the bible, cover-to-cover that year.

"Wuz wrong wit' her?" a man a couple of years my elder, who was a permanent hire, asked his friend. My despondency was apparent.

"Leave her alone," she laughed. "You know how it is when you want a job after you graduate."

But she agreed with him. The consensus was that I should be happy to be drawing a salary for doing nothing.

Talking around me was frequent. I showed little interest in cutting up with colleagues who possessed English degrees and spoke of teaching as if it was beneath them. They had higher aspirations, such as attaining law degrees or screenwriting credentials. I was a trained professional, yet I was the building sub. Their jokes were never funny. I read my bible and sought solace. My mother, Grandma Betty, and even my father seemed to see something in these words, and I thought I would, too. Maybe it would show me why I was close enough to taste happiness, but far enough to have it snatched away right when it was on the tip of my tongue.

Four months later, in February of 1997, Brent, his friend Darryl, his wife, and I learned of a job fair for teachers in Orlando. When I was hired by Detroit's public schools, a human resource personnel person told me that I was lucky. Jobs were scarce. She informed me that there would be an outpouring of employment in about ten to fifteen years when Baby Boomers began retiring, but as of that day, people my parents' age remained as teachers and weren't budging. Playing substitute and sitting in the English department warehouse until the end of the school year was fine but not for ten years. For me, the choice was simple. The four of us rented a van, alternated driving, and arrived in Florida overnight. The four of us, each in our twenties, each newlywed, and wide-eyed, envisioned a charmed life in the South, where we would educate the masses beneath the warm Florida sun. But neither of us had read the fine print. We were underqualified, including me. The job fair was designed for finding community college professors. Neither of us met the minimum requirements, which were master's, with eighteen hours in a content area.

An older man explained this to Brent and me when we visited his booth. He was the president of a community college campus in Jacksonville. "If you move here and get a master's, then I can hire you at FCCJ," he said.

We exchanged information. Instead of sitting in the English department's warehouse, I used the school's library and computer to maintain frequent contact with the community college's president. All Brent and I had to do was move to Jacksonville, and all I had to do was attain a master's, something I knew would be easy.

Brent and I lived on the heels of spontaneity and impracticality, and as he always said, *we could do this anywhere*. By the summer of '97, we'd packed up our clothes, dishes, and television, and moved one thousand miles south. The week we arrived in the balmy city, the community college president relocated to South Florida. He never mentioned his potential new job, and he never helped us, but it didn't matter. Brent and I maintained our plan. He worked at a news station, and I taught high school in a rural community, outside of Jacksonville, while pursuing a graduate degree focused on education. We flowed with life, doubted nothing, and trusted everything would be okay.

Within a year I'd cobbled together a crew of friends in Jacksonville; women who either lived in our apartment complex or taught with me at the high school. A woman who rented us our apartment and I became fast friends. She was a Latina woman, who served in the Navy. Within our first year in Jacksonville, she became pregnant with twins.

"You should have a baby," she suggested, rubbing her belly.

Brent and I visited when my friend's babies were days old. As soon as we entered the apartment, a blend of adobo and sazón wafted through the air. Her mother had traveled from South Florida and a pot of arroz con pollo simmered on the stove.

"Take your shoes off," her mother instructed.

We kicked our shoes off, one by one, and followed our next set of instructions to wash our hands and use hand sanitizer. She hovered to ensure we didn't skip a step. We'd visited this friend and her husband several times over the past year, but their apartment held a warmth that it hadn't before. I sat on an armchair, near my friend, who sat upright in the bed. Guests' conversations hummed in the living room.

"Do you want to hold her?" my friend asked, her mother stood at my side.

The white blanket covered a set of light brown cheeks; the remainder of the baby's body was tightly wound like a burrito.

"No. No, thank you," I declined, fearing I'd break something. Hers was the first newborn baby I'd ever seen. Later, I'd learn this was the wrong answer. Her mother saw it as a sign of disrespect as if I didn't want to touch her granddaughters.

Her mother left the room, picked up empty drinking glasses, and greeted new visitors. Observing my friend and her mother aroused something in me. I wondered what it would feel like to be cared for with such fragility.

The next day, I approached Brent with an idea. "We should have a baby."

Brent trusted my choices when it came to most schemes. If I said I was flying to the moon, he would search for the best polycarbonate helmets and rocket ships in an attempt to help me travel 238,900 miles, never questioning why. But when I wanted to have a baby, Brent scratched his head and disagreed.

"We're not ready for a baby," he said.

"That's what you said when we were in undergrad. Now, we're grown. We're married. We both have good jobs."

It was the next logical step. *First comes love, then comes marriage, then comes…*a baby that would complete our family, so Brent acquiesced. I was pregnant the next summer.

When it was time for me to give birth, my grandmother agreed to live with us for one month. She arrived two days before delivery. Grandma Hunny sat in the corner of the hospital room, while Brent held my right hand. She conversed about minor matters; and every now and then, she'd check on my well-being.

"This is haaaard," I moaned, as the baby's head crowned.

"Yeah. That's why they call it labor," Grandma Hunny laughed.

Our daughter, Kimeiko was born in 1999. Post-partum, my grandmother wondered what she was supposed to do. Homecooked meals still weren't a part of her repertoire. Her own home was less than pristine. Family members who visited her found themselves mopping her kitchen floor or washing dishes. Aunt Lillian once suggested she buy new curtains because my grandmother's drapes had hung there for thirty years. But I had ignored the details of her life and how she'd operated in mine. She wasn't the type of grandmother who baked cookies and shared her sweet potato pie recipe. She was quick to tell you that in the 1960s, she drove Martin Luther King Jr. to his west side apartment as part of her duties in the civil rights movement. Domesticity wasn't a priority. Her friends made baked goods and brought them to her house, not the other way around. I'd ignored all of this and returned to my fantasy world, where the grandmother I dreamed of lived; Fantasy grandmother's instincts would kick in at the sight of her first great-granddaughter. However, her four-week presence in our home snapped me back to reality. Instead of cooking for us, Brent and I made dinner for ourselves and her. She didn't scrub toilets or bathtubs; she left that for Brent or me. My grandmother did what she knew and provided material things.

"What do you want for your birthday?" she asked. "Everyone is going crazy about this dumb-head baby and forgetting all about you. What can I get you?"

As the "baby" in her family, my grandmother had noticed what no one else had: I was no longer the center of attention. I let her offensive comment slide and thought of what she could do to be more involved. At delivery, I was forty pounds overweight. Kimeiko only weighed six. "A bike," I replied. It would help me feel more like my pre-pregnant self.

Brent's mother arrived shortly after my grandmother left. However, what I expected of her was also built in a world of make-believe. I thought thirty days in a townhome would force her to hold a conversation with me or help us to bond. When we lived in Detroit, we'd visit his parents at least once a week. His father would sit at the kitchen table and recount his workday repairing people's refrigerators and air conditioning units. His mother would stand at the counter and chop vegetables or season the day's meat. Their home was always fragrant with a recently cooked or reheated meal. She rarely spoke, and if she did, it was to convey information. *Farmer Jack is having a sale on chicken*, she might say. At night, she headed a team of custodial staff at a Detroit high-rise. Not only was the downtown facility spotless, but so was her home.

Brent's mother decided she'd be called Nana. Kimeiko was her first grandchild, so she doted on her and spoke baby talk. She used words I'd never heard her utter, like *tootsies*. She smiled at Kimeiko in a way I'd never witnessed. Her arrival was synonymous with fresh meals and proper house cleaning. Nana did so much that at one point I asked Brent if I was expected to live in a constant state of gratitude. It seemed a necessary but redundant act to continuously say thank you each time she fed us or cleaned.

I informed Nana of my decision to breastfeed. There would be no heating up of bottles. I would be Kimeiko's sole provider of food.

"I bought nursing bras when I was pregnant with Brent," she said. "But I never used them."

Her voice trailed off in an unfinished story. Kimeiko was slow to latch, and when she was only hours old, the nurses pressured me to try formula. Once she finally learned to suckle, the angle was wrong; she stretched and pulled so hard that my nipples turned bright red and burned afterward. Sometimes, Kimeiko would turn her head in the opposite direction when it was feeding time, eventually surrendering when she'd realize my breast was her only source of nourishment. I understood Nana's silent story. But because neither Nana nor I were knowledgeable about breastfeeding, she wouldn't always make nursing-friendly dinners; however, hunger led me to gobble them up anyway. One night, after eating and breastfeeding, Kimeiko was inconsolable. Her face turned red, and her blood-curdling cries persisted for hours.

"Maybe it's the breast milk," Nana said.

I'd nursed Kimeiko for weeks before her arrival, so I couldn't conceive of it as an issue. It wasn't until Brent fed her formula that I admitted my role. Weeks later, I researched possible reasons for our baby's sudden colic. Gassy foods, such as the Brussels sprouts I'd eaten that night, could indeed be passed on through breastmilk, thus interrupting a baby's delicate digestive system. I silently berated myself for not being a good mother. I should've known better. I should've protected my diet, her diet. By the time Nana left, Kimeiko was on a formula regimen, and I'd determined I was the worst mother ever; I couldn't even do something innate, like feeding my child.

Though I was appreciative of Grandma Hunny and Nana, their presence underscored the bitterness that kept my body tense. The hatred was deep and niggling and continued to resurface at times when a mother figure's attendance would have been appropriate. I was motherless and it hurt whenever I didn't have one to show up for me.

My mother, like her mother, wasn't nurturing, but she was smart and organized. When Papa Henry had a heart attack and had one of the first defibrillators installed, my mother is the person who researched the side effects of medications and mailed them to him. I am certain she would've studied what post-pregnant mothers and their babies should eat; she wouldn't have prepared inappropriate vegetables, ruining the nursing routine I'd established.

My mother taught me to read before I entered pre-school. Even if she wouldn't have nestled

Kimeiko deep in her arms, I know she would've purchased and read books to her before she could murmur her first coo. My mother wasn't obsessive about cleaning; however, we had a Saturday cleaning ritual that included Lemon Pledge and Prince. Had she been there, our apartment would have been clean enough for Brent and me to rest. But deep down, I knew her attempts at grandmothering would have also fallen short of my made-up expectations.

I thought I wanted a baby. But what I wanted was a mother like my friend's. My adoptive mother, chose motherhood, but she wasn't the type of mother I craved; there are no photos of her holding me in a snug embrace, close to her heart; there are no memories of her providing comfort, soothing my pain, yet I longed for this type of connection. I wondered what it would be like to have the type of mother I envisioned. I wanted someone to nurture me, to grow worried over whether I was eating or sleeping as my Jacksonville friend's mother did. I wanted this ideal so badly that I tried to cobble bits and pieces from others' mothers. But piecemealing a mother always left me with a pile of disappointment and the realization that it was unattainable.

I had a baby, when what I needed most was a hug deep inside my mother's bosom, the type of hug that is so tight, your body softens and melts into the other person's; the type of hug where I'd have no choice but to drench my mother's blouse with my tears, while she rubbed my back and told me *everything would be okay* and reassured me that *adoption was painful, but she was here to pick up the slack.*

I longed for something impossible.

My daughter finally gave me biological ties to someone, and ironically made me a mother, while I held deep resentment for my own, who adopted me and left me in a family that didn't seem to know what to do with me. I had to succumb to these truths, but I didn't have the desire or time. I followed the strategies I'd been taught—convinced myself these emotions were irrelevant, packed them away where they couldn't be touched, and raised the baby I'd birthed.

Eight weeks after our baby was born, there was no Grandma Hunny and no Nana. Brent returned to work, and family visits dwindled. The remainder of the summer consisted of long days with Kimeiko and the deep mother wounds I refused to face. The baby slept. Boredom set in. One summer day, completely sober—I hadn't had a drink in a year—the light switch flipped up. The urge returned; I had to show my body to anyone who would look. I found something revealing: a brown, sleeveless blouse that stopped mid-thigh. It was loose before I'd given birth, but now it was snug. I put it on with no bra, no panties, and no pants. I slipped into a pair of matching shoes. I left Kimeiko asleep in her crib and walked three minutes to the nearest gas station, where I bought a bottle of water. The compulsion of being seen half-naked took precedence over mothering.

"You're a pretty girl," the cashier said.

"Thank you," I replied.

And just like that, the light switch flipped down. I returned home and waited for Kimeiko to wake up.

PETULIA

2001

Kimeiko was an undeniably beautiful baby with curly hazel brown hair. She was the kind of pretty that stopped passersby in their tracks. When they stared at her, she met their gaze with alertness and eventually a smile. From the time she was born, my grandmother would loudly announce, "Kimeiko looks just like her nana." Sometimes she'd add, "Like Brent's mama," to reiterate what she meant. My stomach tightened with each assertion and the absence of ever knowing who I looked like in the world.

Brent's parents sent photos of him as a newborn; he and our daughter shared traits. New feelings emerged about my ancestry with each picture I viewed. Not only did I not have a biological family to compare myself to, but I also didn't look like the baby I'd birthed, who was my only biological family. I wanted to know if I, too, looked like my mother because, in some ways, Brent favored his. What were my newborn traits? I didn't know, and it hurt. For years, I had been able to ignore that I was adopted, but having a baby made denying the circumstances of my birth impossible.

When I was six weeks pregnant, I'd asked Brent if he loved Kimeiko.

"She's not even here," he said. "I have to get to know her."

Unlike him, I didn't have to get to know our daughter. Motherhood holds a distinct membership. Kimeiko and I were not only connected through an umbilical cord but also a constant presence in one another's lives. My organs made space for her as she developed near my heart. Her cravings dictated my meals; for ten months, I ate tuna fish sandwiches with extra mayonnaise, something I loathed pre-pregnancy, but she enjoys to this day. While in utero, she slept much of the morning, and when the bell rang for fifth period, she'd awaken and push her elbows and feet against my belly, until she settled into a comfortable position. Sometimes, I'd poke her feet to elicit a response; she'd shift slightly and settle back into a spot against my ribs. I read to Kimeiko before she was born; she learned the cadence of my voice and what each lilt meant. Once born, the nurse cleaned Kimeiko off and plopped her on top of me. We were inextricably bound. She was *my* baby.

However, experiencing motherhood brought suppressed emotions to the forefront. Now that I was a mother, I had a clear view of how a woman brought life into the world. Like Kimeiko, I'm sure I kicked and turned in my biological mother's womb. Like Kimeiko, I'm sure I craved food and changed my biological mother's mood. Did she instantly love me, or was she like Brent, who needed to meet his daughter first? Like me, my biological mother had me on a birthing table, under bright hospital lights. But unlike me, she decided I should be raised by strangers. The idea stung. Mother wounds ran deep, and they didn't begin with my adoptive mother. They were baked in during conception and reinforced when I was born. I had to find out what happened to her and me. It was time.

First, I called Grandma Hunny out of courtesy. She deserved to know about my decision.

"What are you gonna do? Walk up to people and ask: *are you, my mother?* Like that book? Have you heard of that book? I think it's a duck and it keeps walking up to people asking *are you, my mother?*" She chuckled into the receiver.

"I've heard of it," I said. "I'm gonna contact DCFS."

"Your mama always said she wouldn't want you to know who they are. She always said she wouldn't want you to find them. Besides, if somebody's family wanted to find them, they would."

My family had spoken about my adoption twice during my childhood. The first time was when I accidentally discovered I was adopted, and my mother urged me to get over my sadness about the situation. The second time was when Grandma Hunny raised the issue after moving to Covert. For the rest of my life, my identity in my family was treated as a natural birth, as if my adoptive family *was* my family, no questions asked. I knew this decision rested with me and no one else, so weeks after Kimeiko's birth, I reached out to the Illinois Department of Children and Family Services.

"Why do you want to find your birth family?" the social worker asked.

"I want to know if I have any illnesses or anything to worry about."

"You're almost thirty. Any illnesses would've appeared by now. DCFS is not in the business of reuniting families. We're in the business of moving children to loving homes."

Once the DCFS worker realized I wasn't hanging up, she provided information for a place called the Midwest Adoption Center; they *were* in the business of reconnecting families. The social worker listed information required to search: birthdate, adopted parents' names, year of adoption, official birth certificate, and birthname.

"Birthname?" I repeated. It never occurred to me I had another name. I called my father for details.

His smile shone through the phone as he reminisced. "She had named you Petulia," my father recalled. "Your mom and I always thought, who would name a baby Petulia? Maybe she liked the singer Petula Clark. But still. Petulia?"

I agreed. My whole name was Petulia Belcher; however, my parents had changed it to Katherin, after my father's favorite cousin, and Elizabeth, after my mother's grandmother. The name change reminded me of a building renovation. Gentrification requires contractors to change the face of a building—to portray newness: same homes, different neighborhoods. They replace the door, the roof, and the windows. They give the building a fresh coat of paint, and it looks shiny and new. But what about the inside? Sometimes, bad plumbing and light fixtures remain; other times, it's a challenge to remove the heart of an area. Katherin Elizabeth was a beautiful name, but it never reflected who I thought I was. Adoption always seemed like a pet project my mother took on. Kind of like the "bucket list" I assumed she created—raising a baby was another bullet point. Changing my name, which adoptive parents have the legal right to do, no matter how old the child is, seemed like another fabrication. Nothing about my life was real, and my two names proved it. Katherin Elizabeth was reserved for the queens of England, while Petulia Belcher aptly described who I was: an ugly little girl no one wanted; an abandoned child, three times over, who snuck away to the shadows to show off her body to strangers and couldn't keep her legs closed.

Information flowed quickly after I worked with the Center. By August of 2000, the counselor had found my birth records and mailed a five-page report. I read it with the eagerness of a child on Christmas day. When I was younger, I'd developed a pretend biological family. In my head, my "real" family was wealthy, and my "real" mother had shamed the family by being a young, unwed mother. She had to have a baby, but her parents made her give me away. The letter from the center would reconnect us and all would be well. I would live happily ever after with my "real" mother. But the document was further from my imagined truth than I was prepared for: My mother, Joyce Belcher, had considered abortion several times before having a second child. This was noted by her social worker.

I could have been aborted! I could not be here? This first realization was overwhelming. I knew firsthand about the details of abortion, how you could end a growing fetus's life and then go about the business of your life hours later like nothing life-altering had happened. Except for my last abortion with Brent, I'd never given the procedure a second thought. I'd only perceived abortion as something that saved me and preserved my aspirations. Now, I was on the other side of a woman's choice. My biological mother's choice to not have an abortion saved my life. I read and re-read that line and let awareness linger. I was lucky to be alive.

Joyce had been diagnosed with acute schizophrenia: undifferentiated type. Up until my birth, neighbors saw her walking up and down the sidewalk talking to herself, pushing an empty baby carriage. After giving birth, she would lay on the sofa doing nothing most of the day, "laughing hysterically."

I immediately got online and searched *acute schizophrenia: undifferentiated type*. The phrase "undifferentiated type" is no longer used; considered antiquated. But as I scanned the remainder of the results, the words *psychosis, hallucinations, and delusions* floated on the screen.

Shit.

The acute part of the diagnosis meant that the condition ebbs and flows. Schizophrenic people have times when the mental illness is bad, like Joyce walking up and down the street with an empty carriage, and times when it almost doesn't exist.

Schizophrenia is hereditary the internet said.

Shit. Shit. Shit. Am I crazy? I asked myself. All this time, I thought I was "different." Am... I... crazy? I'm not crazy.

The internet said it can skip a generation. *I'm the skipped generation*, I convinced myself. *Shit. What about Kimeiko?*

When I was five months old, Joyce left me in an apartment building. According to the report, a janitor found me and contacted the police. I'd been there several days. Joyce named the janitor as the father, but he denied it. Shortly after, she surrendered her parental rights and continued to parent my older sister, who was five.

I was like those people you read about in the newspaper. Like Tupac's Brenda's Got a Baby? But instead of a trash heap, I was left in an apartment.

There is a term educators use called cognitive overload. It's the reason you don't teach the scope of British literature in two weeks. It's the reason you chunk information into digestible bits and pieces over time. Brains can only handle so much. And when there's too much information, the brain shuts down. *All* of this information was too much. Emotions engulfed me, and like an overheated cellphone, I shut down.

My brain said, "No more," it didn't want to retain anything else. Beads of sweat formed along my hairline. My heart beat quickly, and then my stomach began to ache as if I was going to vomit. I turned off my computer and shared the document with Brent. He hugged me, but he wasn't equipped to provide the tight embrace I needed. So, I called Shaquita. She bawled after hearing this tragic narrative.

"Why are you crying?" I asked.

"I'm...I'm just so sorry for you. Girl, this is terrible."

"Don't cry for me," I ordered. "Everyone has a story of how they got here. Mine just happens to include being abandoned in a building."

My soul knew I needed empathy. That's why I'd called her, but my brain wasn't in a space to receive it. Years of conditioning had taught me to not empathize with my circumstances; my pain and trauma. It didn't matter that I was adopted. It didn't matter that my adoptive father had molested me. It didn't matter that my adoptive mother died. And my schizophrenic birth mother's abandonment didn't matter either.

Two more letters followed the report.

Joyce drowned when she was twenty-eight years old, not long after I'd been placed in foster care. I'd lost not one, but two mothers, and I lacked training on what to do with that information as well. So, I fell back on what my adoptive mother and grandmother had shown me: I forbade myself to sit with the details and feel the pain. I ignored the obvious hurt that one might associate with learning they could've been aborted. It was distressing, but I refused to cry about it. I was here and so was my Kimeiko. At five months, she learned to hold her head upright; self-sufficiency didn't exist, yet I refused to acknowledge the insecurities and subsequent trauma a baby may develop, not knowing when her mother or food might arrive. I quashed the pain the same way I had when I first discovered I was adopted. And I dared not allow anyone else to offer compassion for me.

The counselor, however, was sympathetic. She suggested I take time to think about my options, which were to contact any other living relatives. I chose to store the physical report in a box under the bed. I kept the emotions associated with each detail in an inaccessible space and focused on creating the family and life I desired.

∞

Brent was offered a position in Des Plaines, Illinois. It was 2000. Kimeiko had just turned one, and I'd just graduated with a master's. Since giving birth, I'd wondered how we would raise our daughter within the deep, southern racism I'd barely learned to navigate. Some of my white high school students believed interracial dating would produce spotted children, like *a Dalmatian*. Others referred to me as a *Yankee*, as if it was 1865. Moving closer to home seemed ideal.

Brent and I thought it'd be better to live near our families. We'd see them more. We wouldn't have to commute so far for holidays, and we'd have more support. Terry flew down to help us drive our belongings back north. Chicago's rent was over two thousand dollars no matter where we looked, so we settled for a western suburb. It was forty minutes from Brent's job; forty minutes from Aunt Lillian; and fifty minutes from my father and MJ. Although we were centrally located, we commuted more to others' homes than they did to ours, primarily for them to babysit.

With three years of experience and a graduate degree, I assumed finding a teaching job would be easy; however, my job search was unsuccessful. Someone suggested a headhunter, which seemed excessive for gaining school district employment, but I was willing to try. I had to generate income to help pay our rent. After I passed my Illinois certification test, I sat across from a young white guy, with a clean, pressed white dress shirt and black tie. He all but put his feet on the desk as he asked me informal questions and observed my behavior.

"See, I can tell a lot about you," he said. "It's the way you pronounce *aunt*. You said, *awnt*, instead of *ant*."

He never asked me about teaching, and he never helped me find a job.

I secured employment on my own at an alternative high school in a nearby suburb. Classrooms and offices were in a warehouse-type building. Dingy white walls looked more like a 1960s insane asylum than an institution of learning. Training included instruction on how to "take students down." As they explained the process, I knew I would never stand behind a student, grab him or her by the neck, buckle the back of their knees, and twist their arms behind them. I was a little over five feet tall. All I wanted to do was teach.

Students called me *Miss Candy* and sang Cameo's *just like candaayy* when they entered the 169-square-foot space. I taught a twenty-two-year-old male student how to read; I was twenty-seven. I can still see the way his brown beard framed his face when he realized he could sound out letters to form words. A proverbial light bulb lit above his head when he began to recognize words for the first time. *You don't be bullshitting up in here*, another male student blurted out in the middle of a lesson. Every time I entered the building, my chest constricted, my belly swirled, and I wondered what someone as educated as me was doing there. One October day, the in-house counselor asked a simple question, "How are you?"

I responded with the day's events. I couldn't control two students who were gang members. They'd rather swap stories of their weekend, where they punched the first stranger who walked out of a corner store than listen to me talk about similes and metaphors. As soon as my eyes turned red, the counselor rushed me to his office, which sat catty-corner to my classroom. I cried uncontrollably, sucking up snot and wiping my eyes. I described the discomfort of learning about the signs that a fight would ensue at the school. More than one student sporting Timbs signaled the event. They didn't fistfight; they stomped one another's bodies into the concrete. The counselor managed me the same way he managed the students, with strategies. Paraphrase. Summarize. Clarify. Reflect. His compassionate eyes stared, his head bobbled with understanding, and in a calm voice, he said, "Why don't you take a couple of days off?"

It never dawned on me that I was overwhelmed; stressed. Those words were never used in my upbringing. Of course, upon reflection, I know that's what it was, but back then? I ignored obvious signs. During my reprieve, I dropped Kimeiko off at daycare and returned home to do nothing. When I returned to work, another teacher was concerned. He was a former minor league baseball player. This was the first time since Brent and I had married that I found myself actively trying to ignore a man. I knew that if I entertained any part of his conversation or "concern," then I'd slip back into a behavior I'd left in undergrad. Still, I thought frequently about his six-foot frame. I was determined to honor my promise to be faithful. But his concern for my welfare drew me in.

"You good? You never take off."

"Oh yeah. I am. I can't talk about it here, though."

Because he knew I was married, he gave me his number. I called him from our landline during Brent's forty-minute commute from work. He gave encouraging words for how to maintain my sanity. *Don't care too much. Most of those kids will drop out before long anyway.* By our second conversation, he complimented my body. Birthing Kimeiko had left me with a small pooch full of light and dark stretch marks. His praise was easy to receive. By our third conversation, he described the kisses he would give if we were ever alone. We never met, but his words were an entertaining replacement for the dissatisfaction of teaching last-chance teens, something that could land me back into seeking sex outside of my marriage.[1] Our dreamy phone conversations continued for a few weeks until the bill came.

"What's this 847-area code?" Brent asked.

Ours was 630. Family and friends were 773.

"I don't know," I lied.

"You don't know whose number this is?"

"Nope."

"Well, it's on here a lot," he scanned the remainder of the bill's pages.

My heart thumped against my chest. "I have no idea who that could be."

"Well, let me call and see," Brent said as he picked up our home phone.

"Okay. Wait. I know who it is."

I cried through a difficult apology and admitted everything. We discussed who *he* was. I confessed what I hoped to do with *him*. Brent was quiet. He often could retreat within himself. He never raised his voice. He simply scratched his head and sat, contemplating the next steps. Nothing physical occurred, so he forgave me. I promised it would never happen again. We agreed that if I had future urges, he'd be the first to know. I breathed a long sigh of relief, grateful that our life would return to normal.

Apart from having Kimeiko, I'd maintained a regular birth control regimen for seven years. But at the time, it was believed that taking birth control pills increased the risk of breast cancer. As I neared thirty, I sought an alternative and less harmful contraceptive. The gynecologist suggested we use a condom before beginning a different method, but we didn't. I was pregnant by February 2001. A few months later,

Brent's job offered to move us back to Jacksonville. No matter how racist, we agreed returning to the South where it was warm and comfortable was best.

"Why are you moving back there?" my grandmother asked.

Her question confused me. She hadn't visited our home more than once that year. "I want the same doctor who delivered Kimeiko to deliver this baby."

"That's a dumb reason. Anybody can deliver a baby."

"Brent likes his job."

"Brent can get another job here," she retorted.

"He likes the job he has."

"He just wants to be a big fish in a small sea," she said. Again, her response confused me. Jacksonville's population outnumbered Covert's demographic several hundred thousand times over. In terms of area, the city is the sixth largest in the United States.

She rattled off other phrases and I shrank to my sixteen-year-old self, tuning out most of the conversation, internalizing parts, but remaining silent. I could've said *we just want to move back,* but no words would justify our decision with which my grandmother didn't agree. All she wanted to hear is that we would remain nearby.

"No one's gonna keep helping you move," she said, referring to Terry's previous assistance. She didn't know Diamond's brother had booked a flight and was ready to pack boxes and drive down with us.

When we hung up, I decided not to speak with my grandmother for a while. Before that year, I thought she was a woman in control of herself and her emotions. But she repeatedly showed that she was not. As I matured, her inability to use appropriate words to convey her own emotions became more apparent with each conversation. Between mothering an almost two-year-old, moving, and being pregnant, I needed to avoid negative conversations and opinions. All of my grandmother's calls went to voicemail until we settled into our new home. Weeks later, when I finally answered the phone, I envisioned her furrowed brow.

"Don't you ever do that again," she scolded, "no matter how mad you get."

I never ignored her calls again, but that year, my perspective of her shifted, and our relationship changed; my grandmother became someone I couldn't trust with the details of my life.

At six months pregnant, I found a job at a magnet high school fifteen minutes away from our home. The students there were diverse: Black, white, as well as refugees from Bosnia and Sudan. Socioeconomic statuses varied, but the students who gravitated toward me were neither poor nor rich. Their parents worked hard and simply wanted their children to receive an adequate public education that might afford them better futures. It was a long way from the alternative school; I'd found the perfect place for my personality and academic background.

Our baby wasn't due until mid-November, so I planned to give birth and then take leave through the new year. However, during my last weekly visit, the doctor felt the baby's feet at the tip of my dilated cervix and later noticed the umbilical cord was wrapped around her neck. An emergency C-section was the safest answer. She was three weeks early. Her premature birth meant Brent was the only family in the room. We named her Briana.

Briana latched on quickly in the hospital and nursed for months after, spending hours in a bubble of bonding, leaving a two-and-a-half-year-old Kimeiko to play or fend for herself. Her portable crib sat in the living area, against the wall, next to the kitchen. She slept a lot, and if anyone accidentally bumped it, she'd wail, prompting me to pick her up and rock her back to sleep in the small space of my lap.

"You have to hold her like that until she goes to sleep?" Brent's brother asked. He and his wife had visited to meet their niece.

"Yeah. Otherwise, she won't."

Though my grandmother and Nana visited as they had before, Briana's reliance on me shielded others from an immediate connection. The two of us merged. I showed her that her new world was secure. She showed me I was important.

I was unsuccessful at building a mother but excelled at creating a life worthy of the moniker my parents had bestowed upon me. Katherin Elizabeth had a model husband, whose mere presence provided a sense of calm, two beautiful biological daughters, and a suburban house bigger than any of my childhood homes. I'd even materialized the dog that was once a photo taped on my lilac walls. I finally felt the normalcy I lacked as a child. Katherin Elizabeth had attained a master's, and in addition to finding the ideal high school to teach English, had begun teaching part-time at the community college. I exhaled my family's thoughts—*I'd made it.* I believed what they did— achievements are proof of wellness. I'd pieced together a life of joy, despite my background and proclivities. But like the exterior of some remodeled buildings, my insides started to crumble. Petulia Belcher began to emerge, curious about the world Katherin Elizabeth created, wondering where she fit into this perfectly constructed life. I'd pushed Petulia down my entire life, and she was tired of suffocating.

TRAPPED

SHANE

2003

It had been two years since I thought about having sex with a man other than Brent. My urges returned as I began my eighth year as a high school English teacher. The academic year started in the auditorium, where the principal explained new policies. I sat in the front row with Carmen, another English teacher, and Tasha, an assistant principal. New faculty stood near the stage, waiting to be introduced. One teacher stood out. My friends and I tittered and snickered about his dark skin and sexy eyes as if we were high school girls. The new teacher squinted and assessed the faculty, like a *Bachelor* contestant. The principal ended his introduction with *Does anyone want to show him around?* With little to no shame, I jumped up.

Tasha grabbed my arm and yanked me back to my seat. "Sit yo ass down. You married," she whispered.

With the new teacher around, I not only forgot I was a teacher, but I also forgot that I was, indeed, married.

Some days, I woke up thrilled to be with Brent, happy to be a mother to our four- and almost two-year-old daughters. Other days, I woke up wondering how I ended up married with two kids, as if the universe had handed me a life, I had no business living. Marriage was overwhelmingly monotonous. I worked, drove the girls to daycare, waited for Brent to come home from tennis, graded papers, and had sex about twice a week. Many days, I wondered if this was all there was to life. Was this the adulthood I sped toward in my baccalaureate speech?

"You act like you don't want to be here," Brent said once.

"I want to, but I don't feel like I deserve to be here," I confided.

Petulia clawed her way to my surface. She reminded me that I wasn't who I said I was, no matter the image. *Remember*, she taunted, *no one wants you. If your own mother could leave you unattended in an apartment, then what will Brent do when he discovers who you really are?* She wouldn't let me forget the subsequent trauma. *If you were worth being taken care of, then your adoptive mother wouldn't have died. Why do you think she left? Even she knew you were worthless.* She reminded me that life could be upturned at any moment. *Brent appears perfect, but he's not. He's like your father. He'll wait until you're asleep, and instead of kicking you out, he'll leave.*

The new teacher stood on the periphery of my unhappiness. His name was Shane. A month had passed since the first day of school, and nothing out of character had occurred. We acknowledged each other in the hallway and sat near each other in faculty meetings. Like most Black faculty in the South, we knew we had to band together in white spaces. However, the more he spoke, the more I noticed how he spoke to me. His gravelly voice was low, his words drawn out. It sounded like, "Heeey, Mizzz Gaaarland." I thought I was imagining the innuendo, so I checked with Tasha.

"It's obvious, he wanna fuck you," Tasha said when I sat in her office asking what she thought. She had invited Brent and me to a birthday party, one Saturday, and afterward, we became fast friends. Many Saturdays, I traveled thirty minutes to her house and stayed well into the night, drinking liquor, with her and her childhood friend while our daughters played. Her garish personality was too much for Brent, so he stayed home.

"You think so?" I replied.

"Girl, yeah. It's the way he looks at you."

I wanted her to be wrong, and I wanted her to be right because I was definitely interested. I asked another teacher friend as we sat grading papers and griping about students.

"Do you think Shane likes me?"

"Uh, yeah Gardenia," she said without hesitation. It was a nickname one of our colleagues had given me that stuck. "You can tell by the way he looks at you. It's in his eeyyees."

Shane and I stood at the teacher's mailbox: a narrow space big enough for two or three people. I thought if I cleared the air between us, then the tingle I felt whenever he was nearby and the general sense that we needed to be together would fade into oblivion. After our regular pleasantries, I opened a different conversation.

"My friends seem to think you like me. Is that true?"

He laughed, squinted his eyes, and stared. "I do admire you, but you know, I'm married. I admire you though," he repeated. "Maybe we can be friends."

I returned the smile. "Right. I'm married, too. I was just wondering. Yep. We can be friends."

By November, Shane had discovered my classroom —a trailer outside of the main building. The principal moved me to the portable so I wouldn't have to share a room with other teachers. Aside from the small, rectangular window on the door, you couldn't easily see in or out.

"This is where you teach?" Shane asked.

"Yep," I replied. "Wanna see it?"

Daily visits became the norm. He told me about growing up on the West Coast and playing college football. That's how he was able to become a coach for the high school. He and his wife had been married for the same length of time that Brent and I had. He had two small children: each a year older than mine. Commonalities drew me nearer, just like with Will in undergrad. I looked forward to his visits. I looked forward to staring into his eyes as he talked about his marriage and what his wife would and would not do.

"You know I like you, right?" Shane said after a month. He walked toward the resource closet.

"Yeah, I know. I like you, too, but we're married. And I don't wanna fuck nobody's husband 'cause I don't want nobody fucking mine."

He laughed. "I hear you. But you gon' be my boo," he said with confidence, pulling his pants and underwear down.

"Come here," he said, extending his hand.

When I joined him in the closet, he put my hand on his penis. "You got me standing here naked in a closet. How much longer you gon' make me wait?"

I guess he thought if he showed me what he was working with, I'd break down and consummate our feelings. But I didn't. I shut down his advances that day and every day thereafter. Plus, I didn't want to tarnish my reputation as a "good" teacher with a possible scandal of having intercourse on campus... in a trailer.

I didn't have sex, but I knew Brent and I had to talk.

"I feel like I'm about to cheat," I began. "I'm attracted to a teacher at work."

There was no pause in the conversation. No scratching of the head. No inward meditation. "You need to handle it, then. I'm not going to keep going through this. You have to figure out what to do. If you cheat, I'm leaving."

I didn't have the language to explain what was happening. If I could have said I am a sex addict, someone who has the compulsion to use sex to medicate unresolved trauma, then maybe Brent and I would have understood "cheating" is the effect of the compulsion, not just an immoral decision. Conversely, I'm not certain using psychological terminology would've changed anything. Many people in society, even professionals, see sex addiction as merely a preference that describes someone's sexual appetite.[1]

I'm not sure Brent would've reacted any differently. Who wants their wife to have sex outside of their marriage, whether studies support the concept or not?

Therapy seemed like a good idea, so I met with a thin, white woman.

"Why are we here today?" she asked.

"I think I have a problem. I always feel like I want to cheat on my husband."

She peered over her readers, and said, "If you want to cheat on your husband, then you need to get a divorce."

The therapist's response, though blunt, was understandable. Sex addiction was recognized and named in 1983,[2] but only one study outlined characteristics in 1992.[3] Research about sex addiction began to evolve, around 2001,[4] well after I'd developed the addiction and right around my fifth year of marriage. In hindsight, it was unfair to expect this woman to have known about sex addiction. She would have had to have studied this specific area of marriage and family counseling to be able to adequately help me. Furthermore, sex addiction, though once added to the DSM, was removed, and to this day, has never been re-added.[5] Therefore, instead of expert advice, she fell back on her personal view— perceiving sexual pleasure as a preference, not a problem.

With an ultimatum from Brent, and a decision to make from the therapist, I enlisted Tasha, next, to help me sort through the situation. She sat on the edge of her seat as I described Shane's afterschool visits, conversations, and penis showings.

"I don't know what to do."

"I'd fuck him," she said.

She was no help.

Although we hadn't spoken in six months, my father was my last hope. Once again, he had converted to a new religion. Now that he was with MJ, he had recently become an ordained deacon at her Baptist church. I thought he'd have some pithy scripture that would lead me toward a path of righteousness.

"Don't do it, Baby," he said. "What if it's good? Then, you're going to be running around trying to see each other all the time. What if you like him better? Then, you might break up your family."

My father spoke with too much authority on the subject, and I didn't want to know how. A story from my childhood had floated around my mother's side of the family, something about him helping a woman move to Moline, Illinois, while my mother recovered from her kidney transplant. Regardless, he made good points, but I still didn't know how not to cheat or what to do next, especially because Shane knew I liked him as much as he did me.

This shit is boring.

Shane texted me in the middle of a faculty meeting. It was January 2004 and the first time someone sent me words on a phone. Now, we had a secret form of communicating. Texting confirmed whether it was okay to stop by the portable, or if students were around. Texting allowed us to talk throughout the evening, but never too late, agreeing to respect one another's family time.

Tasha is having a birthday party on Saturday. I'll be alone, I texted.

Come by. My wife and kids will be out of town.

My stomach fluttered. I wouldn't want a woman
to meet my husband at my house, so why was I
planning to do so with Shane?

"I've never done this before," he said leading me
to a back bedroom.

I didn't believe him. His overt willingness to meet
with me seemed familiar; common. I was nervous,
while he was eager. Something told me *this* referred to
allowing a woman inside his home, not cheating on
his wife.

But it didn't matter. Before the month ended, I
officially became an adulterer. My father was right. All
Shane and I talked about was how and when to meet
up again.

Seeing Shane was easy. One way we snuck around
was to call off from work.

I would leave the house like normal, drop Briana
off at pre-k and Kimeiko off at elementary school.
We would meet at a hotel a few blocks away from the
school and split the cost. He'd put his gun on the
nightstand and then undress. Initially, the idea that he
carried startled me.

"People out here are crazy, Baby," he said,
sounding like my father. "You gotta be ready to
protect yourself."

We'd spend the hours of the school day together,
exploring each other's bodies and my favorite part—
talking. He would rub my scalp and run his fingers
through to the bottom of my hair and praise my
beauty.

"You don't look like you had any kids at all," he
said.

"I don't?"

"Well, like maybe one but not two. You don't look like you had *two* kids."

His compliment electrified me. I knew what he was saying. Photos of women's post-partum bellies shocked me. Some looked mutilated. Having a C-section with Briana had destroyed my body and sense of sexiness; the lower half of my stomach hung like a flap and fit sloppily into my jeans. I was happy a man thought it looked decent. I delighted in his admiration.

I enjoyed getting to know him, who his wife was, and why he cheated. According to him, he and his wife rarely had sex. And when they did, there was no adventure. She laid on her back, and according to him, he *did what he knew best.* Depersonalizing his wife, permitted him to cheat by making something wrong with her.[6] There was nothing wrong with his wife; there was something wrong with us, assuaging our unresolved issues with sex.

He showed me a picture of her.

"She's pretty," I said. The way he'd gone on about my looks, I assumed she was an ogre with three heads.

I learned more about his two sons, who appeared to be mini versions of him. I wondered if they'd grow up to be cheaters too. I wondered if Kimeiko and Briana would be like me, planning trysts outside of committed relationships. Discovering cheating was genetic would have diminished some of my guilt and given me another type of permission. It would've been much better to learn that there was a cheating gene than to succumb to the idea that I simply lacked morals.

His eyes glazed over as we talked more. Finally, he said, "You need a friend."

I hit him playfully on his chest. "I have friends."

"You need somebody to talk to," he clarified.

His comments bothered me. I was with him because I liked him, and I thought he liked me, too. What were we supposed to do—have sex all the time?

But that's what we did. We frequented hotels and sometimes used a classroom at the school. Eventually, Shane bought a new house five minutes away from Tasha's, and I developed a new habit—stopping to see him before I saw her. I thought it was serendipity, as if God, himself, wanted me to have this extramarital affair. If I wasn't supposed to be doing this, then why would it be so easy? Why would seeing Shane be so accessible?

I had developed a secret life, something that is common with female sex addicts.[7] By day, I was a teacher, wife, and mother. On the weekend, I was a side chick. Saying I was going to Tasha's house didn't feel like a lie, because I'd always end up there. When Shane moved, I'd let him know I was on the way, and then he'd meet me behind a gas station or in the community college's unlit parking lot. We'd park our SUVs next to one another, and I'd hop in his. We never did anything in mine. Usually, we'd leave right after. But this time, my feelings began to shade our agreement.

"We've been doing this for a year, and you don't know anything about me," I said while pulling up my pants.

"I know you like to *fuck*," he said.

I stared at him, signaling I was serious. The problem was, *he* was serious.

"What else do I need to know?" he asked.

"You don't know my middle name. You don't know when my birthday is. You don't know anything. I know yours. It's in January." Suddenly, I was crying.

Shane rolled his eyes and looked out the window.

"I gotta go," I said. "I told Tasha I'd be there by now."

"A'ight," he said.

Later, he texted and asked when my birthday was. But it was too late. There was an insurmountable knowing; he didn't care about me, no matter what he said. However, just like in undergrad where I'd collected men like trophies, I couldn't let him go.

AUNT CATHERINE

2004 - 2006

"Life's good for you," Aunt Diane said. My family and I were in Chicago for our biannual Christmas trip.

I screamed inside. I wanted to reveal everything that had occurred since my mother died. I wanted to confess the challenges I'd had with sex, men, and relationships. *I'm having an affair*, I wanted to yell. Instead, I told her about my latest academic endeavor. These were the types of updates my mother's side of the family appreciated.

My long-term goal was to be a university professor. Ever since undergrad, the profession had called to me, so by the fall of 2004, I was accepted into a doctoral program at a state research university. My family, especially my grandmother, was overjoyed by the idea. College was a place where I excelled. No matter what else occurred in my life, I always managed to shine academically. Except for the one semester when I had several boyfriends and an abortion, undergrad was easy.

However, I had underestimated the challenges of pursuing a doctorate, while teaching, married, with children, and commuting to the university twice a week. It was different than anything I'd ever experienced. In year one, I developed a chalazion, a small bump inside my eyelid. Before removing it, the ophthalmologist listed reasons it may have developed. Stress and anxiety were two. That was the first time a doctor had suggested I may have stress or anxiety. At the time, those two words meant nothing to me. But in the sex addiction world, they're relevant. These comorbidities, having two or more illnesses at one time,[1] are common for female sex addicts.[2] Oftentimes, those who are addicted live with stress, anxiety, or depression, and do not know how to deal with it, which leads to acting out sexual compulsions.[3] Though my affair with Shane seemed like a moral misstep, sex itself still served as a relief; a coping mechanism on which I'd learned to rely on well after senior year and college. The chalazion should have been a sign for me to slow down; however, my lack of self-awareness led me to pile on.

That Christmas, my family and I sat around Aunt Lillian's living room, just as we had holidays past. Her artificial white tabletop tree sat in the corner. A train set, equipped with a fake town and cotton for snow lived in front of a window with blinking lights. Everyone shared the good news of their life's happenings. I wanted to reveal another major decision. I was in the process of looking for my biological family. I'd contacted the Midwest Adoption Agency and asked for something called a Request for Non-Identifying Information. You can only ask for these details one time, from one person. I had chosen my birth grandfather. As the family's patriarch, it seemed he would know the most. But I thought about Grandma Hunny's previous reaction and decided against sharing.

∞

My biological grandfather contacted me at the beginning of the New Year in 2005. His name was Mose. He was eager to provide specifics about our family, including pictures, a letter, and his phone number. Each of his seven children had been a part of the Illinois foster care system. Only one of his five adult daughters kept in contact with him. Her name was Catherine. Aunt Catherine returned my call on Sunday, during the first quarter of Super Bowl XXXIV. We chatted back and forth like longtime girlfriends. She wanted to know everything that had happened in my life, beginning with the adoption.

"I always thought you might've been raised by some rich Black people," she said.

Me, too, I thought. "Nope," I said. "My mom was a stay-at-home mother with kidney disease and my dad was a pharmacy tech. We didn't have a lot of money."

I could hear the disappointment in her *humph*. "I tried to get you, but the State wouldn't let me. They told me to leave you alone and not ask about it anymore. I tried. I worried every day about where you were…all this time. So, when Dad said you'd called, I couldn't believe it!"

Her confession eased years of rejection that had taken residence in my body. To know that one family member thought about me was enough to prove my existence wasn't an irrevocable error. I mattered. We continued to catch up on the past three decades. I described school, marriage, and the girls. I imagined her cheeks beaming with pride. She told me about her two daughters and grandchildren.

"If anyone calls you, it'll be Crystal. She's the outgoing one," she said. Later, Crystal would tell me that Aunt Catherine would do more than worry about my whereabouts. She and her sister would endure their mother's countless drunken nights, where she'd lament about where Petulia was.

Aunt Catherine described our biological family's mental health. My biological grandmother had a nervous breakdown, resulting in hospitalization. It wasn't clear if she had an anxiety disorder or depression, just that one day life's happenings were too much for her to bear. Mose suffered from depression and had molested four of his daughters, my mother included. Aunt Catherine had clinical depression. Her daughters lived with panic attacks and medication. Her brothers had been imprisoned, one of them for murder. Each sibling had been separated from their parents and raised in foster care.

Hearing these stories helped me to understand myself. I'd always felt different. There was a constant swirl in my belly when life overwhelmed me. Trivial things upset me as a child. When I was younger, I cried frequently for all reasons. One time I swelled up with sadness because my cousins, who had visited from North Carolina, planned to drive to Bolingbrook to visit another cousin. The thought of not being invited sent me spiraling into a surge of anger, sadness, and eventually, crying until my family consoled me and assured me that I'd be right there with them. I was ten. When I was twelve, my parents told me my father had diabetes. The thought of his impending death caused me to bury my head deep into my pillow and cry for hours until my mother came into my room and ordered me to stop. She said it was an excessive emotion for just a diabetes diagnosis.

Aunt Catherine dismissed these connections. "Don't try to be like us. You don't have to try to be like us," she said. "Depression is like a deep hole you can't dig yourself out of. You want to but you can't. It's not something to want."

Since then, I've learned that there are several types of depression, not just the most common one that is described in pharmaceutical commercials.[4] Depression is not always diagnosed as a disorder; sometimes, depression and anxiety are tied to a sensitive nervous system, which is hereditary.[5] During our conversation, I didn't know how to explain my feelings, just that I understood. I didn't know how to tell her that since my adoptive mother had died, I'd only pretended not to feel anything. Inside, I was a bundle of unhinged emotions firing throughout my body with no salve in sight.

Aunt Catherine had recently moved from Memphis to Atlanta and was planning another move to Georgia.

"Savannah?" I almost screamed when she named the city. "That's only two hours from us!"

The synchronicity of us sharing a name and soon living only 157 miles apart meant our reunion was kismet.

Aunt Catherine and I spoke once a week, and she began to notice the waves of my moods, simply from the tone of my voice.

"You don't sound so good today," she'd say, reading my downward spiral over the radio waves of our cell phone connection.

The next week, she'd observe a change. "Whatever you did, you need to keep doing it," she'd say, not knowing Shane and I had just met up.

When she moved to Savannah, my family and I drove to visit. My stomach seized as we approached the gas station where we agreed to meet. Phone conversations were one thing but meeting a live human being to whom I was biologically related plummeted my nerves. My family and I sat in the car and waited. As soon as I saw her light brown skin, small frame, and big floppy straw hat, I knew it was her.

I got out of the car and smiled, "Aunt Catherine?"

She laughed and wrapped her skinny arms around me. "I know it's you because you have our smile. You have our teeth. You look like *us*."

We had the same caricature-like, wide, big-toothed grin. I remembered how my grandmother ordered me to *not smile so hard* on my wedding day. Seeing the smile on her face made it okay for me to grin as wide as I pleased. I was mesmerized. I examined her stature, her hair type, her eyes, and her laugh. Finally, my physical self was reflected in something other than a mirror. I was biologically related to someone other than Kimeiko and Briana.

Brent confirmed what I thought, "That lady looks like you."

For the remainder of the day, I was physically present, but my mind wandered to future holidays and aunt-niece trips.

We walked on River Street and meandered through Savannah's touristy downtown area.

"I'm not supposed to have any beer, because of this stint in my heart, but one is okay," she justified after ordering a pint during lunch.

This woman was an older version of me. I'd disregard the doctor's orders, too.

She stroked Kimeiko's braids, which resembled her long, soft hair. "You know I thought you were going to be tall and skinny."

"Why?" I asked.

"Because I went to visit Joyce one time when she was pregnant with you. I asked her one question. I made her answer one question if she was gone have a baby. Who is the father?"

My eyes widened. "What did she say?"

"She pointed to the janitor and said, 'him.' He was a long, lanky, white man. That's why I thought you'd be taller."

Visions of the State's report flashed in my mind. *The janitor found you and called the police.* Was the janitor my father? Should I look for him? I dismissed the idea as it had already taken too much time to find Aunt Catherine. I'd be content with our relationship.

We perused a candy shop for the girls and before long, our time together ended. We talked throughout the remainder of the year and well into the next one.

I'd promised to visit again soon. But before I did, Crystal, her youngest daughter called.

"Kathy, I hate to call you like this, but Mama passed away. They found her in her apartment. We knew she had been talking to you, though, so we knew she'd want you to know."

It was June 2006. I internalized Aunt Catherine's death. Any relationship I'd had that I'd deemed important ended in death or desertion. Something *was* wrong with me.

"Passed away?" I repeated. "How?"

"They think it was probably a heart attack. You know she had that stint."

"Right."

Mose died a year later.

There was one more possibility for maternal kinship. Before Aunt Catherine died, she told me my sister's name. A simple Google search gave me her address and phone number. My sister knew I existed, but according to her, didn't know how to find me. Our mother had left her with her paternal grandmother, and although our aunts and grandfather lived blocks away from her in Chicago, they ignored her existence. I frequented home often, so we met twice. I assumed the least we could do was develop a bond over our abandonment. But my sister, a darker-skinned, taller, thinner version of me, seemed more bothered with how much I resembled our aunts and mother, than with establishing a relationship.

See, Petulia mocked. *I told you. You deserve to be alone.*

The emptiness remained.

∞

One night, Brent and I wrestled on the floor in the family room, play fighting, our legs and arms intertwined. He overpowered me as I lay on my back. His legs straddled either side of mine and he pinned my arms down.

"Are you cheating on me?" he asked, catching me off guard.

Two years had passed since Shane, and I began our affair. In the beginning, guilt held me hostage. I desperately wanted to confess to Brent what I'd been doing, but his words echoed in my mind: *If you cheat, I'm leaving.*

For a moment, I thought I would reveal everything. But I didn't know how. How would I tell him I was in a long-term affair? Wouldn't it be worse to confess to two years, as opposed to in the beginning when it was fresh, new, and could be dubbed a "mistake?" One or two times can be labeled an error; two years was a conscious choice. How was I supposed to tell him that sometimes when he thought I was at work, I was in a hotel up the street from the school, with another man? The betrayal alone would end our marriage. How would he be able to trust me to go anywhere, if he knew there were days when I pretended to go teach? How was I supposed to describe the constant sexting, another form of exhibitionism? That another man had photos of my body on his phone?

With my arms and legs pinned down, I stared back into Brent's eyes, and said, "No."

I loved Brent. Being with Shane didn't change that, but that was also something I didn't know how to explain. There was a cosmic pull toward Shane I couldn't ignore. Shane did things Brent never would, which is part of what kept the affair ongoing. One year, Shane and I agreed to attend Grad Night, an overnight event Disney hosted for all of Florida's seniors. We were chaperones, but eighteen-year-olds entering young adulthood need little supervision. Shane and I texted throughout the night until we found a place to meet. Behind a nonworking rollercoaster, next to an abandoned vendor's cart, we had sex.

I'd constantly tried to coax Brent into my exhibitionist world, but it never worked. For our first trip to Las Vegas, I intentionally bought and wore a denim mini skirt that, while I was standing, stopped mid-thigh. From the right angle, you could almost see my panties when I sat down. It was perfect Vegas attire.

"Let's go do it in that bathroom," I said to Brent as we walked through a casino.

"What?" he asked as if I suggested we do lines of coke on the curb. "I'm not doing that."

"Why noooot? We're *in* Vegas!"

"I don't want to get arrested. That's why not."

My smile faded into anger. I didn't want to be at the casino. I didn't want to be walking around with Brent. I just wanted to return to the hotel. Brent was too level-headed for my antics, but Shane wasn't. He was like a male version of me. Nothing was ever too wild for him, leading me to believe we were addicted to one another; we both seemed to have compulsions, which we acted out together.[6]

But even things with Shane shifted. It was my birthday and my last set of seniors' graduation day. Shane had learned of my birthdate the previous year, and I thought he'd cared enough to remember. We'd already had a conversation about how important this day was to me. I waited to see if he would say something. I sat through graduation rehearsal. Nothing. I watched through tear-filled eyes as the students I was most fond of walked across the stage. Nothing.

Then, this: *Meet me in the parking lot when this is over.*

Shane wanted sex.

I pulled up beside him in the arena's parking lot, just as I had many nights before.

"Are you fucking kidding me?" I asked. I stood outside of his car. Heat rose from my belly. Tears formed in the corner of my eyes. I tried to hold them back, but it was impossible.

"Today is my birthday. Today is my birthday, and you didn't even fucking remember! You don't care about me!" I shouted. "You don't care about me at all. All you want is pussy. That's all I am to you."

Shane looked at me, probably the way he looked at his wife when she nagged and complained about him leaving the house or staying out too late, leaving her at home to take care of the boys, or "coaching" into the night, when a game was well over. He looked at me like Brent did when I was in a deluge of emotions. It was too much, and he needed an escape chute. But there was no ripcord to slow his descent into the well of my emotions. There was just us in an empty parking lot, lights shining on both of our flaws.

"I do care about you," he started. "You mean a lot to me. You're the best thing I have in my life right now," he continued.

"How come you didn't remember?" I asked.

"I just forgot, but I'ma get you something. I'll have it tomorrow."

"You will?" my eyes brightened.

"I will," he promised. "Come here."

He sat in the driver's seat, and I stood there, while we hugged.

The day after my birthday, Shane gave me a gold ring. I showed it to Tasha.

"What you thank 'bout that?" she asked, her southern accent heavier than normal.

"I don't know."

"That looks like some shit you get off Soutel."

I'd never been off Soutel, but after growing up on the West Side of Chicago and visiting hoods across the country, I knew one thing, and that is every ghetto neighborhood is the same. From seventeen until twenty years old, I wore what we called truncated jewelry, trunk jewelry for short. I had a ring on my middle three fingers on each hand. You could buy these "gold" rings at the mall or sometimes in little shops off major streets. They never turned my fingers green, but it wasn't wedding-band gold either.

That's what Shane gave me the day after my birthday —a trunk ring.

"What you gon' do? I'd leave him the fuck alone," she advised.

I couldn't leave him alone. I didn't want to leave him alone. But I grew to understand who I was to him. Shane and I were, indeed, just fucking.

CLUB GUY

2007

In my third year of doctoral studies, stress continued to present in my body in new ways. The dentist said I was grinding my teeth so much that a crack had formed from the top of my back molar to the bottom. The only solution was a root canal and a metal filling. Later, I wore a night guard. But I ignored each stress-related issue and thought of the manifestations as singular, unrelated incidents. As an alternative, I jumped at the opportunity to return to a familiar practice—partying. Michell, a co-worker, turned friend suggested we go to a place called Plush. I hadn't been to a club since college, but I was game. Tonya, my hairdresser, joined us.

Nervousness and excitement intermingled. The music was so loud I could feel it vibrating on my skin, throughout my body. I drank vodka and cranberry after vodka and cranberry until I was brave enough to join others, who seemed much younger, on the dance floor. First, I rocked back and forth alone, then with a man who came up behind me close enough for me to feel his erection. He matched my rhythm with unbridled eroticism. I lost myself in the moment: I wasn't someone's wife, mother, teacher, or doc student; I was just me. I belonged here in this wild environment. Michell, Tonya, and I became friends, who frequented clubs on the weekends.

"You better not be cheating on me," Shane said as I recounted how much fun my friends and I had.

At first, I laughed. He couldn't be serious. But when his narrowed eyes met mine, my smile faded.

"I always cheat on you, every time I'm with Brent, about twice a week," I laughed.

His squinted eyes were usually sexy. This time, they looked dangerous. I knew Shane carried his gun for safety, but I thought of it often, especially after he began showing glimpses of possessiveness after the first year of our affair. When I got a tattoo of a B and a K in a heart on my right booty cheek during a girls' trip with Tasha and her friends, Shane took a pen and crossed the B out and replaced it with a faint, blue S. Now, we were discussing if I was "cheating."

I certainly wasn't going to tell him about any of my birthday weekends in Atlanta, with Michell and Tonya, where one-night stands had become the norm for me. Cheat on him? Ever since he forgot my birthday, he'd made it clear we were *not* in a relationship, so I was unsure of from where his bravado derived. How could I cheat on someone with whom I wasn't in a committed relationship, with someone who couldn't even tell me my favorite color?

Inside, I chuckled. He thought I was a "good girl." For him, that was part of the appeal. He'd said it before: *I'm smart. I'm pretty. I'm not like other women.* But I told him a couple of years ago, he didn't know anything about me. None of this was his concern, though. Ultimately, I told him what he wanted to hear.

"You're the best. I would never cheat on you."

Going out with Michell replaced weekends at Tasha's house and freed me from the structure of our week. In my life, the event dictated the day. Mondays, I sat and watched Kimeiko master backstrokes for summer swim team competitions. Tuesdays, I'd cheer Briana on as she flipped forward and backward on blue gymnastics mats. Wednesdays, the girls and I grocery shopped. Friday nights were reserved for my friend Sofia and her husband; we'd guzzle Chardonnay and argue over Bill Maher's rhetoric. Unless Brent made plans, Saturday night became the time I left the house and lost my inhibitions. As long as I came home at a reasonable hour, Brent seemed unfazed by my activities.

Michell and I always found ourselves at a club. Even if we went somewhere else first, like moths to a flame, we landed at someone's door, hands getting stamped, ordering drinks at the bar, like the one time we went to her cousin's graduation party. After having a couple of glasses of wine and doing a round of congratulations, we headed out to where the real fun was.

Five minutes in, a guy approached me and asked if I wanted a drink.

"Sure. Chardonnay," I answered.

He brought that drink and the one after. Minutes later, the room spun. I was on the dance floor trying to pull his penis out of his pants as if we were the only two people in the room.

He dragged me away, yelling at Michell the whole time. "Did you see ya, girl? Ya girl is wildin'!"

He stopped yelling when we left, and I agreed to sit in his car for a while. Michell parked next to us, and time moved in a slow-motion blur. My next memory was when Michell helped me to her car and drove me home.

"I don't know how I got this drunk. All I had was wine and not a lot of it," I slurred.

"Girl. That man was strange. I think he put something in your drink 'cause you were not acting like that before he brought it to you. You were just fine."

"Think so?" I asked, then passed out.

I could barely walk or talk when she pulled up to my front door.

"I should've watched her closely. I shouldn't have let her get that drunk," she kept saying to Brent. "I'm sorry."

I walked a few steps to the living room and lay on the floor, in front of our loveseat.

"I'm soooo drunk. My head is spinning. I just need to lay here."

"What happened?" Brent asked.

He sat on the loveseat looking down at me as I stumbled through a partial explanation.

"Why are your panties in your purse?" he asked.

His discovery was a mystery to me, too. I wouldn't have taken them off, and if I did, I wouldn't have put them in my purse. I had no idea; however, I had to convince Brent that my panties being in my purse had nothing to do with having sex with another man. At the same time, I knew I couldn't tell him the entire story because it was irrational, and I wasn't entirely sure that another man didn't have sex with me.

I bumbled through parts about club guy and emphasized that all I had was wine. I repeated Michell's theory about being drugged.

Brent sat on the loveseat, staring down at me.

"You have issues and they always come out in sex," he said finally. "Your issues always come out in sex or men. You have to fix it."

So, Brent had noticed. His analysis was right. But bringing awareness to the "issue" was akin to telling me the sun shone in Florida. I had no more control over my sexual impulses than I did over the sun's constant heat, and in 2007, I didn't know what to do with our "new" realization.

I'd first heard of sex addiction when I read Zane's book, *Addicted*, well before I began cheating on Brent. It always felt fictional. Years later, the erotic novel still didn't match my experiences. *Addicted* read like a Hollywood rendition of a real problem, and it depicted sex addiction as *only* about sex. Off-screen, sex addiction was more of a compulsion that led me into dangerous situations like possibly being drugged in a club. The book, with its sensationalized sex scenes and heightened drama, seemed a distant portrayal of who I'd become. I didn't cheat because I had a vanilla sex life. I cheated to escape the discomfort of trauma.

I was even more disappointed when the term resurfaced with Eric Benét and Halle Berry's divorce. I paid attention to how people reacted; friends and late-night comedians found the concept laughable, and eventually, after attending group therapy with actual addicts, even Benét realized he was not addicted, and that there was a difference between sex addicts and people who may have just "made some bad choices."[1] Since Zane's book and Benét's confession, there has been a perpetual debate in the mental health community focused on if sex addiction is real and whether it should be included in the DSM-V.[2] But a lifetime of challenges centered on sex and my husband's acknowledgment of those struggles led me to believe that maybe I should consider, *perhaps I am a sex addict.*

One of the first diagnostics to determine who a sex addict is was created in 2001; it described behavioral, cognitive, and emotional symptoms so that professionals could begin to identify people like me as living with a condition. The creator of this framework noted that at least five of the characteristics should be present for a sex addiction diagnosis.[3] Years later, the internet offered several adaptations of the tool in the form of online quizzes, so I found and took one similar to this:[456]

Have you made repeated unsuccessful attempts to stop thinking about or engaging in sexual behaviors?

Yes. Ever since I married.

After having sex (with self or others), do you sometimes feel depressed or regret it?

In undergrad, I always felt worse after having sex with someone. Brent is the only person I haven't felt like this with. I've hated sneaking around to see Shane or having sex with random men, but at the same time, it feels good.

Thinking about real-life interactions, do you pursue some sexual behaviors or forms of sexual release anonymously or with complete strangers?

Yes. I've met a man at the club before and had sex with him that night. I don't do it as much as I used to, but it has happened more than once.

Do you ever think your sexual desire is stronger than you are?

Yes. My friends think I cheat because our marriage lacks intimacy. Shane assumes I'm with him because Brent isn't as great as he is. Neither of these statements is true. The fact is there's never enough sex.

Does your preoccupation with sex interfere with life responsibilities or relationships?

No. I always take care of my family, work, and school.

Do you ever have obsessive thoughts of a sexual nature that you struggle to get out of your mind?

Yes, when exhibitionism is involved.

Does your sexual behavior potentially offend others, violate community standards, or place you in danger of arrest?

Yes. Exhibitionism is illegal, and I was almost arrested for it during our anniversary trip in Savannah. We partied in a hole-in-the-wall bar. On the way home, white men drove alongside us. The men and I had

back-and-forth banter, then they asked me to pull up
my shirt.

"You dare me?" I asked Brent.
"No. I know you will."
I was offended and we argued on the way back to
the hotel. When we parked, he went to the room and
passed out. I stood outside the hotel keyless. The
receptionist wouldn't let me in because I was also
shirtless and braless. They called the police.
"I can't go to jail," I begged the officer. Bright red
and blue lights blinded me. "I'm a teacher. I'll lose my
job."
They confirmed my room number, and someone
knocked hard enough to wake Brent up.

**Did you experience abuse, neglect, or other
serious trauma as a child or adolescent?**

Yes. I was abandoned in an apartment building. I
was hit by a car. My adoptive mother died. My father
gave up his parental rights. I was in a car accident,
resulting in a head injury.

**Were you sexually abused as a child or
adolescent?**

Yes. There was the child-on-child molestation
with Trina and the molestation with my father.

**Have you previously sought help for negative, or
damaging sexual behaviors by, for example,
going to a therapist?**

If the terrible therapist counts, then yes.

Have you tried and failed to stop specific sexual behaviors?

Yes.

Has anyone been hurt emotionally because of your sexual behavior?

Yes.

Do you keep certain elements of your sexual behavior hidden from partners and/or friends?

Yes. I always have. There was a night my friends and I hung out in a parking lot after a party. A guy who graduated from our high school said he always wanted to be my boyfriend, but he settled for another girl because she looked like me. It was me he wanted. All ears and all smiles, I followed him to the backseat of his car, where we stripped from the bottom down. My friends waited outside.

"Did you have sex with him?" one of my friends asked.

By then, I'd learned what was socially acceptable and what was not, so my response was, "No."

"We saw the condom on the ground," one of them said.

Have you neglected parts of your life – at your job, at home, time with friends and family – in pursuit of your sexual desires?

No. I would never do that unless calling off from work counts.

Would you regard sex, or the pursuit of sex, as the most important thing that drives you?

No.

Have you felt humiliated or devalued by your sexual activity?

Yes. In undergrad, I had a threesome. I performed fellatio on one man, while the other one had sex with me.

Did your parents have trouble with sexual behavior?

I don't know. (I clicked no.)

Have your sexual behaviors ever caused your friends, family, or sexual partners to become upset?

Yes.

Has sex been a way for you to escape your problems?

Yes.

Have you maintained multiple romantic or sexual relationships at the same time?

Yes.

Do you feel like your sexual appetites have a grip on you?

Yes. Most of the time. Once I feel like I need sex, I have to have it.

Have sexual behaviors ever caused issues in relationships with friends or family?

Yes.

Your results indicate that you are at high risk of suffering from sex addiction.

I stared at the screen for several minutes. The result confirmed what I'd already suspected and what Brent had pointed out. The website said I should schedule a consultation, but how would I explain where I was going? Should I tell Brent over dinner or during our Friday night movie? Would he immediately leave or stay and help me work through it? Legally, adultery is considered grounds for divorce,[7] and depending on the country, women who commit such acts can face death,[8] primarily because the law is interconnected with patriarchal religious edicts.

Three major religions cite adultery as an unforgivable act. *Thou shall not commit adultery* is one of The Ten Commandments wedged in between telling Christians not to murder people or steal others' property, signifying the severity society places on the behavior. The Qur'an calls adultery Zina; offenders can be stoned to death.[9] Judaism defines adultery as only "sexual intercourse of a married woman with any man other than her husband;" placing the onus on the woman, and also noting it as a cardinal sin.[10]

Brent wasn't raised with a religion, and I'd given up on Christianity somewhere between being ambushed with an intercession and reading the Bible cover-to-cover. Still, most men don't want to be married to a woman who has committed adultery, much less one who has been diagnosed and proclaimed to have uncontrollable urges to do so. So, even though I was informed, I kept my findings to myself.

OTHER MEN

2008 - 2010

It was year four of my doctoral process. While the world celebrated the meteoric rise of the United States' first Black president, the chair of my committee returned my dissertation proposal with scores of tracked changes, comments, and re-writes. To conduct research and graduate, I had to meet what seemed to be unattainable expectations. One morning, I awoke but couldn't move my body. My arms and legs were heavy and frozen to the bed. My eyes were open, but I couldn't form words or speak. After a couple of occurrences, I learned to take deep breaths, until each part of my body awoke one limb at a time. This condition, sleep paralysis, is caused by stress and anxiety. But I dismissed it as just another part of life I had to accept.

Hanging out with Michell and Tonya slowly decreased, so I snuck out of the house as if I were a teenager living under my grandparents' thumb in Covert. After a few drinks, Brent would fall into a deep sleep, and I would go to my favorite club and sit alone. One night, I called Tasha.

"Bitch, you sitting at the club at the bar *dranking* like they do on the TV?" she asked.

"Yep."

"Is it fun?"

"Nope."

"Take yo' ass home, girl! You can do that at home."

When I opened the garage, Brent's car wasn't there. The girls were asleep in their room. After calling him five times, he answered the phone. "Where are you?" I asked.

"Where were *you?*" he questioned. "I can't keep doing this."

"You not gone tell me where you are?"

"No. And I'm not coming home."

"Tomorrow is Mother's Day! What am I supposed to tell the girls when they ask me where their daddy is?"

"Tell them I left because their mother likes having sex with other men."

He hung up.

Their mother likes having sex with other men. That's what he thought. At some point, for a person in a committed relationship, who is addicted to sex, cheating isn't a conscious choice. It's muscle memory, like driving a car. It is common to get in a car and drive toward a destination, without remembering how you got there. Your favorite DJ's voice lulls in the background. You tune in and out as he or she banters with guests. You bop to your favorite playlist. You pass the grocery store or a sign that begs you to call a lawyer if you need one. You remember none of it. You zone out, and before you know it, you've arrived at your job, the doctor's office, or your kid's school. Did you consciously drive there that day, or did you do what you've done for years? That's how addiction was for me.

When I met Shane, the void I lived with was vast but invisible. It was impossible for Shane to fill it, and naïve of me to believe that he ever did. Once Shane showed me that I didn't matter in the way I'd built up in my head, I sought *other men* to take his place, not understanding that Shane wasn't the problem. I was. I didn't want to have sex with *other men*, especially not with those who were unfamiliar. Strangers' hands on my body felt slimy and wrong, but I saw no alternative to feel the type of love I craved, the deep intimacy that the guise of sex can mimic.

I imagined how different Brent's words would have been if he understood what was happening. Understanding may have yielded this phrase: *Their mother likes having her nervous system regulated. Their mother learned that sex calmed her nerves.* I liked having sex. But I didn't prefer sex with *other men*. I desired, more than anything else, to not be filled with so much stress that I ground my teeth at night, to not be so consumed with worry about a doc program that my body seized before I awoke, leading me to believe I was near death. *Their mother learned that sex was a fleeting fix for the unresolved issues with which she lived.* Having sex with *other men* had always proven I temporarily mattered in the vastness of the world or the microcosm of my world, but I didn't like to do it. I'd learned to have sex with *other men*, as opposed to dealing with the emotions of any situation.

Brent returned home on Mother's Day morning. I assured him I'd only sat at a bar. Similar to my parents, we never discussed what seemed to be a relationship-shifting event ever again.

A year later, I concluded that confessing my affair would add accountability; however, it is never an ideal time to tell your spouse that you've been sleeping with someone else for four years. It will always ruin whatever is happening at the time, and for Brent and me, something was always happening. We were either celebrating a birthday, going on vacation, or driving to family's houses for a holiday, and neither of those were perfect moments to say, "By the way, I've been living a double life." But I held my breath and chose to admit to an affair during our biannual road trip for Christmas.

"I have something to tell you," I said, somewhere outside of Tennessee, while the girls napped.

"With who?" he asked, staring at the road.

"The teacher at school."

"Who knew?" he asked. "What did they say?"

"Tasha."

"Bitches," he sneered.

Brent never described women that way. The heat from his anger filled the car. I'd been living a secret life —a façade. We weren't the couple others thought we were, and it was because of me. When we'd married over a decade ago, one of Grandma Hunny's friends said we looked like someone *made us for one another*. She saw what we, too, believed—our relationship was written in the stars. Brent thought I wanted to have sex with other men when all I had ever really wanted was to live our version of happily ever after; to exist as we did the summer we met in our twenties. I never wanted my imperfections to be the cause of our destruction. But I was.

"We can't keep doing this," he said. "I can't keep doing this." He'd planned to drop the girls and me off at Aunt Lillian's, then return to Florida, where he would pack his belongings and leave.

Brent quieted himself, then asked, "Why?"

"He chose me," I said. "I was happy he chose *me*."

Stretches of highway dragged as we rode in silence. Brent didn't understand my answer. He had chosen me, too…for life. Why wasn't his love enough? I didn't know the answer. Memories of the sex addiction quiz surfaced. I didn't want to share that having multiple partners was a common characteristic or that each sex addict has a unique behavior pattern. For me, the reoccurring pattern was that I desired— wanted other men's attention and affection, especially when stress and anxiety were exacerbated, which seemed to always be the case.

Hiding the extent of my behavior was also consistently present. I lived in a sea of half-truths and partiality. I spoke about the affair as if it were in the past tense. *I had an affair*, I told Brent, and that wasn't completely true. Shane had moved to South Georgia, so we saw each other less frequently. But if he texted, I appeared. I didn't know how to explain my feelings, and nothing I said made sense. If Brent didn't understand what I meant by, *he chose me*, then how would he ever understand that Shane's attention was something I believed was necessary?

In year five of my doctoral studies, I'd returned to drinking myself into oblivion at Tasha's house. I danced in the middle of the living room floor, spilling my drink all over the place as I tried to drop it low. When I grew tired of that, I stood in Tasha's narrow hallway and talked to her friend's man. She stared at us before walking our way.

"Oops," Tasha's friend said, bumping into me and knocking my drink out of my hand. Red punch and liquor created a small puddle on Tasha's floor, splashing the bottom of our legs.

Tasha called the next day.

"What's up?" I asked.

"Hold on a minute," she said, clicking over. This signaled I was on a three-way. In the past, I'd been the silent third person on one of her conference calls when she wanted me to bear witness to someone's foolishness. Now, I was the offending party.

"I'm back. I just wanted to say we are worried about you. You get too drunk. We all get drunk, but you get *too* drunk."

My grandmother has always said that I've been drinking since I was three years old. When we lived on Central Park, her father used to keep a fat jug of Mogen David on the floor next to his side of the bed. The story my grandmother retells is that I used to open up the cap and drink straight from the bottle. I'd exposed myself one day when I asked, *why'd you put the cap on so tight, Papa?* My grandmother loves retelling that story; each time, my family laughs at the thought of a three-year-old drinking wine. *You've always liked to drink*, my grandmother says, just like Brent says, *their mother likes to have sex with other men.*

Drinking has always liberated me, and it didn't take long to realize it. There was the time I drank too much in undergrad before my friends and I went to an off-campus party. I didn't want to wait to get out of the car, so I climbed through Ami's sunroof and jumped out onto the concrete. I danced the whole night while my left knee bled. Once I began to lose girlfriends, I would sit in my dorm room and drink forty-ounce bottles of beer by myself, while studying for exams.

As I aged, all celebrations included libations. My birthday, friends' birthdays, holidays, new jobs, lost jobs, divorces, and marriages. Each event involved a mandatory bottle and mixer, or a happy hour. Then there was the time I drank too much for one of our wedding anniversaries. I sang karaoke in Daytona, and in between, downed whatever the bartender served. I almost left with a group of white men.

"Were you just gonna let me go off with them?" I asked Brent the next morning.

"You know nobody can tell you what to do," he said, "especially if you're drunk."

As I entered my sixth year of the doctoral program I drank even more. Brent didn't mind my working on a Ph.D.; however, support mostly included well-wishes. Many times, his job wouldn't permit him to take off an hour early to pick up the girls from school when I needed to meet with professors. Oftentimes, Kimeiko and Briana rode with me to campus, and sat on the floor, outside of my professor's door, completing worksheets and coloring. I grew resentful. Drinking relieved the bitterness.

I've yet to admit to being an alcoholic. However, my relationship with alcohol is just as sketchy as my relationship with sex and men. The two go hand-in-hand; alcoholism is another comorbidity for sex addiction.[3] But I'd convinced myself I wasn't a substance abuser. My mother's cousin was an alcoholic. He drank so much that his face grew puffy and red, full of the water his body retained. That's never happened to me. I wasn't drinking alone. I was like many adults: Michell and I drank on the weekends; Brent and I drank on the weekends; Tasha and I drank on the weekends. If I was abusing alcohol, then we all were. Drinking alcohol didn't control my life; however, having sex did. So, when Tasha said I drank too much, all I could do was agree and continue to listen.

"And then you act kinda catty, too" Tasha continued. "You remember when Stacy knocked that drink out of your hand?"

"Yep."

"That's 'cause she thought you were trying to slide up on her man."

"Me? We were just talking."

"It didn't look like it. And then you was dancing all wild. I mean, my aunty and 'nem was there. It's like you ain't got no shame. Like you got a demon on you or something. Maybe you need an intercession. That's why I stopped inviting you over for a while in the first place. If Brent is with you, then you act halfway better, but if you're by yourself, you be too wild. Think of this like an intervention."

I was losing girlfriends, just as I had in college. Women rarely understood me, and justifiably so. I lived outside of what everyone considered "acceptable" behavior. Michell and I barely partied anymore, and I assumed it was because she couldn't trust my behavior. Who wants to bring someone's wife home a sloppy, drunken mess? My intention was never to hurt anyone, but that, too, was a consequence of sex addiction. With no friends and no outside sexual relationship, I focused on finishing my degree and finding a job. I had no plans to remain in Florida, so in my estimation, these events would soon be a memory. Just like when I left Covert, I believed I'd start over in a new environment.

This time, I'd be a professor in a brand-new state, and all of my problems would evaporate.

∞

Weeks before graduation, MJ called. "Your dad wants to know if your grandmother can come a little later, so we can stay at the house and spend some time with you?" she asked.

Negotiating time and space between my father and grandmother hadn't become easier as I aged. The dysfunction continued to exist and cemented the way the three of us related. We all seemed to be stuck in a behavior cycle. My father lacked the courage to call and ask to spend time with me, and at thirty-seven years old, I was afraid to approach Grandma Hunny with the request. In my final year of doctoral studies, I had quit teaching high school to focus more on studying. I kept several part-time jobs and struggled financially. My grandmother had sent me thousands of dollars to cover a range of expenses. In my mind, she'd financially earned the right to come when she pleased and stay as long as she wanted. But she agreed. Papa Henry had died years prior, and Terry and my aunt had divorced, so she, Aunt Diane, and my aunt's children had planned to drive from Michigan. They delayed their arrival by two days, giving my father what he wanted.

My father hadn't visited me since Kimeiko's birth eleven years prior, and it was the first time he'd seen the house we'd purchased. A ball of anger was always reserved just for him. I wanted my father there, but I wondered how he could act as if we had a wonderful father-daughter relationship. I wondered how he could *walk around here frontin'* as he'd accused me of doing years ago.

"You know, your mom would've been proud of you," my father said. "She didn't think you wanted to go to college. I remember telling her, 'College isn't for everyone,' and now, here you are with a Ph.D!'"

When I graduated from Western, he'd mentioned something similar. He didn't think I was going to graduate from high school, which was the reason he sent me away. I stared blankly at the absurdity of his words. Academics were never the issue.

I had my dissertation printed and spiral bound to help my family and friends understand the weight of what I'd completed. My work, centered on literacy practices, was dedicated to my mother, who'd introduced me to reading at an early age, and I'd mentioned specific family members in the acknowledgments. I handed it to my grandmother as soon as she arrived. She read the part where I thanked her for financial assistance, and then looked directly at my father and MJ and said, "Oh yeah. Kathy would call up and say, 'Grandma, I need a thousand dollars…and I can't pay you back this time,' so I'd send it to her, no problem." These spurts of pettiness framed much of my life whenever I was required to share space with the two of them. There was a niggling feeling that I'd always be a perpetual sixteen-year-old girl, who'd just lost her mother.

I graduated on August 7, 2010. Kimeiko, Briana, and I moved to Middle Georgia on August 8th. I began my first job as an assistant professor of education on August 9th. Brent stayed in Florida to complete his contract and to sell our house. Excessive drinking, partying, and acting out had no place in my new life as a professor. I didn't want to risk losing everything I'd worked hard for. I gathered up the same discipline I'd used to complete college degrees and focused on working, taking care of the girls, and being academically published. I believed a new life in a new city was all I needed to be a new person.

When Brent joined us in Middle Georgia, it was the first time during our marriage that he didn't have a job, and the university for which I worked reneged on its promise to help him find a position. This southern state was also more mired in racism than I initially comprehended. I quickly learned that club hopping in Atlanta was not the same as living in rural Georgia.

Brent would arrive for jobs that were listed in the morning but somehow filled by the time he drove to meet with employers in person. Sometimes, he was the only person waiting in the lobby for an interview. The receptionist would call his name as if he couldn't possibly be the person they'd just spoken to over the phone and considered hiring. The four of us lived on my paycheck, which was three thousand dollars a month. We had just enough money for rent, utilities, car insurance, gas, and to eat. Our one redeeming quality was that both of our cars were paid off. Sleep paralysis returned.

One December day, I went to get Briana from school. The parent pickup line reflected the small, military town's efficiency. Cars lined up an hour before dismissal and once the bell rang, children bounced in their respective backseats, and parents sped off. There were no hiccups in this process. That afternoon I inched closer to the door where she normally stood. As soon as the teacher read her name over the walkie-talkie, the car shut off. My SUV was six years old, with over 200,000 miles on it. It had gotten me through graduate school commutes and weekend rides back to Florida. I should have maintained it better. Parents jumped out of their cars to help push it out of the way. Eventually, someone's cables jumpstarted me long enough to return home. I needed a new engine.

Repairs cost over two thousand dollars. I was paid once a month. To fix the car, I had to wait until the end of December. Even if I waited, using two-thirds of my check would leave only enough for rent and utilities. We wouldn't have food. I had to buy a new engine, so I could get to work. Brent's mother wired us a thousand dollars. Grandma Hunny mailed another thousand. I never expected to have a doctorate and an assistant professor job that I'd risked moving my family for, just to be classified as poor. Regardless, I always had enough money for a thirteen-dollar bottle of Smirnoff. On the weekends, flavored vodka erased the pain.

Christmas neared, which added to my angst. Buying real trees that filled the air with fresh pine was a tradition I'd held onto since adolescence. Eventually, I passed the ritual on to our family when we bought our first house. Brent would decorate the windows and bushes with strings of multicolored lights. Decorations symbolized a perfect holiday and reminded me of better times. But in this new life, the Norman Rockwell-ish Christmas I wanted was impossible. There was no tree. There were no lights. There was no way to cover the gloominess of our circumstances. Brent took what money he had and bought dollar store bows and ornaments.

I sulked.

"It'll be alright. It's just temporary," he reassured.

What he said was true because I was willing to do anything to improve our living conditions. At the turn of the New Year, Brent was offered contract work at a major bank in Jacksonville.

"Should I take it?" he asked.

The answer was clear. "Hell, yeah!"

Brent's return to Florida brought many firsts. It was the first time we'd lived apart for longer than one month. We'd been a constant presence in one another's lives for seventeen years. My sex addiction antics were an intermittent part of our lives, but it wasn't our total life. Like many couples, we had developed a marital rhythm. I cooked; he cleaned. I raised the girls; he maintained the exterior of the house. For the first time in years, I sprinkled Comet in the bathtub and washed rings of dirt away in between driving the girls to get their hair done or taking them to the skating rink. It was the first time I'd noticed how heaps of dust piled up in the kitchen if no one ever swept.

Trauma had taught me to be hyper-independent, to not trust anyone's help unless I had to. *I've got it* was a common phrase. I'd rather struggle to do something myself than for someone else to do it and mess it up. It was the independence I'd once spoken about in an ignorant adolescent way. Living in Middle Georgia without Brent showed me the distinction between what I thought I'd craved, what I'd developed, and what I needed.

Single mothers surrounded me. A six-foot Black woman lived next door. Her son wore glasses and rarely looked up from his book; her daughter, long and lean, whispered with Kimeiko. She'd trained her children on the ins and outs of when and how to answer the door when she wasn't home and showed me how to do the same. Another woman, with flawless Black skin, was former military; her husband was a convicted felon. Ace Hood songs were her life's soundtrack as she raised her only daughter to clean with the efficiency of an enlisted soldier. Her daughter played with Briana and when she visited, she vacuumed as if her mother would spot-check. Another girl lived in a different complex; her mother was in a relationship, but not with her father. She and Briana basked in being two of the only brown girls in a gifted program. I leaned on this group of women, who raised their children alone and learned the difference between being a part of an interdependent community and relying on a man and his attention to see me through life. But it wasn't how I'd intended to live.

My time in Middle Georgia marked the first time since I was a child that I had extended periods alone. For someone who hadn't learned who I was or how I could spend free time without men, living in a town that closed at nine o'clock was dangerous; it left me with my thoughts, which culminated into pessimism. I wasn't going to leave my six- and nine-year-old at home for sexual satisfaction but being by myself left me no choice but to face myself. Petulia crept back in and whispered in my ear. *I told you. See how you always end up alone? You moved here. You did this. You told Brent to leave.*

Ever since I'd moved to Covert, a boy or man was by my side, so it was the first time that I wasn't connected to someone of the opposite sex and sharing physical space daily. Reality set in. Negative emotions arose. I sank. A general sadness rested in the pit of my stomach. If someone would've suggested I had situational depression, I would've heavily denied the diagnosis and laughed; however, the first semester in Georgia is where I explicitly felt shitty and recognized the feeling as eerily familiar.

I internalized current conditions: *Why was life so hard for me? I couldn't even get a doctorate and be happy. Why was life such a challenge?* I was no longer cheating, but my husband and I lived three hours apart. *Why couldn't I do anything right?* I attained a job, but it only paid fifty thousand dollars a year. I doubted my decision-making skills. Although I was academically gifted, maybe, I lacked common sense. I spiraled deeper and deeper into an abyss. *Is this the feeling Aunt Catherine had described? It couldn't be. She said, she couldn't get out of bed.* I crawled out to ensure the girls made it to school, were fed, and were happy. But even that wasn't good enough. Briana announced she'd never like living in Georgia. She was accustomed to her and her father's nighttime routine —sitting on the couch and watching *Justice League*, something I refused to do. One evening, she snuggled up in the bed with me.

"Don't you miss Daddy?" she sobbed.

"Of course, I do," I said. Then, my mother and grandmother's voice and tone slipped out of my mouth. "But what do you want me to do sit here and cry about it?"

Briana's contorted face showed me the inappropriateness of the answer. She wiped her face, slid out of my bed, and went to her room. Conversely, Kimeiko didn't complain or show sadness, instead, her face was stoic, her demeanor detached. She didn't express disappointment or joy. She walked around in silence, unless she needed something specific from me, like a signature on new school documents. The biological representations I so badly wanted were now walking, talking manifestations, who mirrored my sadness and suppression.

Acknowledging how challenging it must've been for the girls to suddenly leave our Jacksonville home and start anew in an isolated town with no friends and no father was the least compassion I could offer. After all, I had intimate knowledge of all three. Allowing space for tears was the least I should've done. It's what I should've allowed the three of us to do—to burrow under blankets and melt into a big pool of tears, not forever, but long enough to admit and name our emotions.

ZAIRE

2011 - 2013

When Eddie and I added one another on social media, I expected nothing more than to catch up. Initial conversations consisted of descriptions of kids, spouses, and jobs. He raised three children, suffered one baby mama, and lived in an unhappy marriage. But regular conversations aren't possible for a sex addict, who is in denial and stuck in an unconscious cycle. DMs grew longer, and eventually seeped over to Skype, where interactions turned virtual and intimate. Even though we hadn't seen each other for years, familiarity made an emotional affair easier. Opening my laptop seemed to be a safer alternative than carousing clubs or having a physical affair with a new man. However, my feelings hadn't changed. Like senior year, Eddie was something to do during the week when Brent and I were apart.

My connection to Shane was similar. He had moved from South Georgia to the Atlanta area, two hours away from me. It had been two years since we'd seen each other.

"Lost weight, huh?" he said. "You look good, but you gotta have *some* meat on your bones, damn."

"Got some grays, huh?" he said, noting the silver that glistened in places I didn't know gray hair grew.

"You seem tired," he said.

I was. I could never quite find satisfaction. There always seemed to be something preventing me from achieving happiness. I had the highest degree attainable and the lowest paychecks I'd ever generated in my professional life. I made more money fifteen years prior when I was a building sub in Detroit. I was living in a rural city, with no friends or family. My decisions had created a situation I'd avoided in my teenage years: I was a "single mother" raising two pre-adolescent daughters. Loneliness urged me to meet with him. A married man, who'd confided the reason he was with me was because I was available. I was exhausted. What was once an escape for both of us, was now a chore, including a laundry list of flaws he perceived I'd acquired. That was the last night I saw Shane.

In my estimation, the unhappiness I sensed was solely related to a lack of relationship with my father, not the sex-addiction diagnosis that had flashed on my screen years prior. Either way, I didn't want to take whatever my issues were into another decade of life, so in 2011, for the second time in my life, I sought therapy. My friend, Amitra, was now a PsyD. We'd spoken at length one evening about our post-high-school lives. I couldn't seem to maintain friendships, and I was convinced my in-laws hated me. She suggested I see a Black psychologist with a doctorate because *someone who looked like us understood our issues.*

The doctor's office was outside of Atlanta in College Park. If I could drive two hours to see Shane, then I could drive four hours roundtrip to find healthier ways to relate.

Dr. Aminu curled up on her sofa, legs underneath her bottom, pen, and legal pad in hand, locs flowing around her neck and down the front of her chest.

"Why are you here?" she asked.

Tears welled up when I confessed to cheating on my husband. I kept my sex addiction a secret. Like most women who live with the disorder, I thought I was the only one suffering.[1]

"Do you think he's cheated on you?" she asked.

"No, but you only know what someone tells you," I replied.

"You know that doesn't make sense," she said, scribbling on her legal pad.

It did to me. That was my modus operandi. Whatever I told anyone is what they knew. Only I understood what I'd hidden. I recounted the most prevalent issues: my mother's death and my father's abandonment.

"What do you want from your father?" Dr. Aminu asked.

"Nothing," I answered, but she wouldn't accept this as truth, mentioning I wouldn't be sitting across from her if there was no preferred outcome.

What I desired sounded too simple: I wanted my father to show he cared about me, by doing plain things, like calling, visiting, and being interested in my life. I'd rationalized that if this would happen, then monogamy would miraculously occur.

For the next three sessions, I described people and relationships. Why couldn't I get along with anyone? Why couldn't I keep friends? Why didn't my cousins call and check on me?

"Do you realize every time you talk about someone, you end up saying they don't care about you?" she asked.

Dr. Aminu introduced me to cognitive behavior therapy. She pulled out a blank piece of paper and drew a triangle. At the top, she wrote the word *thoughts*. At the bottom right corner, she wrote the word *feelings*. In the bottom left corner, she wrote the words *actions/behavior*. This cognitive triangle was intended to help me not only understand others' feelings and behavior patterns, but to also provide a foundation for acknowledging how thoughts dictated my behaviors. Cognitive behavior therapy helped me to pay more attention to my thinking, to make more sense of life outside of my mind, and to stop thoughts from spiraling into oblivion.

But just when Dr. Aminu and I were making progress, I was offered a position at a research university in Florida. Our sessions ended with my decision to move, and Dr. Aminu didn't have a suggestion for another therapist.

∞

My new job was perfect, but there was one obstacle. It was 175 miles away from our Jacksonville home—a three-hour, one-way commute. I knew driving there was unreasonable after attending just one faculty meeting. But I agreed. Accepting the job was proof that I was intelligent, the one positive sense of self I'd held onto. Working at the highest university level validated my sense of identity. People were generally pleasant when they found out about my job at the liberal arts college in Georgia, but disappointed.

"This is just a stepping-stone," Brent's father once asked. "Right?"

His rhetorical question embodied most people's sentiments. But when I announced I was working at a research university, people's eyes brightened; their ears perked up; and they verbally praised my hard work and efforts. It was the same validation I'd felt decades ago when people found out where I attended high school. Now, friends and family personally knew someone who taught at a prestigious place. Their accolades stroked my self-esteem. This caliber of university was where I was supposed to be, even if it took a six-hour round-trip commute to prove it.

Brent said it was too far, but I ignored him. Packing up the girls and our dog for weekend trips back and forth between two states had gotten to be overwhelming. Moving to the city where the university was, required that he take a severe pay cut, and neither of us wanted to live through another financial struggle. We both deserved to have equally satisfying salaries and careers at this phase of our life. We'd already wasted money living and maintaining two households and we knew we didn't want to live separately again. This was how I justified driving six hours to teach.

Then MJ called.

"I just thought you oughta know," her Arkansas drawl dragged the remaining words. "Your dad has stage-four throat cancer."

My father and I hadn't spoken in nearly a year, and I hadn't seen him since graduation, two years prior. I had only had four therapy sessions, and we hadn't delved into what to do about my relationship with my father. Left to make my own decisions, I was determined not to talk to my father ever again. MJ's phone call about my father's illness came at a time when I'd liberated myself from the emotional burden of our dysfunction. The cognitive triangle wasn't enough to demonstrate how I should handle a dying father, who for twenty-three years, had ignored my existence unless it suited him. Furthermore, it was ironic that my father wanted what I'd longed for the past two decades—care. Memories of where I ranked on his to-do list had hardened me. How could I give what I'd never received even in the face of his impending death? I didn't realize it then, but my father's prognosis returned me to a sex addiction cycle, and I unconsciously dealt with it as I had implicitly learned to do in years past: suppress, fantasize, and seek sexual satisfaction.

∞

His name was Zaire. He was a trainer I met at the gym. Pretending I didn't see his five-eleven frame was impossible.

"C'mon let me work you out," he'd beg.

"Nope. I'm good."

"Let me take you through a workout," he persisted.

"I know what I'm doing."

"You ready to work out with me?"

I gave in. "Yep." It was free, I reasoned. *What could it hurt?*

"I love your natural hair," he doted while I finished my last reverse crunch. "So many sisters are stuck in weaves or perms. They hate themselves and it shows. I ask them all the time 'Who wants limp hair?' Our hair is strong."

Zaire would talk about the plight of Black folks with the intensity of a 1960s civil rights leader, and I would listen as if I was the next Betty Shabazz. He was too motivated to stay in his Memphis hometown. According to him, all Black people wanted to do there and everywhere is work for someone else. His personality was too driven and energetic for a desk job, so he worked part-time and spent the remainder of the day as a personal trainer and entrepreneur. When he wasn't doing any of that, he worked on a children's book about autism.

"If you ever need someone to edit the book for you, let me know," I offered.

We exchanged numbers to discuss his project and texted for the rest of the day. Our conversations ranged from Black empowerment to my growing dissatisfaction driving up and down the interstate. We talked about his mission to help children with disabilities, my being married, and his reasons for being single. The chats were endless, the topics exhaustive. But only through texts.

We have a lot in common.

I know. We're the same. Intellectuals with a unique paradigm, he confirmed.

I looked forward to seeing him at the gym, and when he was there, my stomach fluttered, like it did when I'd met Brent. This time, I was aware of what was happening, and I wanted to share it with my husband, just as we'd agreed. Maybe telling him would create accountability.

"Finally worked out with the trainer," I confessed while crunching a baby carrot.

"Oh yeah. How'd that happen?" Brent asked.

I described the day's happenings. I wanted to tell him more but then I remembered the consequences: he'd leave, and we'd divorce, so I ended the story by telling him about editing Zaire's autism book and never mentioned him again. My gym workouts continued.

"You wanna make sure you squeeze those glutes when you stand up," he coached.

"Like this?"

He checked behind me and laughed. "Yeah. Like that."

Brent worked at the bank past seven, came home, ate dinner, and worked more. He'd scratched his hair into a thin layer on top of his head as he figured out the institution's billion-dollar dilemmas. Although he was naturally thin, his face sunk, and his frame grew skeletal. Our friends commented on his weight loss, which he hadn't noticed. He ignored his health and me, while Zaire and I texted.

A year passed and I still looked forward to those rising and falling grey ellipsis, signifying Zaire's impending conversation. We exchanged memes. I once sent him a picture of a Black woman whose hair was shaped like Africa. The caption read: *Know thyself.* His Black conscious ego loved it. And so did mine, his appreciation invigorated me. We cared about the same issues.

After George Zimmerman was found not guilty of shooting and killing Trayvon Martin, I asked Brent, "What do you think we can do? How can we stop this from happening again?" *We* referred to Black people, like us, like our daughters, who could've been holding Skittles and wearing a hoodie.

"Nothing," Brent answered.

"You don't think we can do anything at all?"

"I don't see how we can do anything. This is just gonna keep happening."

Delving into deep conversations and solving the world's problems was no longer a part of our relationship. The time had long passed since he and I would spend hours answering one another's hypothetical questions. Now, I was like Shane, implicitly blaming the decline of my marriage on my spouse. Brent wasn't conscious enough, I decided.

I texted Zaire about Trayvon Martin and the future of American race relations. In between, he described his upcoming trip to my home city. He was going to help with gang violence. The next day, he sent me a song, Isaac Hayes, "I Stand Accused."

For me? I asked.

This is how I feel, he replied.

I hit repeat and listened to it for an hour. It was the confession of a man who had fallen in love with a married woman. New questions formed: *What was happening? Why is this happening? How did this happen?* I didn't even want this to happen, whatever *this* was, or did I? *Is texting him cheating?* We never saw each other, except at the gym, and we had no physical contact. Sometimes he'd answer the phone on my commute home, but most of our communication was virtual. This "relationship" confused me, because it wasn't physically cheating, but it was dishonest.

Six more months of intermittent texting continued until I decided to end my gym membership and join a new one. He noticed.

You need to come get a workout in?

Oh, I changed gyms.

What? You weren't gonna tell me? It's 'cause of me, isn't it?

No. I need a change. That gym is too small.

Cowardice kept me from admitting that it *was* because of him. Flipping my phone over and dimming the light whenever Brent was nearby felt extra-marital. And I was trying so hard to be "good."

"Why did you change gyms again?" Brent questioned.

I repeated the reason I'd given to Zaire. "It's like everyone is too close and knows all of your business. People talk to me too much and all I wanna do is work out," I went on and on. It was a truth. There was no need for him to know I felt like I was in a relationship with the trainer.

We kept texting. Some mornings, Zaire was the first virtual voice I heard. He talked extensively to me about not following society's rules, including self-imposed expectations for what I should be doing after receiving a doctorate. He helped me feel more positive about myself, like Dr. Aminu, minus the triangle. We celebrated our likenesses. We were the same sign; our birthdays were two days apart. He loved poetry and I was beginning to write creatively again, something I hadn't done since elementary school. When my first personal essay was published by a well-known blog, he was the first person I shared it with. Sometimes he'd read drafts and marvel at my talent. He created nutritional products to match his growing brand. When he launched his new fitness drink, he sent me the logo and marketing strategy.

Wyd? I asked.

Reading The Souls of Black Folks again.

He believed he and I were a part of Du Bois' "Talented Tenth." He stimulated my mind, and that made me desire his attention even more. We would text through the night while Brent slept. He was always there. Virtually present.

Two years of sporadic communication passed, and I knew it had to end. I defriended him from social media several times to sever ties but added him back just as many. Though being desired was fulfilling, our "relationship" solidified the idea that I couldn't control seeking out new men. If I could establish and maintain a pseudo-romantic connection with someone via text message, then that meant a deeper problem existed.

THE TRAINER

2014

My father's death lingered.

"You could send a card or something," MJ judged.

"Are you sure you don't want to do something?" Brent echoed.

Financial support replaced care and concern. Brent and I loaded a pre-paid debit card each month to help with my father's medication, and we found a final expense insurance plan to supplement his five-thousand-dollar policy. I thought it irrational for him to want more from me than he'd sown.

Chemo and radiation captured his voice and health for six months, but the following year brought frequent communication. He whispered through conversations, many times asking me to recount tales of the girls and what they were into. The doctors felt hopeful that reconstructive surgery would repair his vocal cords and help avoid a tracheostomy. My father's confident nature kept our family encouraged. His optimism led us to believe that the future would hold sounds of his renewed speech.

Emotions I'd buried, stirred. Towards the end of that year, my family and I trekked to Chicago. Years of tradition dictated that we stay at Aunt Lillian's house, spend Christmas day with my mother's side of the family, and then travel to the South Side to visit my father and MJ at night.

"It's like you just do a drive-by," MJ once commented. "I mean you come by, but then you don't never stay long."

She was right, but I'd always thought the reason was obvious. Her home didn't hold my childhood. Her name graced the deed years before we met. My father moved there after their nuptials. Each wooden step that creaked under my feet held her nostalgia, not mine. Not ours. He was my father, but *he* made memories under her blue roof, not me. Most years, I did well just to stop by at all. But this holiday, I grew more concerned. It mattered not where he lived, but rather that he survived cancer and post-ops. We created a new ritual. Brent, the girls, and I arrived at his house during the daylight hours.

A smile spread across his face as he opened the door. He hugged each of us through our winter wear bundles. A white patch protected his throat's incision. Later, he described the careful process of cleaning this wound. Blue and white cans of meal-replacement shakes sat on the kitchen table, some empty, others waiting their turn. Before I could sit down, he cupped my face in his palms as if I was a child.

"You and I need to have a talk," he whispered.

I rolled my eyes, "Alrighty."

He winked at my family, who sat single file on the white, faux leather couch. "Just a little daddy-daughter talk," he reassured them.

I followed him up the rickety, narrow staircase to their attic's makeshift office. The black swivel chair swooshed air as I plopped down. He sat across from me on a black folding chair and leaned over. His eyes were already watery.

"I feel as if you've been mad ever since your mom died."

I maintained indifference. "I used to be. But not anymore."

"What did you want me to do?"

I reminded him of how he'd packed up all of my teenage belongings and thrown them in black trash bags in the middle of my bedroom. He wanted to know what he could have done after he sent me to live with my grandparents in another state. What could have been different after he gave up his parental rights when I was a year shy of legality?

"You could have called to see how I was doing," I said.

His eyes no longer held the tears. He removed his glasses and wept. "That's all?"

"Yep. That's it. You left me there and didn't look back."

Tears crawled down his face. "*Who* put your stuff in black trash bags?"

In the medical field, the effect of chemotherapy is called *chemo brain*. It can leave patients with selective memories. While I could never forget how my clothes and stuffed animals rested haphazardly in those garbage bags, now he couldn't recollect who'd filled them. He attempted to recall why his former self would've engaged in such an egregious act. Eventually, he determined that he must have been "really mad."

Our talk continued. I did my best to explain the loneliness of losing one parent to death and another to desertion. It's a challenge describing experiences to a clueless perpetrator. Tears ran down his cheeks, down his chin, and onto his bandaged throat. I tried to disassociate but couldn't. For two decades, I'd approached him with these concerns through emails and letters. This wasn't new information. In the past, he'd promised to maintain contact and visit when money allowed, but something else always took precedence, leaving me to undo any fantastical idea of the father I'd constructed in my dreams.

Puzzled, I asked one question, "Why did you decide to ask me now?"

He cleaned one lens, then the other. He placed his glasses back on his face. "It's the threat of mortality, Baby. Death makes you see things differently."

His response wasn't comforting. *The threat of mortality* seemed a selfish reason to seek forgiveness and understanding. Forty-five minutes later, my father made a new promise—to spend the rest of his life making sure I knew he loved me.

He was a twenty-four-year-old trainer at the new gym, where I'd run to evade Zaire. A professional bodybuilder. I found this out after succumbing to his stares. We found a reason to exchange numbers. We texted for a week until tiny words on a screen weren't enough. He wanted to see me in person outside of the gym. I agreed.

I was steeped in a sex addiction cycle; however, I felt something I hadn't before—guilt. I knew meeting with him was wrong before I arrived. That day, I worked out, meditated, and wrote in my gratitude journal, a new practice I'd heard about on *Oprah's Lifeclass*. During meditation, I asked a specific question: *Should I go through with this?* Unlike previous meditations, I heard a voice reply, *no, but since you're not going to listen, be careful.* At the time, I was studying the Law of Attraction and believed this voice to be my inner being or higher self. Today, I know it to simply be intuition. Whatever its name, I ignored it and proceeded with what I wanted.

I knew it was wrong because I was nervous. Before heading toward the directions he'd sent, I stopped by the liquor store at one in the afternoon to buy four miniature bottles of vodka. I devoured one before I arrived at his brother's house, the second as I sat in front of the home, and the third when I walked in. He asked me for the fourth, which I handed over. He turned it upside down, emptying the bottle.

I knew it was wrong because as I lay there, under his pronounced biceps, I realized I knew nothing about him, and if he wanted to, he could kill me, or at the least rape me had I changed my mind. In the past, I'd never felt an impending sense of danger, even when I stumbled upon a stranger in an alley. Something here was off. Only one friend knew about my plans, but she didn't know where I was. My frame, not too small, but not big enough, was no match for his professionally trained muscles. This man could end my life with one snap, and no one would know.

I knew it was wrong when Briana texted me.

Where are you? she asked.

Since we'd moved back to Florida, I'd developed a clear routine. Each afternoon, I sat at the computer, grading papers, ready to greet her when she arrived home.

Out running errands. Remorse was immediate for lying to my daughter.

I knew it was wrong.

After we had sex, he admitted to falling in love with me. According to him, he loved everything about me.

"Tell me you love me," he begged.

"Huh?"

"Tell me you love me," he repeated.

I love you! "You don't even know me," I said.

He texted for the remainder of the day. I knew it was wrong. Not only did I not love him, but I also didn't even like him. All interest had vanished.

I stopped responding to his texts, in hopes that his sudden infatuation would fade away.

When I returned to the gym, we stood in front of a row of treadmills. The thud-thud-thud covered our conversation—the relationship he wanted. I refused. We didn't need to be with each other.

"You used me," he said.

Before I could respond, a former co-worker and her brother walked up.

"Gardenia!" she shouted. I hadn't seen her since we taught high school.

They both greeted him with matching smiles, "Hey, Pastor!"

My eyebrows raised and eyes bucked as the three held a conversation about church happenings. Once they left, I stared at him. "Pastor?"

His eyes lowered, "Yeah."

"Why didn't you tell me?"

"I didn't want you to treat me differently."

I'd told people the same thing about my professional identity. Whenever strangers found out I was Dr. Garland, they suddenly straightened their backs, cleaned up their *ain't's* and *fixin' to's*, or began telling narratives of

223

why they never went to, or finished college. That's when I saw it; he and I were the same. We didn't share a vocation like Will or an ideology like Zaire; we had parallel issues. Still, he pressed on, wanting to develop and maintain a relationship outside of our marriages.

"So, are you the stereotypical preacher who is fucking all the women in the congregation?" I asked.

He rolled his eyes and scrunched his lips.

"You don't want to be that guy. Do you?"

He never answered. In retrospect, I knew the reply. I wasn't talking to him at all. I was talking to myself, and the answer was clear. *I* didn't want to be the woman who was having sex with all the men outside her marriage while personifying implied morality as a university professor. I couldn't do this with him or anyone else ever again. More importantly, I had to figure out what was wrong with me that, at the age of forty-one, I would willingly jeopardize my marriage, family, and life by having sex with a man I didn't even know. This time, change had to occur, if only because of what happened next.

I'm pregnant, I texted my friend.

She was hours away in another country but FaceTimed immediately.

I showed her the two pink lines.

"I thought you used a condom?"

"We did. The first time. I'm . . . such . . . a . . . fucking . . . idiot," I cried.

"You are not an idiot."

"I am. This is so stupid. How could I be so stupid?"

"You are not stupid," she said. "We're gonna fix this. You just have to get an abortion."

"I have to tell Brent."

"NO!" she screamed. "DO NOT TELL BRENT! If you tell him, he's going to leave you."

I wanted to disappear into the walls of the clinic's tiny hallway. A woman, approximately thirty years old was in front of me and a woman, approximately nineteen years old was behind me. I constantly reminded myself that who was here didn't matter; we were all there for the same reason. I waited for the nurse to call my name. She weighed me. She took my blood pressure. She pricked my finger to find out my blood type. She asked me to pee in a cup.

And then, a few minutes later she said, "Oh, yeah. You're *very* pregnant."

Another gravelly voice told me to take off my clothes from the waist down, to get on the table, "and cover yourself with this." *This* was a thin sheet. It didn't take long for her to complete an ultrasound, but she couldn't see anything. It was too soon. She decided to do a sonogram. That didn't work either. It was too soon.

It was too soon for action. They must see something before they can remove something.

"Come back in two weeks," the nurse told me.

"Two weeks?" I nearly shouted.

The nurse mumbled something. The cashier gave me a partial refund. I rescheduled.

As soon as I closed my car door, I sobbed. How could I have been so reckless?

Typically, I disassociated with ease; however, pretending not to be pregnant with a husband and two teenage daughters was challenging. Brent, the girls, and I went to breakfast one morning, and my mind was on a constant loop of how undeserving I was of my own family. Yoga saved me. A few years prior, I'd noticed how my body buzzed after practice and how calm I was the remainder of the day. To keep from bursting into tears whenever I looked at Brent's face or the girls' eyes, I forced my guilt from my body and onto my mat for the fourteen days preceding the procedure.

I was immersed in shame and sadness, but something led me to practice each day for an hour and a half at a local studio. The first day, I rolled out my mat, with my head lowered. I was convinced there was a scarlet "A" branded on my chest. Like Hester Prynne, everyone must've known what an awful adulteress was in their midst. Still, something pulled me out of bed and toward the studio each day. Although yoga was familiar, that first day felt new. When we began in Balasana, child's pose, knees wide, belly and head to the floor, tears welled up. Sweat from the heated room masked the physical manifestation of emotional pain. The deep bass of Bhakti music covered my whimpers. Calm covered me. Balasana forces your body into a relaxed state. The pose is akin to self-soothing, something babies in healthy environments learn to do, a skill Petulia lacked, and something I needed as I laid on the mat and forced forgiveness onto myself for the atrocious acts that peppered my life.

On the second day of yoga, I bent my right leg in front of me, and straightened my left leg behind me, my body pressed close to the floor, arms outstretched —Ardha Kapotasana, half-pigeon pose. Again, I silently wept as sorrow filled my space. Today, it is common knowledge that our bodies can hold the tension of multiple emotions for many years. On day two of yoga, I didn't know this; consequently, I continued with each pose, while reaching for my towel to wipe away the snot and dab sorrow from my eyes. My body released pain, past and present.

On the day of my appointment, Michell met me at the grocery store nearest my house. We rode with trivial conversation.

"Two hundred and ninety," the receptionist said when I approached the window.

Michell laughed. "You know I'ma mess witchu, right?"

"What?"

"Cash only?" She laughed again.

"When you're dealing with my husband, you gotta be extra careful. He notices things when he wants to," I said.

"Yeah, I remember from the last incident," she said, reminding me of the time I arrived home with my panties in my purse.

I finished completing the paperwork and we sat in the lobby. The nurse called my name and confirmed I was still pregnant. "Wait here," she directed.

Here was another room with different colored director's chairs folded and lined up around the perimeter as if we starred in our movies. Around the walls were handwritten notes from other women who once sat where I did: *Don't feel bad.*

But I did feel bad. I was about to endure a fifth abortion, and though multiple unwanted pregnancies are the norm for a female sex addict,[1] it was embarrassing for me.

Everyone makes mistakes.

Not understanding the intricacies of safe sex is a mishap reserved for teenagers who lack sex education; having a fifth unintended pregnancy, especially married, at the age of forty-one, and with two teenage daughters was not a mistake—it was immature and negligent.

It's your right to choose an abortion.

I've always been a staunch advocate for reproductive rights, but as I sat waiting, two visibly pregnant women wobbled in, causing my stance on abortion to fluctuate.

"Is there anyone who is twenty weeks in here?" the nurse asked.

The two very pregnant ladies got up and followed her, and my judgment turned outward. At twenty weeks, I was scheduling gynecology appointments to reveal our babies' sex. Twenty weeks was around the time Kimeiko would shift from one side of my uterus to another. I would never have an abortion mid-pregnancy, and I couldn't think of a reason why these ladies would need to. I judged and justified my abortion as protecting a secret no one could see.

Thanks so much for helping me.

I tucked my judgments away. No matter our gestation period, we were each there for the same reason: we needed abortions to resolve our unwanted pregnancies.

A pasty, skinny young lady sat down. We made constant eye contact. Another young white lady sat next to her. A few other ladies walked in with designer bags but left as soon as they were administered an abortion pill. The rest of us watched three episodes of *The Fresh Prince* and two episodes of *Wayans Brothers*.

Then, the nurse asked us to disrobe and wait. After we changed in the bathroom, one by one, our names were called, and we walked down the short, white hall to our common fates. Finally, I heard my name. I followed the nurse and waited in the room for the doctor. Next door, I could hear moaning, screaming, and yelling.

"Well, that sucks," I said to the nurse.

"That's strange," she replied.

The doctor finally walked in. "How are you, Hun?"

"Good, until I heard the girl next door," I half-joked.

"Well, it's hard to explain to people that when you do recreational drugs, it makes things go a lot different," she said. The screaming girl couldn't get enough medication to help her through the procedure. But I did. The next memory I had was waking in another room with the same ladies, barely able to open my eyes or redress.

The nurse rushed me out and handed me a bag full of medication and pamphlets. Michell drove me back to the grocery store parking lot and followed me a block away from my home.

"Hide that bag," she warned.

Michell didn't have to remind me. I had been hiding my entire life.

SELF-REGULATED

JOYCE

2014

C o-regulation is something that usually happens between parents and their babies.[1] It's how children learn to manage their emotions. When a baby cries and a calm parent coddles and soothes them, they relax. Over time, the child learns how to self-soothe or self-regulate their emotions.[2] But if a baby does not learn how to manage their emotions at an early age, they can become emotionally dysregulated; everyday events can rattle them; they either overreact with excessive tears or anger, or they underreact and show little-to-no emotion when feelings are expected.[3]

Childhood trauma, different types of neglect, and traumatic brain injuries, all experiences I've had, can also cause emotional dysregulation.[4] No matter the reason, when children don't learn how to self-regulate, their mental health can suffer, and they may develop a "maladaptive coping strategy such as emotion suppression that leads to internalizing issues,"[5] abusing substances, or engaging in high-risk sexual behavior.[6] In some ways, I was fortunate to have married at such an early age. Bouts of co-regulation can occur in a healthy adult relationship, where one's spouse is calm; however, unlike a parent, a spouse cannot be expected to constantly co-regulate their lover. The goal is for a person to self-regulate. This is where I was after my fifth abortion: I had to learn to regulate my emotions, while also facing sex addiction head-on.

Sex addiction can be rooted in abandonment, such as losing one's parent, as well as abuse and neglect. My biological mother's abandonment, my adoptive mother's death, my adoptive father's desertion, and the incidents of molestation in my childhood not only caused emotional dysregulation, but they also became triggers for my addiction. Knowing the root cause, I learned how to treat the effect. I had to heal from the trauma I endured within my family, sealing the psychological fissures and fractures that compelled me to come out of my clothes in search of a warm body to serve as a balm that soothed the sadness I'd hidden for so long. It was time to leave the fantasy worlds I'd developed over the years and enter reality with an unabated awareness.

Self-therapy began the day after my final abortion by way of a twenty-one-day guided meditation focused on relationships. Lessons on how to relate to others seemed critical. Meditation had been a part of my life ever since Brent's mother gifted me with a creative visualization book in the late nineties, so understanding how to focus and breathe was easy. However, a guided practice was new. During the first week, the recorded voice instructed me to sit somewhere comfortably. A folding chair on our patio served as solace. Next, I closed my eyes and placed my hands on my lap, palms up. After repeating a mantra, like *Om* or *Om Vardhanam Namah*, there was a journal exercise. I was fully committed to healing whatever it was that caused me to repeatedly engage in reckless behavior and grateful the guided meditation included steps. Following sequential directions toward healing was like attending undergraduate classes; a roadmap helped me to see a clear path.

Days one through four offered simplistic tasks, and there was little-to-no shift in my thought pattern. Day five's journal question, *what are your fears, if any, of truly accepting and loving yourself* threw me off guard. Brent once said he loved me more than I loved myself, and I scoffed. I was the most confident, high-achieving person I knew. How could I have attained three degrees and become "Dr. Garland" if I didn't love myself? Of course, I loved myself. But when it came to providing an answer, my fingers froze. It was a challenge to write an authentic answer that extended deeper than accolades and achievements. Once I decided my answer was private, I exhaled and wrote the following: *I'm afraid that I won't like myself. I believed there was something wrong with me for me to lose so many important people and for them to leave me.* Then, I did something I'd never done—sat with the emotion.

Exploring the hatred that I'd harbored for myself forced me to think about something I'd ignored— being born. I despised how I'd entered the world, and I wished it was different, and it was integral to piece together a picture of who I was as an infant, based on the limited knowledge I'd received. I returned to the contents of the DCFS packet. I re-read each word intent on envisioning my biological mother and my birth.

Joyce had been hospitalized twice in mental institutions; she was diagnosed with schizophrenia the second time. I imagined how fearful she must've been when she became pregnant with me. I knew what it was like to have an unwanted pregnancy without resources to birth a baby and to know that, should I bring a person into the world, she would be my sole responsibility. Joyce was a mother to a five-year-old daughter, mentally ill, poor, and pregnant with me. What was she going to do? *Roe v Wade* had recently passed, and Joyce fit the conditions for many women who seek abortions; however, she was conflicted. With me in utero, she stressed, roaming back and forth to her social worker, arguing with herself over whether she should have a baby she couldn't financially or psychologically support. On a good day, when schizophrenia didn't have a stranglehold on her, she opted for birth. When her mental health declined, she ventured back to her social worker, wondering how she could abort me. The stress of pregnancy caused Joyce's mental illness to deteriorate, and birth became her only choice.

The social worker presented another option: adoption. All Joyce had to do was see my birth to term. Once again, her mind filled with scenarios—*can I raise another baby? I can't raise another baby*. Anxiety filled her mind and body. The safest place for an unborn baby is supposed to be her mother's womb, but it wasn't for me. Anxiety lived there, too. My biological mother fed me her schizophrenia; each stressor floated into my bloodstream and my still, developing psyche. Nervousness nourished me like nutrients. Tremors were created out of my mother's tensions. Her mother passed down an inability to deal with life, and over ten months, she passed it on to me. Acknowledging my biological mother's mental illness was an important step in accepting myself and the circumstances surrounding my birth, but it made my heart ache.

Joyce was afraid as she birthed me with no social or emotional support; and with a toddler whom she already couldn't take care of. She'd agreed to adoption before I was born, but according to the DCFS document, changed her mind after my birth. What I craved to know was there in black and white, but in my haste to suppress emotions, I overlooked the details. My biological mother felt the inextricable connection to me that I felt when I birthed Kimeiko and Briana, or at the least, a sense that it was unnatural for a mother to separate from her child. But her illness dictated the outcome.

When I was three months old, she took me to an adoption agency; however, there were rules. She had to prove she wasn't married, and she couldn't. Joyce tried to do the "right" thing. She tried to follow government protocol, but she couldn't. Joyce was married, but her husband wasn't my father, and even in her psychosis, she knew revealing this would cause further issues for her and me. So, two months later, she left me in her apartment for five to seven days, until a janitor found me. These are the conditions that led to the next part of my birth story that I had to face—abandonment.

I pictured a five-month-old Petulia lying on the floor, hungry and unable to move, while she soiled her diaper and waited days for a mother who never appeared. Instead of being nurtured, I visualized the shock of being scooped up and saved by police officers with rough hands and no affect and then moved to an unfamiliar foster home with other abandoned children of varied ages. No oxytocin. No emotional bonding. No maternal attachment. Emotionally dysregulated. The world is a scary place for a motherless child. Remnants of rejection made a home in my infant cells and cemented into the fibers of my being. This abandonment led to an anxious attachment style, where I internalized rejection and became clingy and codependent,[7] looking for proof that I mattered in the crevices of dark Chicago streets or within the tautness of my relationship.

On day five, I allowed myself to cry for myself, and I stopped speaking about Petulia as a person apart from me. I replaced third-person pronouns, such as *she* and *her* with *I* and *me*. Petulia Belcher wasn't a nasty voice reminding me of my unworthiness. She was me. I owned my story. I am Petulia. I was born a five-pound baby. When the janitor found me at five months, I was only seven pounds. My mother had no other recourse but to leave me in an apartment building. I waited for her to feed and care for me. She didn't. She couldn't. She didn't have the capacity. However, I was *severely malnourished* not only in my body, but also in my mind and spirit. I began life, like most babies, listening for the sound of my mother's voice and never found it, and I'd never stopped longing for her.

Eventually, I did what nearly every self-help book suggests: I reimagined a new narrative to continue the process of self-therapy. As a mother, I knew what babies required. I had to be my own mother. I visualized myself as two entities: baby Petulia and the mother of baby Petulia. In my imagination, I picked the baby version of me up and hugged and kissed myself. I told myself *I love you* and I told the baby part of me I was safe and protected. I also accepted Joyce Belcher as the woman who birthed me, and I attempted to see her as more than her mental illness.

Joyce was a young woman, who lacked the stability of a loving home. For much of my life, I assumed my birth mother abandoned me because of me. As I processed the DCFS document, I realized my birth mother's choice had to do with her and a system that didn't protect women and children. The agency could have cared for me had she not needed her husband's permission to surrender parental rights for a child who wasn't his. There was nothing I could do about who Joyce was or the choices she was forced to make. In coming to this realization, I finally forgave her for leaving me.

Over time, I learned to be grateful for my biological mother's choices, mainly because of my awareness of abortion. Had Joyce made a quick decision like I had, I would not have been born. Joyce did the best she could. But I had to be honest. My biological mother's "best" produced my first trauma. My background was constructed by others, but it was my responsibility to repair it.

NAURICE

2014

While the healing of familial trauma began with putting my birth story into proper context and forgiving my birth mother, I also had to explore the origins of my adoption more deeply than I had in the past. Mothers, whether biological or adoptive, are a child's life force and a vein for all things living, so it seemed fitting to continue with mine. To facilitate my healing, I had to learn about and process who my adoptive mother was, before becoming my parent.

Grandma Hunny had always been forthright about her first marriage to a man, who had enlisted in the Navy and served in World War II for two years. Upon his return, he and my grandmother dated and married in April 1947. My grandmother speaks fondly of how, a year later, my mother, Naurice, was born with *curly hair and sharp gums.* She was also born with a birth defect, congenital talipes equinovarus, otherwise known as club foot. Her feet faced one another, instead of straight out. When my grandmother reflects on this disability, she is blunt and uneffusive as if she were describing the color of the sky.

The same way another mother might remember her baby's first smile is the way my grandmother recalls how *doctors placed tiny casts on Naurice's feet, which stretched up to her knees.* After one month, plaster and bandages were removed and my mother's paternal grandmother, Nana, massaged her soles in a pot of warm water several times a day. She wore expensive corrective shoes for five more years. She also wore glasses. My grandmother always laughs when she gets to this part of the story at the memory of how one of her sisters teased her about her firstborn's odd appearance. In the mid-twentieth century, a spectacled toddler with orthotics was a sight.

However, unbeknownst to Grandma Hunny, her husband had developed a heroin addiction. They divorced by the early 1950s.

"I left," she said, summing up her decision.

Grandma Hunny moved back to her mother's home, which was a few blocks away, on the near-North Side of Chicago with my mother in tow. Devoid of emotion, she recounts riding the city bus to and from a job, during the Jim Crow era to work with racist white women. There is no remorse or self-pity when she speaks of her diligence in saving weekly wages to afford to leave her parents' house, and she never addresses her emotions associated with leaving the person she'd married, who was *addicted to drugs.* I don't know how she felt about her husband choosing heroin over his family. If she was disappointed to move back in with her parents as a single mother of a child, who today would be labeled as having special needs, she's never mentioned it. These events were simply her reality and required no fanfare.

By the time my mother was eighteen, she was diagnosed as having one kidney and would later spend most of her life on dialysis, a common effect of being conceived from a drug-addicted parent. My mother never spoke about her reasons for adopting; however, according to Grandma Hunny, my mother always wanted to have children because she desired to provide a child with the same *wonderful* childhood she'd had. But physically giving birth as a dialysis patient was risky for both the mother and baby and the life expectancy for someone on dialysis is up to ten years.[1] In retrospect, it seems that my mother's impending death may have always been at the forefront of her mind, and becoming a mother may have been one of the first bullet points on her "bucket list." Therefore, I was adopted, fulfilling my mother's dreams.

When I think about accompanying my mother to dialysis, images of how easy she made the process look come to mind. It was routine. Natural. She never lamented the brown fistulas bulging from her arm. After her kidney transplant, her small frame grew rounder, her skin darker, and her hair thinner, but she never complained about the excess pounds she gained from prednisone prescriptions. Even when the transplant failed, she never displayed her disappointment to me. My mother embodied calm. She would say, "If my great-grandmother could lay ties on the railroad tracks, then certainly I can get through this."

Like many Black women, my adoptive mother and grandmother were pillars of strength. These women demonstrated through action how to get on with life, no matter what was handed to them. They personified the phrase: trauma is not about the event, but rather how the person perceives the event. It seems that my grandmother and mother both experienced loving someone with a substance abuse problem and other traumas: divorce, disability, and death. However, it's possible that these events were not traumatic for either of them because they learned not to perceive experiences as negative. However, I did not inherit that optimistic trait of perception. I was not of their biological lineage. I was adopted.

When they court-appointed Naurice as my mother, she agreed it would be a closed adoption, one where documents are sealed both ways. But closed documents don't change DNA. Naurice raised me, but Joyce's blood coursed through my veins. Naurice passed down a pattern of behavior for dealing with trauma that she seemed to have learned from her mother and grandmother: Face the current reality. Show no emotion. Be strong. But Joyce and her mother passed down something to me, too: Everything is a threat. Dysregulated emotions are reality. Spiral when faced with life.

Conflicted versions of how to deal with emotions lived within me from the day I was adopted, and I never learned to manage or navigate the emotional discomfort. I ignored what my body felt, to act out what my mother and grandmother taught, proving that what we learn in our families is as integral to the quality of life we will later have as genetic predispositions.

My emotional discomfort was feeling sorrow and yearning when I found out I was adopted but not knowing how to name and move through the rejection.

My emotional discomfort was feeling sad that my adoptive mother died but not having the tools or support to process the grief. Not receiving empathy or comfort in times of distress is a form of emotional neglect and, for me, led to further emotional discomfort. A psychological state of suffering that had not only been present with me from birth through adolescence, but also one I had explicitly learned to suppress until I found I could use sex to feel better. In the same way, my mother's father reached for heroin to temporarily soothe the internal pain of experiencing an external war, I'd used men and sex to subdue the emotional turmoil that existed in my body due to outside stressors.

To heal, I had to learn to allow my emotions to bubble to the surface and burst, no matter how uncomfortable it made me. Thinking deeply about my adoptive mother's background in conjunction with my grandmother's influence on her, and eventually, my life, was an important next step in learning to sit with my sadness.

For years, I'd carried immense shame in being adopted, some of this derived from my mother, who was uncomfortable admitting she hadn't birthed me. However, much of the embarrassment stemmed from my perception. I envied other people and their families, for no other reason than they looked like their parents. After completing day five of the relationship meditation guide, I accepted my sadness, anger, and envy as valid emotions. I permitted myself to want to look like someone else in this world and admitted how much I envied Kimeiko who favored Brent and his family. I acknowledged that, though Briana's eyes, cheeks, and smile looked like mine, her darker skin tone came from the depths of a family line I may never know. Though some families appear clone-like, that wasn't the case for me; my children's looks reinforced that I was adopted and heightened my shame.

But shame breeds bitterness and they fester and rot both body and soul. I had to release them. There was no reason to be ashamed of being an adoptee. Although I disliked Grandma Hunny saying that sixteen years was a long time to have had my adoptive mother, I knew what she meant. My adoption was miraculous in many ways. It was a miracle that I didn't die on the floor of an abandoned apartment. It was a miracle that DCFS gave me to a Black family because that wasn't and still isn't common; white babies are adopted at twice the rate of Black ones.[2] To this day, some Black people act as if they are confused by the concept of adoption. They assume Grandma Hunny and I are biologically related and that my mother passed me down to her. It takes effort to explain that my family *is* my family, but they also are not. This, too, is something I've had to learn to use: my voice. It was a miracle that my mother was able to raise me for as long as she did due to her disability. My mother surpassed life expectancy by two decades.

I am grateful that I was adopted, especially with a clear understanding of the generational trauma passed down through my birth family; however, my adoption and my mother's subsequent death produced added layers to an existing abandonment wound. In addition to being anxiously attached to family and friends and constantly worrying over their impending departure, I also developed an avoidant attachment style.[3] My adolescence proved that people would leave me; consequently, creating the idea that I could not depend on anyone,[4] not the husband I chose, the children I bore, or the flux of friends who flitted in and out of my life. Expecting to be betrayed was a constant fear that competed with my desire to be loved.

TONY

2015

By the time my father gave up his parental rights, the idea that people leave was deeply entrenched in my psyche. I shifted between an anxious and avoidant attachment style from adolescence and beyond young adulthood, simultaneously pushing everyone away and pulling people close, especially if it was a man. Though Brent frequently professed his love for me, I rarely believed him. I never expected anyone to stay, and when it was time to leave, I couldn't, because I feared being alone. As I suspected when I met with Dr. Aminu, healing my relationship with my father was an important part of moving forward and healing the addiction because he, too, was a part of my origin family.

My father and I had spent the last three years actively working to repair our relationship. He assumed more of the onus of our bond. Consequently, the scales balanced toward parallel understanding. But a new barrier surfaced. Having diabetes hindered his previous throat operation from properly healing. He had to have tracheotomy surgery, which would allow him to eat solid food. However, he'd have to learn to use a tool to talk. We Skyped. We could see each other, but his words were garbled. We called. We could hear each other, but phrases were unclear. When he could've used his voice to repair our dysfunction, he didn't. Now that he wanted to restore our bond, his voice disappeared. I suggested texting. He often forgot to power his phone, and sometimes he would take several days to return a message. But overall, we communicated more. Conversations centered on my family, my endeavors, his health, and when Brent and I would reload the prepaid gift card.

He reminded me of his promise. *I'm going to spend the rest of my life making sure you know that I love you.* Though I'd carved out a space for hope, my abandonment wounds were slow to heal; a large percentage of distrust remained. Kimeiko was a year shy of when I'd lost my mother. Briana had little knowledge of who "Grandpa Tony" was and secretly called MJ by her first name, instead of Grandma. It seemed too late for the type of mending he wanted simply because of the *threat of mortality.* But my father remained committed to repairing our relationship, while I struggled to embrace his repentance. I had one foot in therapeutic overhaul and one cautious foot out.

The relationship meditation had shown me the importance of leaping forward. One of the days prompted me to *think about a hobby I'd abandoned.* Writing was my only answer. By May, I'd outlined my broken history with my father via a personal, but public, blog. Descriptions devoted to my father's role in my teenage life and lack of participation in my adult life characterized him as negligent. He was an avid reader and my words hurt. He wanted me to write about how he taught me to drive when I was sixteen. I reminded him of twenty years of deficient relationship; we'd only recently begun mending decades of dysfunction. He thanked me for the clarification and didn't reach out for three weeks.

Grandma Betty had once explained what happened to my father's father: her husband had agreed for her to travel from Newark, New Jersey to Chicago with their three children. He promised to meet her in their new city and never did. Like Grandma Hunny, there was no self-deprecation involved in the retelling of this narrative. Grandma Betty dusted herself off, independently raised three children, and attained a master's in nursing.

My father never spoke of his abandonment or how it may have impacted his life, but the consequence was obvious. One cannot be what one does not see. I turned forty-two with no communication from my father and began to wallow in old emotions. His lack of contact confirmed what I'd suspected—he couldn't be trusted; it was just a matter of time before he'd abandon me again. I was grateful for the noncommittal foot. When I didn't hear from my father, I was aware enough of my emotions to recognize I was upset and felt unimportant, so I didn't feel the urge to suppress or soothe the pain with sex. However, I used another coping mechanism that had worked throughout the years: detachment, which is commonplace to prevent further hurt.[1]

But this time, when I decided to disengage, my cousin texted: *Mom wants to talk to you.*

Alrighty, I wrote back.

My father and MJ had moved five hours away from me to Atlanta, something no one had shared.

Another message glowed from my cousin. *Did you ever hear from Mom, Uncle Tony, or Aunt MJ?*

I talked to Auntie, but not Daddy.

Do you want me to tell you, or do you want to wait? They have something they need to say, but they don't want you to worry.

I braced myself. *Tell me.*

He has cancer in his lungs now, and it's hard for him to breathe.

Just when I'd learned to honor my emotions, life flooded me with more. Each feeling melded into one glob and froze into a block of familiar detachment. That night, I slid under the covers and slipped into an unsettled sleep. The next morning, I awoke around five. Worried about my early rise, Brent stared from the corner of his eye as I brushed my teeth.

Thoughts thawed and spilled into a river of rumination. Our family was scheduled to vacation overseas. *What if he dies while we're there? They can't bury him without me. Oh no! He's gonna die for real. This means the opportunity for a father-daughter relationship is over.* I slipped back into childhood disappointments. *Why couldn't I have had parents devoted to raising and being with me? Where were my quirky mom and dad who embraced grandchildren, family vacations, and me?* Compassion cracked my heart open as I realized time was limited. My father had lived with cancer without me. There was time and space for me to choose a different path.

Silently, I stood in the middle of my kitchen and wiped my face dry of tears. I said a prayer that his spirit and soul be at ease through the transition. Then, I consciously put both feet into the relationship renovation. I wanted my father to know I cared. My will to forgive became greater than decades of resentment. He was right. The threat of mortality could shift perspective.

Brent, the girls, and I visited my father two weeks later, before our overseas trip. But I was dismayed. A brown bag of bones stood before me.

"Never thought you'd see me this skinny, huh?" he joked, revealing several missing teeth.

His receding mini afro had turned a snowy shade of white. He shuffled around showing me his room, bathroom, and patio. Having mastered the talking tool, his words, broken and robotic, were now comprehensible.

MJ's weariness was a visible part of the room's energy. Her voice trailed behind as she described new cancer developments in his lungs. They had found out right before they'd packed up a new life 700 miles away from years of familiarity. She needed directions to Emory. I wanted to ask why they hadn't mentioned the move. But somehow, it seemed irrelevant.

Brent, the girls, and I moved a few boxes to and from the outside storage. People walked directly past their porch. Third-floor dwellers peered down, invading their space.

My father frowned. His New Jersey and Chicago instincts kicked in. "We need some iron bars out here."

I laughed. But sadness filled my heart. I promised to try a little harder. They were only five hours away. I had no idea how long he would live, and it didn't matter. They were close enough for me to offer more help.

He cupped my face in the palms of his hands.

"Come back," he whispered and kissed me on the forehead.

"I will," I promised.

But my newfound commitment was too late.

Fourteen days later, when we returned to the States, my father rolled a green oxygen tank behind him. He couldn't speak without coughing, spitting, or gasping for air. Shortly after, doctors refused him chemo. Frailty wouldn't allow it.

He refused to eat.

Seventy-two hours later, the hospital moved him to hospice.

The next day, he was unresponsive.

When my daughters and I returned to Atlanta, the nurses' soft, overly kind voices coupled with sunset lighting cued me for the end. The girls and I entered his room. HGTV blared. The deterioration had set in and left a shell of his former self, absent of spirit. He lay among white blankets and pillows: limp, mouth open, and body angled up enough to appear as if he was actively breathing. He wasn't. His connection to a sugar IV gave us time to make funeral arrangements. Although MJ had warned me about his coma-like state, I still tried.

"Daddy," I said above a murmur.

His breath was belabored: In. Out. Gasp.

I handed the girls my car keys. There was little reason for them to witness the moment. I held his skeletal hand and regretted that I couldn't have healed sooner, in time to accept his apology. I wished we both could've done better. More acceptance set in. He was the father I had been given.

The following morning, all the patients' doors were open, except his. The sun's light shone through cracked blinds. Quiet filled the remaining space. No apparatus. No wires. No machine. The blankets that kept his body warm just a day ago, and the white fluffy pillows that had propped his body up, were neatly folded and stacked one on top of another near the window. His mouth was still open. His body lay flat; the woven white covers neatly folded across his chest.

My father transitioned on July 5th. He seemed to be at peace and now it was time for me to be. His death released me from years of suffering and wondering when he'd meet love with action the way I wanted. The permanence of death meant he never would. Instead of burying the pain under another man, I wept, and I wrote.

∞

The year after my mother died, I told Grandma Hunny I was going to write a book.

"Oh yeah? About what?" she asked.

"My mother's death."

"You think you're the only one whose mother died?" she replied.

Face current reality. Show no emotion. Be strong.

Decades ago, my teenage self didn't know how to respond to the stress of losing my mother. I was told not to cry about it, and then I felt mocked for wanting to translate my pain into words. Instead, I acted out and used sex to relieve stress, only to find that on the other side of orgasm, I was empty inside and felt worse than I did before. This reoccurring cycle created more anxiety and increased my stress. There was no way I could dismiss my grandmother's words when I was sixteen. I looked up to her and assumed she knew more about how to navigate life than I ever could. Every so often, she'd confirm the idea by reminding me that she'd always know more than I did, simply because she'd been on the planet longer. If writing about my mother was a bad idea, then so be it; however, I wasn't offered an alternative way to deal with the stress. I dismissed my dreams and filed writing about my reality under something whimsical and insignificant, like owning a pet unicorn.

Decades later, the relationship meditation permitted me to write. I'd begun publicly sharing true stories to release myself from a self-imposed bondage of shame, a byproduct was that I also uplifted others.

Unlike my mother's death, where I muffled tears and felt large pockets of loneliness, I grieved my father's death openly with an international audience. In between helping MJ prepare for my father's funeral, I sat in her spare bedroom and shared each conflicted emotion through a series of blog posts and felt a collective embrace from an understanding community. Daughters who'd suffered open abandonment wounds via their fathers sent me virtual hugs of empathy. Discussing our challenges, which didn't culminate with Hollywood bows, provided relief for them and me. A return to writing helped me to manage stress and emotions and I was content because this form of creativity wasn't entangled in extra-marital affairs, self-destruction, and secrecy. I was learning to self-regulate one word at a time. It was the beginning of liberation from the sex-addiction cycle.

GRANDMA HUNNY

2015

"What do you want from your grandmother?" I imagined Dr. Aminu would have asked.

At this phase of my healing journey, I wanted a grandmother who provided vulnerability, the kind that Iyanla describes, where you feel safe enough in the person's arms to *let your heart break*. I've been in Grandma Hunny's arms. My heart tightens and shields itself from the daggers of her words. There is no warm embrace emanating from the depths of her soul. Her arms wrap around me like dollar store greeting cards, filled with obligation and offered with salutations. I wanted a hug that ached with the anguish of losing my mother, a physical lamentation of the pain that poets have penned, or that artists outline with thick brush strokes. I wanted to hear the details of how she grieved the loss of her child, my mother.

I once tried to access the emotions I was sure my grandmother held about my mother's death. I was still nervous to ask her meaningful questions but believed talking with her was necessary for my healing. I found a quiet place in my home and dialed her number, secretly hoping she wouldn't answer.

"I have a question," I casually said after pleasantries. "How did you feel losing your oldest daughter?"

My voice trembled.

"Kathy," she started. "Like I told you. Keep your mama in your heart. Your mama has always been in my heart. Before she died, she said, 'Make sure Kathy's alright.' So, I did. No questions." Her voice trailed off into a new topic unrelated to our shared family history.

Everything about my grandmother's actions seemed dutiful, including her rationale for why she picked up the slack of caring for me. She had stories about my mother, but none of them conveyed the love of a mother and her child. I wished for a detailed narrative of Grandma Hunny's hopes and dreams for her daughter. Every mother has them. What were hers? Did she wish for more than forty-one years with her? I wanted her to communicate that she chose to take care of me out of love, not out of responsibility. But that is not the way of many elders. They're called the "greatest" generation for a reason. Many of them value commitment and loyalty, such as taking care of family, with *no questions*. Those who were coming of age through the Great Depression or World War II, like my grandmother, learned resiliency; they experienced a range of life-altering situations but didn't have time to cry about any of them. Perseverance took precedence over pain. Grandma Hunny exemplified these characteristics; however, before we hung up, she did offer some hope. She promised to send a letter to further answer my question. But when that letter arrived, my heart sank with disappointment; she scribbled long explanations for everything, except how she felt about my mother's death. So, I left the topic alone and attempted to process the reality of who my grandmother has been.

My grandmother has lacked the emotional acuity to offer what I need. She has shown me this lack of capacity several times in the past, but I'd dismissed it as a personality flaw. I thought she was being mean when she told me I shouldn't write about my mother's death. I thought she hated my father when he asked to walk me down the aisle at my wedding. I thought she was manipulative when she responded with sarcasm about seeking out my biological family. But I now view how my grandmother related as a matter of both/and. Oftentimes, her reactions and words were mean, and she didn't have the skill set to function any differently. She knew no other way to interact when faced with negative emotions. Like my mother, Grandma Hunny's strength was linked to her upbringing and to her grandmother laying ties on the railroad and not breaking down into a pool of vulnerability. But her comments invoked what a therapist would characterize as a type of emotional abuse, resulting in a constant dismissal of my emotions, bullying, and inappropriate reactions.[1]

Still, I longed for a deeper connection with her. I wanted to have an honest conversation with her, where I could confide that, while sixteen years was a long time for me to have my adoptive mother, sixteen years was not a long time to have *a* mother. I wanted her to understand the abyss that was formed from losing, not one, but two mothers. However, the longer I processed who my grandmother had been, the less I desired to talk with her. Our conversations were once melodious, filled with mutual back-and-forth cackling judgments, but over time, these diminished to intermittent, thirty-minute, dry diatribes where Grandma Hunny talked about fleeting subjects that came to her mind to fill the gaps of my silence.

"Yeah, I was telling Norma that you found your . . . what do you call them? Your sister and the lady in Georgia and them? What was the lady's name?"

"Catherine," I said.

"Yeah. And she was who?"

"My aunt."

"Yeah, but what do you call them?"

"My biological family."

I hit mute, turned on the kitchen faucet, and squeezed bright blue liquid on a sponge.

"Yeah. I was telling Norma that Kathy likes people. She likes to know all the people. And I'm wondering whatchu gonna do with all those people? I told Norma, you know Diane's girls found their other mother. She's short and kinda stocky just like Sheri, and I think Sheri was trying to kinda get to know the mother, but Shemika said she got a mama, she got a daddy, and I guess she said she don't need to know those folks. Sheri was gonna go to the family reunion, but I guess she said nah, I don't think I need to do that. But Kathy? She talks to those people. That's what I told Norma. You like people."

I turned off the running water and tried to simmer the anger that boiled inside. I counted to ten. I inhaled deeply.

"Grandma, that's the difference between me, Sheri, and Shemika," I said, finally taking the phone off mute. "Every adoption is different. Every person is different. They still have a mother and father; I don't. That's what's different here."

"What?" she asked.

She couldn't hear me, so I repeated myself, but the conversation she began about the choices adult adoptees make was over. I told my grandmother I had to make dinner, even though Brent and I had already eaten.

I have wanted to have an open conversation about what is going on in my life, so I've tried to meet my grandmother where she is with stories of our trips abroad or new accolades. These are the only conversations where she can hear me.

"Have you heard of Chicken Soup for the Soul?" I asked.

"Yeah."

"The franchise created a special edition for Black people, and the editors chose 101 Black women writers to participate. They chose one of my essays."

"Are you gonna send me a book?" she asked, anticipation sparking through each fiber.

"Of course," I said. But I didn't feel loved by her pride; I was annoyed, then ashamed that I was annoyed because I could not and have not accepted her for who she is. The achievements mean something to her that they don't to me, and I don't know how to meet her in the middle of our misunderstandings.

Grandma Hunny was overjoyed when she received her copy. She enjoyed the anthology not only because I'd written about race relations in academia, but also because *her* granddaughter was a contributor.

"I'm coming down there," she announced a few months later. "I'm gonna fly to Norma's in South Carolina, and then we're gonna drive to your house. Can you order some more of those books for me? Ten of them . . . order ten of them."

I complied.

My grandmother eased one leg at a time out of Norma's sedan, offered a dollar-store hug, and pecked me on the cheek.

"There's my baby girl."

A woman I once cowered to look up to, had shrunk to my height, and I was able to do something impossible in the past—look her in the eye. Her blouse and trousers hung from her body like drapes. She and her quad cane inched across the driveway and over the threshold of the house, where she was grateful to plop down on a nearby couch.

"Whew!" she sighed. "You have the books?" she asked, handing me a check for the ten I'd ordered, plus ten more for a subsequent order.

"Right here, Grandma," I said, sliding the box toward her and presenting a stack of lilac covers.

"You got my bag?" she asked Norma.

Norma, twenty years her junior, shuffled back to the car and brought her tattered carry-on. Grandma Hunny dug through the bag, until she found a white piece of printout paper, with scrawled cursive writing.

"Here. Read this," my grandmother said.

She had written a letter to the Black women in her life to whom she was going to send a copy of the book. In it, she'd described how important Black women were and she'd directed them to the page where they could find my essay. She'd planned to sit on the couch and prepare the letters for delivery. Later that day, she instructed Norma to drive us to a place for her to photocopy the letter. When we returned to my home, she sat on the couch and wrote each woman's name at the top, signed her name, folded it up, and stuck one in a book, ready to be delivered like a personal assembly line.

"You didn't know I was gonna do this, did you?" she asked.

Indeed, I did not. I thought she was coming to Florida to visit with me, to ask me about the contents of the essay, or to discuss how times hadn't really changed for Black people like her or me. Instead, she sat glued to the couch, signing and folding.

The following day, we spent one hour at the UPS store sending books to women she loved that showcased me, who she loved. But I didn't feel loved. I felt as I always have with my grandmother as if I was in the room, but not within her full vision, like a circus animal whose discontent the audience ignores because lions don't have tears to symbolize the pain of repeated performance. Mantacore the Tiger didn't attack Roy Horn because of a miscue; I believe he left his trainer in shreds because he was tired of being put on display. The one aspect of our relationship with which I thought we could bond—relishing in external validation—is something I'd begun to relinquish and resent.

I'm embarrassed to feel what seems like ingratitude from the one person who was willing to pick up the pieces of my life. Sixteen years isn't a long time to have a mother, but over forty years is a lifetime to contend with a grandmother who is not only unaffected by emotions but also oblivious to them. I'd much rather have had tenderness from a matriarch who asked me about how I'm faring in the world, than one who used my achievements as proof that my background didn't matter. Adoptees are supposed to be grateful, and Grandma Hunny reminds me that sometimes, I am not. The perception of being an adoptee is that one is lifted out of a horrendous situation and gently placed into a more loving one. Many times, adoption has felt as if I was taken out of a frying pan and dipped into the fire of life's trials and tribulations, culminating in being passed around and landing with one of the least compassionate people I know. I got the short end of the adoption stick, and I hate that no one seems to understand this. Even Brent reminds me that I received an undergraduate degree, paid for in full by my grandparents, as if emotional abandonment and abuse shouldn't matter. His reminder shows me Grandma Hunny gave me what she could—loyalty and self-sacrifice—but I needed someone to co-regulate my emotions, not ignore them. As an adult on a healing journey, I learned that was my work to do.

Yoga taught me how to self-regulate. Two years following my final abortion, and on a journey to heal my family of origin wounds, I often practiced yoga in thirty-day increments to center myself whenever guilt arose. The peace I experienced during and after yoga became the barometer for my body at rest. The more I recognized sensations of ease during each pose, the more I noticed sensations of discomfort off the mat. Anger raged and rumbled in my abdomen. Anxiety fluttered and flitted below my navel. Fear of speaking gathered in my throat.

Yoga instructors explained how poses correlate with life.

"Sthira-Sukha," one teacher reminded me as I stood in a triangle pose. It means, *there's strength in softness*, which is the opposite image of a Black woman laying ties on a railroad track.

Yoga taught me *how to feel* my emotions--which is necessary for healing as a sex addict--and how to release past and new emotional discomfort. My teacher encouraged me to relax my body to become stronger, especially if a pose was challenging. It is impossible and hurtful to try and hold my arms at an angle for several seconds while locking my knees. The flexibility and power required to practice nudged me to develop a level of gentleness with myself I wasn't raised with, which equated to self-compassion. Garudasana, eagle pose has helped me to give myself what my grandmother could not, a hug that embodies security. Like external validation, I had to give up looking for others to enact care in ways I valued; I've learned to have empathy for myself. Being in tune with my body in each moment forced me to become aware of where I should be softer. Poses aren't intended to be conducted while clenching my teeth and holding my breath. Neither is life. Off the mat, I learned to give myself the permission I'd been waiting for—permission to feel and release grief and never suppress anything further. The moment I begin holding on to negative emotions is the moment I return to a sex addiction cycle.

KATHERIN ELIZABETH

2016

The year my mother had a kidney transplant, I wrote a book called *On the Farm*. It was the story of a little boy whose father died. The boy had to learn how to survive and how to take care of the farm and his family. My fifth-grade teacher, Mrs. Patterson submitted it for a citywide competition, associated with Gwendolyn Brooks. I didn't win, but I remember the satisfaction of having expressed myself in a creative way through writing and the thrill of being invited to a citywide celebration with other young writers.

Decades later, Julia Cameron's *The Artist's Way* revealed that I'd not only become a blocked artist, but I'd also blamed my mother, father, and grandmother for not nurturing my talent. From my childlike perspective, they each knew I was a writer and could've done something to support my gift. As an adult, I saw my faulty logic. My mother fought to live each day, and her mother devoted time and energy to provide a "normal" life for me, such as taking me to the ceremony. My mother's life-or-death circumstances took precedence. Their priorities were understandably elsewhere. Consequently, it was my responsibility as an adult to nurture this part of myself; writing became an integral part of my recovery.

I maintained the blog I'd begun after my father died, coupled with a self-made rule: I would share personal stories, but the platform would not serve as an online diary. Essays would only encompass carefully crafted topics to help readers. I wrote about my mother, but only from the angle of universal concepts of mothering, such as how we parent based on our backgrounds. I wrote about being an adoptee, but only from common bonds, such as a sense of belonging, which is challenging for those of us who live with abandonment wounds. Several posts focused on my upbringing, my feelings about my upbringing, and stories about romantic, familial, and platonic relationships. As a sex addict, I'd created my identity and self-worth through sexual activities, so I needed to learn who I was when the pattern of addiction was removed.

My healing was contingent on replacing sexual outbursts with healthier options. Blogging provided a new coping mechanism and allowed me to reach an international audience. On the platform, there was a sense of camaraderie in the conversation I had with my readers about each new topic. Their engagement and comments ignited something in me I hadn't experienced in my family: being seen and heard. Readers saw themselves through my words and experiences. Blogging gave me a way to process the emotions yoga helped me feel within a caring community that affirmed my words, voice, and experiences, without having to announce to the world: *I'm a sex addict.*

The friend to whom I'd confided about having the last abortion noticed my new authentic personality. "Are you gonna ever tell Brent what happened?" she asked.

"I don't know."

No matter how much I healed and released past trauma, the guilt of cheating remained, with most of the remorse stemming from the final affair. A couple of years after my last abortion, I published an anthology called *The Unhappy Wife.* I interviewed eleven women about the dysfunction of their marriages and fictionalized their stories; a twelfth story focused on me. Creating this anthology was the closest I came, at the time, to publicly sharing about my marriage; I wasn't ready to disclose a story about having an affair that resulted in pregnancy. Instead, I included the story about Zaire and our emotional affair. Before publishing, I confessed the details to Brent. The essay outlined low-stakes content. Having an emotional affair is rarely perceived as the same as physically engaging with another person, though the act and betrayal are similar.[1]

Our conversation was brief. Brent said he understood. He knew adultery wasn't solely about the adulterer and admitted to not being fully present during that time of our marriage. He, too, was culpable in how we related to one another. Relationships require the work of two people. His acceptance removed some of the angst in my stomach, but my new work of releasing past trauma and not suppressing new pain, made living with a lie difficult; my conscience constantly nagged me. But there was more work to do before I could confess. I had to figure out who I was if I wasn't living a double life and using sex to cope with emotions.

∞

Growing up, books were my sustenance. We had a bookcase in the living room, a bookcase in the dining room, and I had my own. Words fed my only-child soul. Like many seventies' households, an encyclopedia set lined one of our shelves. Ours were *World Book*. Their dark and light green spines were alphabetically aligned and within reach. I spent several days looking at pictures of animals I thought I'd never see and studying terminology for which I had no context. The encyclopedia was my best friend when we had elementary school research projects. It's part of the reason I still remember that Addis Ababa is the capital of Ethiopia and Haile Selassie was its emperor.

My favorite adult book was my mother's, *Our Bodies Ourselves*. This book discussed health issues and was written by women about women. Inside held treasures of prophecy. The best page was the one filled with images of what the female body was supposed to look like. It illustrated women's bodies from birth to late adulthood. Because of this book, I knew budding breasts were normal and flabby bottoms occurred around fifty. This book affirmed me as a woman.

I read in my bed or laying on the floor. When I wasn't ravenously reading my mother's books, I devoured my own. *My Book about Me: By Me, Myself* was a favorite. It encouraged self-love well before the concept gained mainstream traction. The book was interactive and promoted introspection. Young readers were prompted to add pictures and fill in the blanks of what made them . . . them. My weight, height, gender, hair type, and handprint completed each page's narrative. Even though this book was for someone in primary grades, I kept it well into upper elementary, changing the picture annually, as well as erasing old answers to re-fill in the blanks.

I was the first person in my elementary school to read *Charlotte's Web*, a thick chapter book. I can still see the librarian's pride when she announced it to the other fifth graders. Her praise sounded like, *why can't you aspire to be a reader, like Kathy?* As I aged, I graduated to Judy Blume and visited our neighborhood's public library. The library was the only place my English-degreed mother would allow me to spend countless hours. I kept up with Run DMC and New Edition through issues of *Right On!* When I moved to Covert, Stephen King's novels helped me escape to a world scarier than my own. During undergrad, I traded my business major for English education, not because I loved teaching, but because I loved reading. Classes focused solely on Shakespeare or Chaucer stimulated me. I read novels cover-to-cover, and sat in the front row, prepared to discuss language use and style.

But when I met Brent, I slowly replaced reading with his hobbies, specifically watching movies. We went to regular-priced movies, and after marriage, we consumed "dollar movies," where you could watch films that were no longer popular for a cheaper rate. Once we had children, we frequented theaters every weekend, but instead of *Leaving Las Vegas*, we watched *Finding Nemo*. The books that lined my adult bookcases, primarily from adolescence and college, slowly collected dust. This wasn't Brent's fault; it was my undoing. Lacking an awareness of my own unique needs based on a clear understanding of what I liked to do was a consequence of having no boundaries, which is a codependent characteristic.[2] Brent and I had been married twenty years, and I possessed little knowledge of who I was or what I enjoyed apart from him. That had to change.

Trips to the beach were sparse, even though we'd lived in Florida for much of our marriage. If family visited, I packed up the car and took the girls and their cousins to play in the sand and wade in the shallow shoreline. However, in 2016, sporadic trips here and there weren't good enough. I felt drawn to the water, much like I'd felt drawn to yoga. When Kimeiko and Briana couldn't go with me, I asked Brent.

We bought matching light-blue beach chairs that sat low to the ground. Brent purchased a new pair of shorts, and I found a cooler. *We were going to be real Floridians*, I thought, unconsciously building another fantasy world.

"How long are we going to sit out here?" Brent asked.

It had only been an hour. We had dipped our toes in the Atlantic once. That's when I confirmed beach-going was an independent activity meant just for me. It was something I enjoyed. Because my academic schedule allowed for four months of summer vacation, I visited once a week, by myself. Planting my feet as firmly in the sand as I could, while trying not to be swept away by the water, revealed my strength as well as nature's. The ocean's waves forced me to relinquish control, while also maintaining control. I'd finally learned what it meant to surrender to something greater than myself; I finally learned the purpose of floating.

Salt water wafted past my nose, while I sat close to the shore, letting the current roll in and around my legs. Once again, I felt calm. Instead of using another person to co-regulate, the beach became a natural way to de-stress and lower my anxiety, healing my parasympathetic nervous system with each visit.[3] My weekly beach trips were timeless; I arrived and left when nudged to do so. Learning to just be, without expectations or obligations strengthened my intuition and became another way for me to focus on bodily sensations. The beach helped me to stop disassociating. Digging my toes into the sand helped ground me, and connected me to earth, and myself. I self-regulated, one beach trip at a time.

Self-awareness illuminated who I was apart from Brent. He watched hours of television; I'd rather read or write. I loved socializing; Brent mingled but preferred to be home. For him, stress rolled like water off a duck's back; I appeared more like the fowl's feet, paddling furiously underneath the water's surface to keep afloat. Once upon a time, I hung onto Brent's every word about superheroes. Now, I grew weary of watching hours-long Marvel sequels. With so many dissimilarities, there was a moment when I questioned if I truly loved Brent. Had I been so traumatized when we first met that any man who paid attention would do? Did I hang onto him the same way I'd done with Eddie, Shane, or the others? Was I afraid to let him go?

Similar to my family of origin, I evaluated our relationship. I spent time reflecting on who he'd shown himself to be over the years and pondered things I'd dismissed. Brent's lack of care was attractive when we first met. In my twenties, I was impressed that he showed little concern for anything or anyone. His lack of emotions matched an unattainable goal I'd striven for, for years. I thought about a story he often retold. His mother was in the hospital, but Brent had displayed no emotion about the situation; his father was angry and had to tell Brent that he should be concerned about his mother and that he should be showing something similar to sadness or worry. In undergrad, when I had my fourth abortion, Brent reacted similarly. He didn't check on my well-being. Like the story with his mother, he didn't say anything.

In 1998, as we began trying to begin our family, the doctor had advised us to wait six months to allow the birth control pills to leave my system. I didn't listen, and a month or so later, we were pregnant. By our first gynecology visit, there was no heartbeat. The embryo had died but had not yet been released from my uterus. We scheduled a dilation and curettage, a common surgery to remove the remains. Brent was with me, but like Grandma Hunny, he seemed to lack the language to provide comfort. A week later, we continued with life as usual and attended his family's reunion in South Carolina, where his mother, instead of offering consolation, simply instructed me to wipe off picnic tables in preparation for visitors. Upon experiencing this, I figured Brent's lack of affectation was hereditary.

Stories like these have punctuated our relationship. One time, I called his mother so she could understand how tired I was while pregnant with Kimeiko. I wanted her to explain to her son how, during pregnancy, small tasks turned into huge feats because, thus far, Brent would laugh and reply that nothing was wrong with me when I'd ask him to iron my clothes for the next day.

Years later, when our relationship became taxing, he'd make clear that he could leave *with the shirt on his back.*

"None of this means anything," he'd declare like a Buddhist monk.

His comments left me to believe the "this" he was referring to, meant not only material things, but also the family we'd built. I'd met and married someone who mirrored my grandmother and mother, someone who lacked empathy, someone who enacted a form of emotional neglect. As I learned to feel emotions, I grew agitated with this trait in him. I'd married an emotionally unavailable man, and I didn't know what to do.

My new way of being—naming and moving through emotions—highlighted how little Brent labeled and shared his feelings. I raised this as an issue, and we parsed out our family backgrounds and compared the two. Brent came from a home where he was taught it was okay to feel, but not in public. His mother once told me that she thought he was going to be the "sensitive one," but he ended up the polar opposite. She said this as if she or his father had no hand in his transition, as if a thief came in the night and stole her sensitive son and replaced him with an insensitive shell of a person who didn't know how to react when his mother was hospitalized. According to Brent, his behavior was learned in ways familiar to most boys. Crying was discouraged. His behavior was learned in ways familiar to most Black children. His father warned that should tears appear in the corners of his eyes, he would give him something to cry about. Eventually, Brent stopped crying; he stopped reacting.

Brent don't give a fuck, a friend of mine used to say, referring to how he could sit in a room full of people and tune out conversations and interactions that didn't pertain to him. Our daughters have often questioned whether *he really doesn't care or is pretending not to care.* However, to suggest that Brent doesn't care is to also offend him. He insists it isn't true.

"So, where is it?" I once asked, referring to the care he claimed to possess.

"I care," he said. "It's just inside."

Becoming aware of Brent's emotional unavailability was as revealing as processing my trail of traumas. Though my addictive behavior wasn't his fault, his lack of emotion had contributed to its progression. In the past, the ease with which Brent had forgiven and then forgotten about each indiscretion had benefitted me. A disassociated partner was ideal when I kept secrets and caroused the streets. Now that I was healing unresolved trauma and quickly returning to my core self, which by and large, was emotional, I craved intimacy in ways that Brent seemed incapable of providing.

My new identity required a fully present husband, one who asked what time I'd be returning from the beach, one who asked follow-up questions about writing events and speaking engagements, not one who sat idly by as I won writing awards and published chapters in anthologies. So, I attempted to change him. I tried to help him access his emotions, even though he hadn't asked for such assistance. If his emotional intelligence could atrophy in childhood, then it could be rebuilt in adulthood, like working out a bicep. *You can take off your mask,* I implored. *It's okay to share how you feel,* I begged. But he didn't seem to be hiding anything. This low-affect person appeared to be who he was. Something I realized a few years later.

Briana's been in an accident," Brent said. "There were four cars. She was the third. Someone hit someone else, that person hit her, and she hit someone."

"What?" I asked.

"She called me a few minutes ago."

"Did she sound alright?" I asked, preparing to drive to the scene.

"She's fine," Brent said. "I told her to wait 'til the police get there, and then go to school after . . ."

"You told her to do what?"

"She's fine!"

An hour later, Briana texted me.

Mommy, my head hurts.

Come home, I replied.

Briana and I spent the next day in a chiropractor's office. He knocked her knees with a reflex hammer, pinched the back of her neck, and diagnosed her as having a concussion. An MRI showed she was fine, but she would have to continue with physical therapy twice a week. Simple words like *theory* escaped her memory, and when she did remember, her mouth moved slowly to pronounce both syllables: *theeee-reee,* she said, her eyes dazed. Her personality dulled, and she walked around as if someone had turned off the lightbulb in her brain. Eat, rest, and take medication, the doctor had ordered. For the next few days, my job was to prepare her lunch, ensure she remained off of all screens, and bring her meds every three hours in between teaching online classes and grading papers. Brent worked at the office.

On day two, Brent arrived from work and packed his tennis bag.

"I thought about going to work out, but I'm too tired," I shared. Briana had virtually presented a school project and refused to finish her food.

"Why are you so tired?" he asked.

My eyes turned red with rage. Brent had communicated with the lawyer and the insurance company; however, he seemed to ignore the severity of the damage to Briana's brain and hadn't inquired about my well-being.

"Aren't you worried?" I asked.

"About what?"

"About your daughter. Her concussion. A concussion is a brain injury," I reminded him. Have you noticed her speech? Aren't you worried whether she's going to be okay?" I was worried. Navigating my daughter's injuries post-car crash inevitably forced me to relive my own. I didn't recall such a long recuperation time after the concussions I'd suffered when I was her age.

Brent explained that he had little concern because he knew she was going to recover. He didn't understand why I was so upset. Everything was going to be fine. Then, he changed into his blue and white outfit, slipped into his matching shoes, and left to hit balls with his friend.

I dreamt of divorce, but quickly dismissed the idea. For years, Brent had accepted the ugliest and most embarrassing parts of my personality, and I had to do the same. I loved Brent, and the least I could do was accept who he'd shown himself to be. I married a man who was emotionally unavailable when I needed a place for sadness to breathe. I agreed to be in a committed relationship with a man, who offered co-regulation by accident, by being his even-tempered self, not because he was a soft place to land. We were two people with different identities, and thus, unique needs and ways of fulfilling them. Acknowledging our dissimilarities was disappointing, but it was a necessary part of not only accepting myself, but also healing our codependency. I finally knew where he ended and I began—it was in the space of detachment, where he and his emotions had learned to live, and I could no longer reside. It was in the tears he refused to cry, and that was his work to do, not mine.

MR. PHILIP

2018

A unt Catherine confirmed that my mother had named the janitor as my father, and she'd added that he was a lanky, white man. Ever since our conversation, I wanted to know if I was, indeed, biracial. Wide hips and curly hair signified the possibility of a "mixed" identity. My high cheekbones resembled photos of Native Americans. When I rode the train home for Christmas one year, a man old enough to be my father sat across from me. His simple *hello* led to more conversation and moments later he was showing me pictures of his wife, a woman who was one-hundred percent Indigenous.

"You're definitely Indian," he said as he compared my cheeks with his wife's.

Adoption connects adoptees with strangers in ways biological families could never understand. His words remained in the back of my mind until I connected with my grandfather Mose. Mose confirmed that his mother and her mother were one-hundred percent Cherokee. He'd also sent DCFS a 1970s photo of his five daughters; it arrived with splotches of correction fluid over everyone's faces, except my mother's. Government privacy rules wouldn't allow me to compare my features to my aunts'. Everyone had big poofy hazel brown manes, like mine. I assumed the huge afros were the products of blended people: African and Indigenous. But blank faces and afros only established my race. I still wondered who I was ethnically. Enter ancestry.com. In 2018, I joined millions of others and delved into the world of genealogy beginning with commercialized DNA testing.

When the small white box arrived, my stomach churned with excitement. It was time to reconcile another part of my identity. Anxiety built. I spat as the directions stated and dripped an additional blue solution into the tube. Droplets spilled down the side, my saliva turned blue, and I quickly followed the remainder of the instructions and rushed to UPS. Although it made no sense, when I returned home, I logged in to Ancestry's site to see if there was a change. Nothing. I sent an email inquiring about details: *How would I know when they received it? How would I know if I'd completed the test correctly?* A website manager replied with a formulaic answer. I'd find out in four to six weeks. Still, I checked my email daily for a week, and then weekly for a month. Finally, I let it go and the results came.

The outcome was seven percent of Ireland, Scotland, and Wales. High school biology taught me that seven percent wasn't enough to confirm a white father. However, the test also showed fifteen percent England/Wales/Northwest Europe. Still, it seemed if there was a white part of my DNA, it would have to be closer to fifty. The remainder of the results showed majority African descent: thirty-eight percent Cameroon/Congo, twenty-nine percent Benin/Togo, and seven percent Mali. Knowing with certainty that my lineage derived from Africa gave me the sense of belonging I'd craved growing up, even if it was tied to an entire continent.

Confirmation that I was not half-white showed when I clicked on a green button called, "View DNA Matches." At the top of the page of my DNA results was a man's name: Philip Johnson. Under his name was a possible family range: parent/child. Under that was a confidence level bar: Extremely confident. And under that was a relationship: *Philip Johnson is your father.*

Brent was the first person I showed. The reality of the situation was unbelievable. I'd never imagined finding my father could be this simple. When I searched for my biological family in the early 2000s, I released the idea of discovering another parent. No one knew who he was, and I never imagined that over ten years later, there would be some futuristic six-week method for locating and confirming paternity. The results were astonishing

Ancestry offered a brief science lesson on how DNA works. Specific relationships can only be linked to certain people. For example, I can only be related to my daughters as their mother, and they, as my daughters. With that information and an *extremely confident* DNA match, I sent an email to a man, who the day before I didn't even know existed. I typed and deleted several messages, with Brent's advice to "not sound too crazy."

Dear Mr. Philip, based on my DNA results, we could possibly be related. I was adopted and have only found my birth

mother's family. So, I was wondering if you've ever lived or grown up in the Chicago area.

I clicked send and returned to the results. Under Philip's name was a woman, whose moniker was phoenixcatherine. She was listed as my first cousin. Perhaps she would know something. Mired in disbelief, I reframed what ancestry showed me. If she was my first cousin, then maybe Philip was her father, and consequently my uncle, thus explaining the whole "father" thing away. I emailed her next.

Hi! I'm new to Ancestry, but I see that we could be possibly related. I was adopted out of my family and have only met my mother's side of the family. Looking forward to hearing from you.

I repeatedly checked the site throughout May. Neither of them responded, nor did they log back into Ancestry, something the site allows you to see. Three months passed. I returned to my regular schedule of teaching and writing. In September, I received an Ancestry email stating another member and I shared DNA. Like phoenixcatherine, this new person was also listed as my first cousin. Because she had recently accessed the site, I assumed she might be a better person to contact. So, once again, I emailed:

Hi Felicia! I'm actually adopted and have only met my biological mother's side of the family. According to this site, we're related, and I'd love to hear more about you. Were you raised in the Chicago area? Do you know who Philip Johnson is? Hoping to hear from you soon.

She responded the following day.

Hi! From my understanding of how this DNA stuff works, you could be anything from a 1st cousin to a half-sibling, so I'm very eager to connect with you! My name is Felicia, and I was born and raised in Chicago, and remain there today. I have several immediate family members on here that are DNA matches for you also, but I am the only one that actively checks my account and does the whole research thing. phoenixcatherine is my sister, and Philip Johnson is my father. What can you tell me about yourself? Not to invade your privacy, but when were you born? What is your bio mom's name? Are you currently in Chicago? How else can I help you connect the dots?

The words sister, father, and half-sibling echoed. Suddenly, it clicked. Oh shit! Philip Johnson really is my father, and these are my sisters!

I responded immediately, detailing information from the DCFS report and what I knew of my adoption. Felicia contacted her father, mother, and sister before replying, something she shared with me later. Once she did, Mr. Philip emailed me back.

I apologize for missing this message -- my youngest daughter brought it to my attention and taught me how to message you back. Yes, I live in Chicago, and I lived in the South Shore & Hyde Park areas in the 70s. My youngest daughter also told me that your mom's name is Joyce Belcher. I don't remember having a relationship with Joyce and did not know I had another child, but based on these results, I would think you are my daughter, and would very much like to meet you if that's what you would like. I hope you respond and tell me about yourself. I have lived in Chicago my entire life and have been married since 1972. You have 3 half siblings— Felipe, Phoenix, and Felicia. I am sorry about the circumstances that led to your adoption and wish I had known about you.

I'd spent four years healing trauma from my background and accepting how my family of origin impacted my life. I'd learned how to feel, name, and move through familiar emotional discomfort, but these were new emotions. This wasn't the anger that surfaced when talking to Grandma Hunny or the pent-up anxiety I'd learned to suppress. These emotions were indescribable. I was faced with an experience I never imagined—finding my birth father.

My emotions outnumbered the new coping strategies I'd adopted. This unexpected layer of my life came at a time when I'd begun accepting who I was and how I'd gotten here: biology and unprotected sex. A living person, called "father" added complexity. Anger, excitement, nervousness, sadness, and confusion overwhelmed me. I practiced yoga and meditated. I blogged about events and journaled. The effort required to meet this hurdle was exhausting. Past coping mechanisms were effortless. It was easier to bundle emotions together and stuff them away than it was to name and process each one. So, I cozied up with familiar and established methods. I was fine and finding my biological father and his family was no big deal. I was back at the beginning of a sex-addiction cycle: experiencing emotional discomfort and not staying grounded.

∞

"I don't know why," Mr. Philip said, "but when I found out I had another daughter, I was just excited."

We began talking on the phone in mid-September. He texted a photo. We shared a nose. We shared similar eye shapes. His hair was wavy, like mine. Each superficial reason I had for finding family was completed at our reunion. Children who are raised by their biological families have the luxury of seeing themselves in their parents. I'd only begun to revel in seeing the likeness of both of mine after this interaction. While I knew my short stature and athletic build came from Joyce, seeing my father completed the picture and provided me with a physical understanding of who I was.

In the picture he sent, Mr. Philip stood beside a woman, his wife. They'd married the same month I was conceived, August 1972, and had remained so for the past forty-six years. I was forty-five at the time, and so was their oldest daughter, Phoenix. She was born in March 1973, two months before me. When he handed his wife the phone, she spoke hesitantly about the challenges of learning about my existence.

"I understand. I'm a wife. I'm a mother," I said.

Her reluctance to accept reality required compassion. I spoke for myself and Joyce to ease her thoughts as she talked to me, about the manifestation of her husband's adultery. Learning that your husband cheated four decades prior is difficult; having proof in the form of a person who looks like his twin and shares the same age as your daughter, is a different level of betrayal.

Phoenix and I chatted a few days later. Mr. Philip had sent me her wedding picture. I stared at her face, the way she held her head, the curvature of her spine, the wedding dress she'd chosen. Mr. Philip had passed my wedding picture on to her as well. Later, Phoenix told me she was suspicious to learn of my existence but comparing wedding photos convinced her that we weren't only sisters, we were practically twins. Our similarities were undeniable. Our histories were different, but the cadence of our voices and sense of humor were the same. We laughed and talked non-stop for one hour. Talking with Phoenix was like talking to myself. I grew excited about the possibility of discovering a sister who sounded as if she was ready to accept another sibling.

Mr. Philip and I interacted for another month. At first, he couldn't recall who my mother was, until I texted a photo of Briana. The image jogged his memory.

"She looks just like your mother," he said.

Four decades after they'd met, he was still mesmerized by Joyce's beauty. My mother and Mr. Philip met while he was renting an apartment. My mother, fleeing her husband, was looking for a place to live. The owner of the building wasn't home, but she wanted to see what a unit looked like. My father agreed to show her his. His memory ended where my conception began.

"So, there was no relationship?" I clarified.

"No. Katherin, I know what you're saying. No. That was it. Just that one time."

Brent and Phoenix found the story odd, particularly the part about meeting a stranger and having random sex. I, of course, did not. It was not only plausible but also, in some ways, affirming. Maybe, I'd inherited more than my big eyes and a wide smile from my mother and father.

According to Mr. Philip, he didn't know my mother was pregnant or that I was born; otherwise, he would've, *raised me with the rest of his children, under his roof.* His words were nice, but by 2018, I had reconciled my birth and upbringing. I was where I was intended to be. No mistake was made.

Finding and meeting Mr. Philip offered closure and provided me with an origin story, which also completed an understanding of my identity. I was the energetic manifestation of two people who engaged in an extra-marital affair. Their union explicitly and implicitly affected my life, as all parents' unions do. This story is not one I would've consciously chosen, but it is *my* birth story. However, typing words of acceptance is easier than actual acceptance. Mr. Philip's existence and rendition of events created a new wound; this narrative was another dismal tale to be added to the overall story of who I was.

Three months after these new revelations, Tonya called me. I hadn't heard from her since the peak years of my infidelity. She had been recently released from jail and wanted to hang out. I agreed to attend a birthday party with her. Cups of rum punch filled my belly and sent me into euphoria. Someone's man and I partnered and won a game of Spades. A woman sidled up next to me and whispered that she'd seen me staring at her.

"I know you want me," she accused, the tang of rum inches away from my nose.

Towards the end of the night, I danced by myself in the middle of the host's living room, and according to her, I announced, "I could take anybody's man in this house."

I was thrown out.

I don't recall saying those words, but I do remember side-swiping my new car as I peeled away from her street in a fury. How I arrived safely home is a miracle. I sulked for weeks. I hadn't drunk that much since I'd bumped into Tasha's friend in her narrow hallway. I returned to self-deprecation and called myself stupid for slipping into a cycle I'd thought was over. Though I was relieved I didn't have sex with anyone, it frightened me that I could have. It seemed to be a matter of time. The key to maintaining recovery was to stay in reality, no matter how painful.

I mailed the host an apology note.

Seven months after I found the paternal side of my biological family, it was clear that, like my adoptive father, Mr. Philip and I wouldn't have a relationship, either. Neither would my younger sister, older brother, and I. Only Phoenix and I would remain close. These circumstances caused an additional trauma wound. Instead of processing how I felt about my biological family and their rejection, I returned to suppression: *I'm fine*, I thought. *This is fine. I'm an adult woman, with a family of my own and a successful career. I don't need them anyway.*

AUNT DIANE

2020

The last time I visited Covert was in 2014. I'd scheduled a meeting with a former professor at the university where I'd received my bachelor's degree. My then job had paid for me to go anywhere in the country for professional development. I chose my pre-professional roots, hoping my methodology professor, the person who taught me how to teach, would impart some wise words on a journey that grew increasingly foggy.

As soon as I entered my grandmother's driveway, the same stretch of land where she'd taught me how to ride a bicycle, my breath quickened. I hadn't learned how to breathe through emotions yet, so I held it and took sips of air when necessary. Despite the irregularity, I slept soundly that evening in the room where I once lived my senior year. The following morning, soft mounds of white snow made heaping hills in the driveway. My grandmother and I shared breakfast, then sat across from one another in the living room, she in an armchair and I on the couch.

"Where's the shovel?" I asked.

"It's in the garage. I'll go get it," she said.

But she didn't. We sat for thirty more minutes as network television blared, audible to anyone within ten feet of the house, her hard-of-hearing status at its beginning stages.

"Grandma, are you gonna get the shovel? I have to meet my professor," I said.

"I'll get it," she said.

My grandmother had a skillful way of controlling situations; by the time the experience ended, it was unclear if you'd given your power away or if she'd taken it. My abdomen burned, but I remained quiet. Time traveled backward: 2014, 2000, 1990. I was no longer forty-one. I was seventeen. I was alone. I was powerless. *Keep your mouth shut and wait for the shovel,* I thought. Sadness overwhelmed me. Breathing became laborious. I focused on the television's volume and waited for her to liberate me from the driveway, whenever she saw fit.

An hour later, we trudged through the snow to the garage, and she handed me the tool. It never occurred to me that I could've found it myself. The anger of being forty-five minutes late to my meeting formed a tight ball in my chest. The repetition of digging and the sting of cold air calmed me. I turned my fury into a social media post about perseverance; perhaps someone would be inspired by my resentment. I never processed this specific incident. I ignored that it even occurred or made me angry.

∞

2020

Aunt Diane's oldest daughter, Sheri, married her husband on September 19, 2020, the same weekend as my mother, my aunt, and I had. Grandma Hunny's chest swelled every time she mentioned that *her girls were all married on the third Saturday of September.* Traditions are part of the makings of family. Each wedding had occurred at St. Matthews, but this September, the world was six months into a global pandemic, thus my cousin's marriage would take place in Covert in Grandma Hunny's backyard.

Sending a gift would have been sufficient, especially in a time of COVID, but I felt compelled to attend my cousin's nuptials. Aunt Diane had named Brent and me as her godparents shortly after her adoption. Even though we were as distant as the miles between us, I wanted her to know we cared. Our family was small and old when I was growing up. Twenty years later, when my cousin and her sister were added, several deaths had dwindled our clan to the size of a basketball team and those who were left were aged. When Sheri wed, Grandma Hunny neared ninety-four, and Aunt Lillian was ninety-eight. While growing up, I was embarrassed to be the youngest person in my elderly family, and I wondered if my cousin felt similar. Either way, it seemed important for Brent and me to be present.

"Could you imagine living here? Or near here?" Brent asked.

We traversed an unfamiliar combination of twists, turns, and trees. Everything was foreign. Roads I used to chase Eddie through and backwoods I'd learned as shortcuts conjoined into unrecognizable terrain. Like strangers, we relied on the cellphone's GPS.

Are you gonna be alright?" Brent asked as we traveled closer to Grandma Hunny's. He'd begun paying more attention to his emotions and mine.

"I'm fine. Everything's fine. I'm a grown-ass woman," I replied as more of an affirmation than a truth.

On the first day, Grandma Hunny wore her mask around her chin, talked about how stupid my cousin and her fiancé were for not setting things up sooner or asking for her help, and demanded we speak up louder, instead of wearing her thousand-dollar hearing aids. Ignoring words and my surroundings worked before 2014. But in 2020, I was hyperaware of sensations. As I sat on my grandmother's couch, emotions piled up and crowded one another in my body.

On the second day, after burgundy and cream decorations hung from picnic chairs, my grandmother announced she was going to get chicken, "but not for everyone, just me and Lillian."

Then, Brent tiptoed over and whispered in my ear, "Your grandmother wants to know if you want some chicken?"

The only person I can control is myself, I thought, practicing a new mantra.

"Grandma, I don't feel comfortable getting chicken for just me and no one else here," I said. "I'll get it if anyone else wants some."

"Oh, *she'll* get it," she said, winking and tapping my mother's cousin on the arm. They both smiled. "I don't care who gets it," she hollered. "As long as everyone knows I'm not the one asking or buying it for anyone else."

Annoyance slid next to my anxiety.

Grandma Hunny and my mother's cousin talked and laughed as we drove to town to pick up the chicken. I faded into the back seat, as I had during the summer my grandparents drove me to Covert, away from my home. I was there in body only. If someone included me in the conversation, then I came to life. Although I was an adult, who paid for everyone's meal, somehow, I felt as if I was living in 1990, where what I wanted was insignificant. We got the food and headed back home, which is when my grandmother decided to stop at her friend's house to "see what she wanted when she called."

"Now?" I asked.

"Yeah. Why not?"

Maybe because we have everyone's dinner, I thought, but as if I was seventeen, I dared not speak.

The food was cold by the time we arrived back at the house. Helplessness set in. I couldn't even pay for and deliver hot food; Grandma Hunny was in charge. Loneliness took over. Aunt Diane had slipped away to her hotel; her introverted personality had had enough for the day. My cousin's bridesmaids were her sister and her sister's friend. Their airtight closeness was evident as they sat on the couch and cackled about something or another. Brent and my cousin's fiancé stood in the basement and held a conversation. The only place left to eat was at my grandmother's table. Grandma Hunny sat to my left; Aunt Lillian to my right; and across from me, was my mother's cousin. I shrank into a familiar child-like status, surrounded by adults.

I'd planned to fade away. *I'll eat these chicken legs and green beans in peace*, I told myself, but all of my fantasy worlds had been dismantled.

My grandmother also had other ideas of how I would be spending my time. She begged me to outline the dullness of online teaching. The fact that I didn't want to discuss the topic seemed trivial. *Just tell her about your day,* part of my mind urged. *I don't want to,* the other part argued. *We're grown,* both halves agreed.

"I log on, and I do work," I mumbled.

"But what do you *do?*" she asked.

I knew what she meant. Whenever Grandma Hunny visited, she started and finished the day with me. She drove with me to work, so she could see the building, meet coworkers I'd told her about, and see me in action, teaching. This was the protocol, no matter the state, school, or status. One time, I didn't have to drive to work, so she opened my bedroom door and slid into the bed with me, on the side where Brent would normally be. What probably should've been a nurturing moment, made my skin crawl with uneasiness. She'd once sat in the back corner of my college class, so she could understand what I was doing. That's what she wanted. She wanted me to create a visual of my day, so she could be a part of it, but I didn't feel like storytelling. Sitting at her dining room table was challenging enough.

"I don't do anything, Grandma. I log on and do work. That's it."

My mother's cousin looked up mid-chew. Her eyes shifted toward Grandma Hunny. I think it was my tone that gave her pause.

"I don't know what the big deal is," Grandma Hunny said. "I just want to know what you're doing. I don't know what people are doing in this century," she said, pieces of fried chicken crumbling out of the sides of her mouth. The permanent wrinkle between her brows furrowed more, signaling her frustration. Finally, she let it go.

I cleaned the drumstick and excused myself.

"I'll be back," I said.

Before Brent and I returned to the hotel, I bought a fifth of vodka and a plastic travel cup.

That evening, I'd stayed up well past midnight scribbling in a journal: writing and processing. It had worked when my father died; perhaps it would work now. I wrote until my eyes were heavy.

"I don't belong here," I told Brent the morning of the wedding.

"Here in Covert or here in your family?"

"Both."

But it was too late for epiphanies. We had a wedding to attend. The only way I could live through the rest of my time in Covert was to remain self-medicated, and to numb current pain with liquor. Forget feeling emotions. Forget pranayama. Forget self-regulating. I didn't want to experience the impending heat that was sure to rise should my grandmother tell me to speak up or beg me to engage in trivialities.

"You couldn't find anything classier," Aunt Diane joked, as she watched me take long sips from the plastic straw of the travel cup.

"I tried," I said. "This was all they had."

I made frequent trips to the car and drank until the bottle was empty. By the time the last car backed out of the driveway after my cousin went from Miss to Mrs., the lights blurred. Grandma Hunny and my mother's cousin lay in the bed, readers on their noses, TV loud. Liquid courage helped me to tell my grandmother she should wear her mask above her nose, as well as her hearing aids.

"It's just me here," she retorted. "When it's just me, I don't need them. I just turn up the TV."

"But it's not just you," my voice cracked. "There was a whole wedding going on here, and you couldn't hear any of it!"

I left her room and scoured the kitchen. The only thing available were libations reserved for college dormitories, so I poured what I could find into the plastic travel cup, with no mixer.

"Bae. Please, don't drink that," Brent said, watching.

I ignored him.

"It's time to go," he said. "Let me use the bathroom, then we can go."

Aunt Diane, her beau, and I waited in the kitchen, the same kitchen where my grandmother convinced me that she was the only one in the world who cared for me, the same kitchen where I'd agreed to stay in Michigan to finish college, even though I wanted nothing more than to return to a home that only existed in my mind.

"So, did you enjoy being back in Covert?" Aunt Diane asked with the innocence of a child.

Did I enjoy being back in Covert? Not only had I not enjoyed it, but I had spiraled in front of her face, and she hadn't noticed, just like when my mother died.

But that's not what I said.

For over two hours, I spouted my likes, dislikes, wants, and needs from all the adults who raised and didn't raise me, including Aunt Diane. I reminded her that she was my mother's only sister, and not once had she asked how I was doing since her sister died. I told her no one cared then, and no one cared now. Her asking, *Did I enjoy being back in Covert?* proved the whole family suffered from an extreme lack of awareness. Not once had she protected me, I accused.

"Protected you from who?" she asked.

"Your mother!" Snot glazed my upper lip. The saltiness seeped into the corners of my mouth as I vomited my life experience at her feet. I purged the pain and left everything in Grandma Hunny's kitchen.

"You're fucked up," I told Aunt Diane. "And so is your mother."

I was happy I wasn't alone in the hotel that night. Brent held me in his arms, and we made love. Had he not been there, I fear I would have texted Eddie, who lived an hour away. As a divorcee, I've no doubt he would've scrambled in the middle of the night at the chance to pretend we were teenagers. The alcohol would've been my excuse, would've clouded my judgment, and would've allowed me to repeat the familiar cycle of using a body to temporarily reduce the pain. In my mind, it was better that my husband served that purpose. At least it wasn't casual and outside of my marriage. But in reality, it further showed I was still in recovery.

"Good talk," Aunt Diane said when we arrived the next day.

There are times when life is clear when someone says something that illuminates everything. Aunt Diane's, *good talk*, showed me what I'd already determined: suppressing emotions was a generational pattern, passed on from Grandma Hunny to my mother, my aunt, and to me. At the time, I couldn't determine if Aunt Diane's comment was sarcasm or if she believed we'd had a *good talk*. Later, she referred to it as a *heart-to-heart*. She'd characterized my drunken diatribe as something revelatory and "good." That's when I knew there was nothing left between us. Like Grandma Hunny, she didn't have the emotional capacity to engage. I sent Aunt Diane a video apology, because even though what I said may have been necessary and eye-opening, how I said it was inappropriate.

Isn't technology wonderful? she texted.

After the wedding, I berated myself and wondered if I was really healed due to how I'd fallen back into the pain cycle. I was relieved to find out that I'd experienced a series of triggers—the way someone speaks, or a familiar scent[1]—which could be a tap on the shoulder. Any of these prompts and more can send someone back in time. I didn't know this when I returned to Covert or when I yelled at my aunt in the kitchen. Unbeknownst to me, I was triggered when I visited in 2014 as well. That winter, I remember telling Brent I felt like I was seventeen, as if time and space converged and no time had passed at all. I felt as if it was 1990, even though I was over forty. The feeling returned when we attended my cousin's wedding, not because I wasn't healed, but because I had been triggered and chose numbing, instead of grounding.

Like Kacey Musgraves sang, "Healing doesn't happen in a straight line." In American culture, therapy is treated like a magic wand. Popular media heals trauma in two-hour films and thirty-minute sitcoms. The instant gratification part of society shows us that everything comes fast, even in recovery. Once you do x, y, and z, then you're "cured," and you live trauma-free. That's not the truth. I've spent years working on myself and as Iyanla says, "doing the work." On most days, my past does not define me or my choices. On other days, talking with my grandmother causes my chest to cave, and I silence my voice before she can.

"If you're mad, you better scratch your butt and be glad," Grandma Hunny says. In her late nineties, it's one of her favorite phrases when referring to emotions that may be uncomfortable or negative.

When she recently said this, I inhaled deeply for four seconds, exhaled deeply for six seconds, and said, "That's not very nice."

"What?" she asked. "Let me turn down the TV."

"It's not nice to say," I repeated.

"Hmmmpph." She changed the subject.

I inhaled one more time, proud of myself for learning how to coregulate, for speaking up; for taking baby steps toward healing my trauma.

KATHY AND BRENT

2021

It is easier to tell five lies than one whole truth. But it isn't honest, and honesty is an integral part of being in a healthy, loving relationship. I suspect that's why my adoptive mother waited to share the truth of who I was and of who she was; it's tricky to tell someone you love that what they thought was reality isn't. That they've been living a delusion. When I wrote *The Unhappy Wife*, a colleague reached out to me and advised that I "not tell Brent about any more cheating." She didn't advise that I seek therapy to understand why I was cheating, just that I maintain secrecy. I'm sure that encouraging me to lie was a form of protection. I knew it stemmed from the same logic my other friend screamed about when I was going to reveal the final abortion: *He's going to leave you!* My abandonment issues caused me to believe the same: If he knows the whole truth, he is going to leave me. So, I lied.

I'd tried to tell Brent the truth a few times. The first was in 2009 when I confessed to sleeping with Shane; however, that partial lie wasn't received well, making me believe Brent couldn't handle the truth. It's not only easier to tell lies, but oftentimes, we'd rather hear falsehoods than have our worlds shattered and realize we've been living a delusion. The second time I attempted truth-telling was in 2014, after my final abortion. I suggested Brent and I have an open marriage. I thought the solution to my uncontrollable urges was to create a different arrangement. Christopher Ryan's Ted Talk on monogamy supported my claim.[1] Ryan explained how relationships are not always "sexually exclusive."[2] He even described the Mosuo, a group in China who are "sexually autonomous without shame," to illustrate how we're currently doing sexual relationships is outdated.[3] I shared these findings with Brent.

"Maybe we should get a divorce," he replied.

The following day, he and I discussed logistics at a bistro.

Our food arrived as we figured out how he'd remove his name from the lease. Black olives and artichoke sat in my mouth, mushy and warm. Brent took one bite of pizza and placed it back on his plate.

"What do you want to do?" he asked.

"I don't know." I swallowed tears.

Stuck in a divorce conversation was the ideal time to confess, but admissions of adultery in that moment would lead to what I'd feared all these years: being alone. He sat, arms folded, peering at me like a disappointed parent.

"You two need boxes?" a waiter asked.

"Yeah. Sure," we responded in unison.

"You two married? he asked setting the boxes on the table.

"Yes," we both replied.

"Oh, good, good," his excitement grew. "So, you can answer this for me. How do you *not* give up?"

Is this a joke? I wondered.

Brent answered. "You realize that this is the person you want to be with and then you work through it. You work it out."

"Yeah, but what if the other person has issues?" he continued. "What if . . . like my girlfriend? The other day we were driving, and you know I'm from the West Side, so I know where I'm going. But she's not even from here. So, she's driving, and I'm trying to tell her where to go, you know, the side streets and stuff? But she thinks I'm trying to tell her what to do. I'm just saying, I'm frooom here, from the West Side, so I know how to get there."

Considering everything occurring in my life, this seemed like an insignificant reason to break up with someone. Plus, I couldn't believe he hadn't noticed my red eyes or my husband's annoyance.

"Well, let her drive," Brent said. "Turn on the GPS. Enjoy the ride. If she doesn't want you to tell her directions, then don't."

Internally, I laughed in disbelief that, at this moment, he wanted advice from us about how to stay together. Brent sat, arms folded, and offered up Zen-like sentiments like he was a mystical shaman with the answers to life.

"I think she has issues with her dad," the waiter continued.

"Well, if that's the case, then those are *her* issues," I began. "And she's going to have to realize she has personal problems *she* has to work out. And if you're gonna stay with her, then you'll have to realize she has these challenges and see if you can handle it."

"Riiiight," he answered.

His smile subsided as he began another story. "Like we were at her dad's house, and I think he's a great man. I think her dad is one of the best men I know. But she haaates him. So, we were at his house, and he asked, 'Which one of these boxes of popsicles do you all want to take?' and she said, 'The ones you didn't pay for.'"

This time, I laughed, the sarcasm familiar. Whatever had happened between this woman and her father, only the two of them knew. And I already understood his girlfriend would have to deal with that herself. The waiter decided they'd break up. He just couldn't and didn't want to deal with her or her issues.

Conversely, Brent and I sat in the booth for two more hours, guided by the waiter's questions. Brent eventually uncrossed his arms and warmed his gaze. By the time we left, we decided not to divorce. The fate of our relationship couldn't be determined over pizza and salad, and neither one of us wanted to give up what we'd developed over eighteen years, even if one of us had an issue that required further resolution.

I decided there was no reason to confess.

Brent and I had grown closer through my self-therapy and sans a confession; however, sheltering at home during the pandemic forced us into an undiscovered relationship zone, one where we spent twenty-four hours together. Prior to the lockdown, our home was my personal sanctuary: I'd left the research institution for a community college and worked primarily from home, waking to silence and making my day up as I pleased. Like the world, by March, Brent was suddenly working from our dining room. Action movies blared in the background when his workload was light. My sense of freedom trickled away, and our home became a coffin. I found myself stifled, physically and creatively. Red wine runs replaced actual running.

But in other ways, we grew closer. Brent began to recognize patterns of behavior, which he'd never seen because he was at work.

"You look like you have to do a lot," he once commented.

He was referring to my exercising four times a week, my eating a strict diet, which included at least three meals per day, and my incense lighting and meditation rituals, all of which were mandatory before I logged in for work.

"If I don't, then things don't go so well," I answered.

Brent noticed that leaving the house was not optional for me, it was necessary, like yoga. One weekend, we drove to Orlando for a day trip and ventured into conversation.

"How does it feel to have everyone you consider family be dead?" he asked.

The question startled me. We'd been married for twenty-four years, and he'd never asked me anything about the emotions associated with my past. He'd done the opposite. Like others, he'd often encouraged me to *get over my mother dying* and stared blankly when I cried over my father's death, with the Clark Sisters on repeat.

"I don't think about it much," I started. "At this point, it's just the way it is. I figured I'm not supposed to have a specific family, especially after Aunt Catherine died. Sometimes I get sad about it, like when I see a movie and a mother is helping her daughter pick out a wedding dress or something. You know I never had that kind of thing. Now, I'm used to the absence."

I grew curious. "What's something you've learned about me that you didn't know when we first got together?" I asked.

"I didn't realize you were so sad and lonely."

It was a fair assessment. My extroversion made it easy to hide behind circles of friends and a permanent social calendar. Only someone who'd lived with me for nearly two and a half decades could have observed how pockets of grief and despondency marinated and influenced my life. I wondered when he recognized this part of me but opted not to discuss it.

Binging on several television series helped numb the stress of the pandemic. On one Saturday, we watched *Modern Love*. In episode 5, Yasmine, a main character, recounted how she'd sought attention from men. She'd taken an adolescent game, making eye contact with male strangers on an escalator, into her adulthood. She relied on the male gaze for approval and self-worth. The show seemed to be a perfect entry point to telling the truth about who I had been.

"I understand her," I told Brent. "Remember when you said I liked the attention from men? We were on our honeymoon," I tried to jog his memory. "You were right."

Brent nodded, with little interest.

The next week, I exposed more. "I hold negative energy in my body. My set point seems to be to suppress."

"You think *you* suppress your emotions?" he asked.

Every friend or family member can retell a story of dysregulation where I've "gone off" on someone. When suppression stopped working my modus operandi was anger. I yelled at incompetent cashiers and spoke rudely to the waitstaff. When I could no longer hold emotions in, I cried uncontrollably and spit venom at family members as I'd done with Aunt Diane. I understood Brent's incredulous tone. Emotional outbursts seem like the opposite of suppression; however, they are the result of suppression, and suppression is the result of not knowing how to manage one's emotions. Most people only saw the effect of suppression, not the root cause.

"I think," I explained carefully, "even if I say I don't care about something, I still hold on to the emotion of it in my body, like with Mr. Philip and them. I said I was okay, but I wasn't. And then a few months later, is when I went to that party with Tonya and got all fucked up."

"That makes sense," he said. "You hadn't even hung out with her for a while."

I continued to inch toward the truth. Weeks later, I shared bits and pieces of a sex addiction definition, hoping an expert's words would soften anything I eventually revealed. Brent looked up intermittently from his makeshift desk and continued our conversation.

"You know I told you that you had issues with sex before, but you'd just look at me like I was crazy. Maybe it was because you were always drunk when I tried to talk about it."

I was on my way to the gym, and ill-prepared for a conversation. "I really don't want to discuss this right now," I answered. "But I will say this. It's kind of like trying to tell a person with a mental illness they need to seek therapy. It won't do any good until the person sees it for themselves. And I mean, you would tell me, but I didn't know what to do. What was I supposed to do with the information?"

"What did you want me to do?" he asked.

"If I came home with my panties in my purse, I'd think that would be a follow-up conversation…when I'm not drunk."

Our conversation wandered and landed where it always did, into a pool of philosophy. According to Brent, the non-addicted cannot help the addicted. The person with the problem can only help themselves. But in the space between Brent's comment and my reply, I breathed a sigh of relief. The fog surrounding what would happen when I talked to him became clearer. Although he could never fathom the magnitude of my so-called secrets, they weren't really secrets, after all. The details were, but the overarching theme that I had a problem was not hidden. He knew it and I knew it, but our backgrounds led both of us to enact willful ignorance throughout our relationship.

A formal conversation was necessary, though. I considered several variations. In one, I'd begin with an apology for lying. I even wrote a poem. *I apologize for not being the person you thought I was*, it began. I wanted to take ownership, but I didn't want to call myself a liar. Everyone has told a lie; however, repeated lies throughout a marriage makes one a liar, and if I were on the receiving end of the conversation, I'd find it hard to trust my lying spouse.

In another version, I explained that, as he'd pointed out, he knew something was wrong, but *I* just had to come to terms with it. We both appreciated analysis, so another option was to explain years of self-evaluation and recovery and assure him that nothing would ever happen again. However, I wasn't entirely sure; like many addicts, it could be a matter of time. How could

I convince Brent there would be no more affairs, physical, emotional, or otherwise?

Brent is smart, and I was hoping he'd put each random confession together, so I wouldn't have to participate in one long discussion. Next, I eased into the topic of adultery and admitted to cheating more than he knew. Brent was not surprised. He listened as I outlined a few experiences and answered my questions.

"Did you think I'd just stop?" I asked.

"I thought it was based on certain liquor and I thought once you had the girls and didn't feel as confident about your body, you'd stop."

"I didn't," I confirmed. "Did you think I was making a choice each time I cheated? No one wakes up and decides 'I'm gonna cheat today.'"

"It might not be a choice, but it is like cake," he said. "It's like cake on top of cake."

Brent's answer was expected. He couldn't get beyond the "sex" of sex addiction. Sex is equated with pleasure, and no matter how I framed it, he couldn't see past the idea that something enjoyable can also be something one is addicted to. Unlike substance abuse, sex addiction sounds like excessive gratification. Don't we all want to be addicted to sex?

"I didn't always *want* to cheat. I wished I could stop," I told him.

"I love you just the way you are," he reassured.

I knew, in my heart, that if I loved Brent, too, then I had to reveal the truth in its entirety. Lying is not love.

In the past, I'd feared Brent's absence. His leaving was tied to my self-worth. However, I'd grown since the day I stood as a scared little abandoned girl in my father's kitchen, wondering who would love me if Brent didn't. I'd developed a sense of identity not predicated on men or family members' choices. I was no longer afraid of the unknown. I committed to a date: I would tell Brent on the first Friday in September of 2021. Nothing would be happening; it would be a long weekend; and he would have time to process. I would put my own feelings and fears aside and rely on one idea: Telling him the truth wouldn't be predicated on his decision about our marriage.

But that didn't happen.

Instead, one weekday in August, I came across a term called "mother wound." After reading about it, it was obvious I'd healed from three mother wounds: my biological and adoptive mothers and grandmother. Each woman physically or emotionally abandoned me in some way. Of the ten ways to heal the mother wound, I'd completed nine. I shared this with Brent, who click-clacked away on his keyboard.

"So, you have a mother wound?" he asked, not looking up, as if to say *now what else do you think you have?* And it bothered me.

"Do you believe I had a litany of undiagnosed, untreated issues when we met?"

"Yes. I didn't realize it until later, though," he said, steadily typing.

"How much later?"

"After we were married."

"After kids?" I asked.

"Yeah. After we had kids. Why?" he asked, looking up from his monitor.

Suddenly, I felt the nudge, the same nudge that told me to do a relationship meditation, the same nudge that led me to Bhakti yoga, the same nudge that pointed me toward the beach, writing, and other recovery methods, except this nudge was a firm hand on my back pushing me to tell the truth. Fear fluttered in my stomach.

"I have reasons for asking, but I don't want to talk about them now. I don't think this is a good time."

We went back and forth about having a conversation. Brent wanted to move on by the time our niece was scheduled to arrive in three days. I'd been processing for seven years. I knew this wasn't a three-day situation. But I took a deep breath and confessed the remainder of what he didn't already know: the five-year affair with Shane and the final abortion.

Brent stared at me.

"So, after me, and the teacher shook hands at that party, you two were still having an affair?" he asked, referring to a time the three of us stood outside of a bounce house at a child's birthday party. Shane stood on my left; Brent stood on my right; the energy was palpable.

I nodded.

Brent stared out of the window into oblivion.

"How did you have an abortion? I mean, there are aftereffects."

"When you say affairs with an "s" what do you mean?"

I answered, until there were no more questions, until we both stood in the silence of truth.

EPILOGUE

Brent decided to remain married to me, but neither he nor I knew what that looked like. It was unfamiliar terrain, one where he saw me for the first time, and not in a romanticized way. Everything was raw.

"Do you know how much you've hurt me?" Brent asked one day. "Do you know how hard it is for me to be here?"

Instead of trying to change him, I was able to be honest. "I don't," I said, "because you haven't told me. I can imagine, of course, but if you don't tell me, then I have to guess."

Brent's feelings showed on his face: *realization, sadness, and fear.* The realization that, although he had decided to stay, he had processed his anger by himself. Sadness that accompanies repeatedly recognizing that part of our twenty-five-year marriage had been a lie. Fear that he could no longer afford to detach. Repairing our relationship relied on him sharing much more about whatever was on the inside than he had in the past, especially because he elected not to do personal or couple's therapy.

This is how our marriage has been. Sometimes it's like intermittent romantic interludes, filled with exciting trysts, and other times, it's watching Brent battle all that comes with betrayal: seeing someone differently, recalling events through a new broken lens, and questioning the concept of commitment. It's understanding the challenges he faces with participating in what used to be regular activities. He wonders if I've been at the beach for hours, or if I've been elsewhere. Either way, we've decided our lives are better with one another in it, and we wake up each day committed to building a new relationship based on truth and clarity.

Life for me has been much better now that I've accepted who I am, a woman who'd lived with undiagnosed mental health issues, intensified by discreet traumas. Foundational people had abandoned me and left me in pain. I wanted to love, but as bell hooks says, I wasn't thinking about love; no addict is. A sex craving was just a desire to be healed. However, sex addiction kept me from engaging in true love, even loving myself was inaccessible. It wasn't until I began to heal the trauma that I was able to turn inward and then express love outward. It feels good to be a healthier version of myself—an honest, authentic version, in recovery and out of hiding.

ACKNOWLEDGEMENTS

Thank you to Nikesha Elise Williams and NEW Reads Publications for seeing the larger vision of this project and understanding the overarching message. This memoir wouldn't be the same without you nudging me toward "digging deeper" and "putting these words to work."

Thank you to Monson Arts Residency for nurturing me as an artist and for showing me how to center writing in my everyday life.

To the WordPress blogging community, thank you for validating my stories and life experience, and to several of you, thank you for becoming colleagues, with whom I can bounce ideas off of, and whom I can rely on for personal or professional advice.

Mika, I appreciate your companionship, which has been woven throughout my life at just the right times. Thank you, Wanda, for being my biggest cheerleader. Calvin, thank you for pushing me toward authenticity.

Lisa, thank you for providing levity whenever I needed it. Duane, I appreciate your candor and contemporary masculine perspective. Camille, thank you for always supporting me as a friend and artist. Mek, thank you for being my sister from another mister. To past best friends: "Shaquita," "Riki," "Sofía," "Tasha," and others not named in this memoir, thank you for supporting me at varied phases of emotional pain; your generosity and grace has not gone unnoticed.

To my former students, turned friends, Ishna, Brittany, and Kotrish, thank you for always holding space for who I am and showing me how to develop symbiotic relationships. Thank you to all of my cousins (too many to name), who have been pseudo siblings, by my side and down to ride out whatever my Gemini brain schemes up next.

To my two mothers, my two fathers, and my grandmother, thank you for doing the best that you could. My life would have been drastically different without your influence.

To Celeste, thank you for being the sister I didn't know I needed, as well as a constant presence and sounding board, and thank you for balancing my pettiness.

"Kimeiko" and "Briana," thank you for being patient as I grew into motherhood and for implicitly motivating me to heal, so I could be a healthier person and better parent.

To "Brent," thank you for committing to the journey. Thank you for seeing me in 1993 and now. Our love is undeniable. Our relationship is inexplicable.

NOTES

KATHY

1. Gabriella Gobbi. "Parental Death during Adolescence: A Review of the Literature." *OMEGA-Journal of Death and Dying* (2021): https://doi.org/10.1177/00302228211033661.

KENNY

1. Gabriella Gobbi. "Parental Death during Adolescence: A Review of the Literature." *OMEGA-Journal of Death and Dying* (2021): https://doi.org/10.1177/00302228211033661.

EDDIE

1. Carole Livingstone, *Why was I Adopted?* (2nd edition) (Lyle Stuart, Inc., 1978), no page numbers.
2. Livingstone, Why was I Adopted?

COVERT

1. Daniele Mollaioli, Andrea Sansone, Giacomo Ciocca, Erika Limoncin, Elena Colonnello, Giorgio Di Lorenzo, and Emmanuele A. Jannini. "Benefits of Sexual Activity on Psychological, Relational, and Sexual Health during the COVID-19 Breakout." *The Journal of Sexual Medicine* 18, no. 1 (2021): 35–49. https://doi.org/10.1016/j.jsxm.2020.10.008.
2. "Are You Using Sex to Cope?" August 24, 2021, Getmegiddy.com, https://getmegiddy.com/using-sex-to-cope.

WILL

1. Carolyn Gregoire, "Why This Doctor Believes Addictions Start in Childhood," *Huffpost,* January 27, 2016, https://www.huffpost.com/entry/gabor-mate-addiction_n_569fd18ae4b0fca5ba76415c?s284obt9=
2. Elyssa Barbash. "Different Types of Trauma: Small 't' versus Large 'T,' *Psychology Today*, 2017, https://www.psychologytoday.com/us/blog/trauma-and-hope/201703/different-types-trauma-small-t-versus-large-t
3. Barbash. "Different Types of Trauma: Small 't' versus Large 'T,'

4. Carolyn Gregoire, "Why This Doctor Believes Addictions Start in Childhood," *Huffpost,* January 27, 2016, https://www.huffpost.com/entry/gabor-mate-addiction_n_569fd18ae4b0fca5ba76415c?s284obt9=

5. Barbash. "Different Types of Trauma: Small 't' versus Large 'T,'

6. Barbash. "Different Types of Trauma: Small 't' versus Large 'T,'

7. "What is Emotional Dysregulation?" *WebMD.* 2021, https://www.webmd.com/mental-health/what-is-emotional-dysregulation

8. Esther Giller, "What is Psychological Trauma," *Sober Recovery,* November 26, 2010, https://www.soberrecovery.com/forums/friends-family-alcoholics/214177-what-psychological-trauma.html

9. Rob Waters, "Addiction Rooted in Childhood Trauma, says Prominent Specialist," *California Healthline,* January 10, 2019, https://californiahealthline.org/news/addiction-rooted-in-childhood-trauma-says-prominent-specialist/

BRENT

1. Heal Your Nervous System, "47 Practices to Heal a Dysregulated Nervous System," Accessed on November 5, 2022: https://healyournervoussystem.com/47-practices-to-heal-a-dysregulated-nervoussystem/?vgo_ee=mlIExAka7FM9MIPQh%2FfqHqyPUFd7JHyq9acdSgULWaM%3D

MJ

1. Marnie C. Ferree. (2001). "Females and Sex Addiction: Myths and Diagnostic Implications."

Sexual Addiction &Compulsivity: The Journal of Treatment and Prevention 8, no. 3-4 (2001): 287-300.

2. Ferree. (2001). "Females and Sex Addiction: Myths and Diagnostic Implications."

MRS. GARLAND

1. Rosemary H. Balsam. "Women Showing Off: Notes on Female Exhibitionism." *Journal of the American Psychoanalytic Association* 56, no. 1 (2008): 99-121.
2. Niklas Långström. "The DSM Diagnostic Criteria for Exhibitionism, Voyeurism, and Frotteurism." *Archives of Sexual Behavior* 39, no. 2 (2010): 317-324.
3. Gülşah Ezgican Kızılok. Sexual Addiction: Definition, Etiology, and Treatment. *Psikiyatride Guncel Yaklasimlar* 13, no. 3 (2021): 394-411 şam doyum ilişkileri (Yüksek lisans tezi)." *İstanbul Maltape Üniversitesi* (2018).
4. Långström. "The DSM Diagnostic Criteria for Exhibitionism, Voyeurism, and Frotteurism."
5. Balsam. "Women Showing Off: Notes on Female Exhibitionism."

PETULIA

1. Gülşah Ezgican Kızılok. Sexual Addiction: Definition, Etiology and Treatment. *Psikiyatride Guncel Yaklasimlar* 13, no. 3 (2021): 394-411 şam doyum ilişkileri (Yüksek lisans tezi)." *İstanbul Maltape Üniversitesi* (2018).

SHANE

1. Gülşah Ezgican Kızılok. Sexual Addiction: Definition, Etiology and Treatment. *Psikiyatride Guncel Yaklasimlar* 13, no. 3 (2021): 394-411 şam doyum ilişkileri (Yüksek lisans tezi)." *İstanbul Maltape Üniversitesi* (2018).
2. Patrick Carnes, Out of the Shadows: Understanding Sexual Addiction (Hazelden Publishing, 1983).
3. Patrick Carnes, Don't Call it Love: Recovery from Sexual Addiction (Bantam, 1992).
4. Kızılok. Sexual Addiction: Definition, Etiology and Treatment.
5. Kızılok. Sexual Addiction: Definition, Etiology and Treatment.
6. Michelle M. Jeanfreau, Angel Herring & Anthony P. Jurich†. "Permission-Giving and Marital Infidelity," *Marriage & Family Review* 52, no. 6 (2016): 535-547, DOI: 10.1080/01494929.2015.1124354
7. (2001). "Females and Sex Addiction: Myths and Diagnostic Implications."

AUNT CATHERINE

1. "Comorbidity," Psychology Today, 2022, https://www.psychologytoday.com/us/basics/comorbidity
2. Ferree. (2001). "Females and Sex Addiction: Myths and Diagnostic Implications."
3. Kızılok. Sexual Addiction: Definition, Etiology and Treatment.
4. John G. Cottone, "Four Types of Depression," *Psychology Today*, 2020, https://www.psychologytoday.com/us/blog/the-cube/202004/four-types-depression

5. Elaine N. Aron, The Highly Sensitive Person: How to Thrive when the World Overwhelms You (Kensington Publishing Corp., 1999).
6. Ferree. (2001). "Females and Sex Addiction: Myths and Diagnostic Implications."

CLUB GUY

1. S2S Magazine, "Was Eric Benét ever a Sex Addict?" 2:46, September 4, 2008, 1:43 https://www.youtube.com/watch?v=0CjEjbHEtW4
2. Kızılok. Sexual Addiction: Definition, Etiology and Treatment.
3. Carnes. Out of the Shadows: Understanding Sexual Addiction.
4. "Sexual Addiction Screening Test," 2022, https://psychology-tools.com/test/sast
5. Michael McGee, "Sexual Addiction Test: Self-Assessment," *Psycom,*. (January 27, 2022), https://www.psycom.net/sex-addiction-test
6. "Sex Addiction Test," *Sex and Relationship Healing*, 2022, https://sexandrelationshiphealing.com/for-addicts/sex-addiction-test/
7. "U.S.A. Laws on Infidelity and Adultery," Infidelity Recovery Institute, 2020 https://infidelityrecoveryinstitute.com/u-s-a-laws-on-infidelity-and-adultery/#:~:text=In%20Florida%20adultery%20
8. Julia Naftulin and Gabby Landsverk, "In Taiwan, Rawanda, and even North Carolina, being Unfaithful can Land You in Jail or with a Hefty Fine: Here are 19 Cheating Laws around the World," July 12, 2019, https://www.insider.com/places-you-can-go-to-jail-fined-infidelity-laws-2019-7
9. Liv Tønnessen and Akram Abbas, "Global Campaign to Stop Stoning of Women," Chr

Michelsen Institute, 2014, https://www.cmi.no/
publications/6644-global-campaign-to-stop-stoning-of-
women#:~:text=According%20to%20Islamic%20crim
inal%20law,United%20Arab%20Emirates%2C%20and
%20Nigeria

10. David Werner Amram, "Adultery," *Jewish
    Encyclopedia*, 2021, https://
    www.jewishencyclopedia.com/articles/865-adultery

OTHER MEN

1. Ferree. (2001). "Females and Sex Addiction:
   Myths and Diagnostic Implications."

ZAIRE

1. Ferree. (2001). "Females and Sex Addiction:
   Myths and Diagnostic Implications."

THE TRAINER

1. Ferree. (2001). "Females and Sex Addiction:
   Myths and Diagnostic Implications."

JOYCE

1. Janette E. Herbers, J. J. Cutuli, Laura M. Supkoff,
   Angela J. Narayan, Ann S. Masten. "Parenting and
   Co-regulation: Adaptive Systems for Competence
   in Children Experiencing Homelessness." *American
   Journal of Orthopsychiatry* 84, no. 4 (July 2014):
   420-430.
2. Nicole B. Perry, Jessica M. Dollar, Susan D.
   Calkins, Susan P. Keane, and Lily Shanahan.
   Maternal Socialization of Child Emotion and
   Adolescent Adjustment: Indirect Effects through

Emotion Regulation. *Developmental Psychology* 56, no. 3 (March 2020): 541-552.

3. WebMD Editorial Contributors, "What is Emotional Dysregulation?" *WebMD*, June 22, 2021, https://www.webmd.com/mental-health/what-is-emotional-dysregulation#091e9c5e8216e0b7-1-3

4. WebMD Editorial Contributors, "What is Emotional Dysregulation?"

5. Pamela Li, "How Co-Regulation with Parents Develops into Self-Regulation in Children," *Parenting for Brain*, Accessed February 23, 2023: https://www.parentingforbrain.com/co-regulation/#:~:text=Co-regulation%20is%20an%20interpersonal%20process,emotional%20state%20%E2%80%8B1%E2%80%80%8B.

6. WebMD Editorial Contributors, "What is Emotional Dysregulation?"

7. Conradi, Henk Jan, Sanne Dithe Boertien, Hal Cavus, and Bruno Verschuere. "Examining psychopathy from an attachment perspective: The role of fear of rejection and abandonment." *The Journal of Forensic Psychiatry & Psychology* 27, no. 1 (2016): 92-109.

NAURICE

1. "Dialysis," National Kidney Foundation, 2022, https://www.kidney.org/atoz/content/dialysisinfo#how-long-can-you-live-dialysis

2. "U.S. Adoption Statistics," Lifelong Adoptions, Accessed November 15, 2022: https://www.lifelongadoptions.com/adoption-statistics

3. Conradi, Boertien, Cavus, & Verschuere. "Examining Psychopathy from an Attachment Perspective"

4. Conradi, Boertien, Cavus, & Verschuere. "Examining Psychopathy from an Attachment Perspective"

TONY

1. Conradi, Boertien, Cavus, & Verschuere. "Examining Psychopathy from an Attachment Perspective"

GRANDMA HUNNY

1. Sherri Gordon, "What is Emotional Abuse: Signs and Red Flags of Emotional Abuse," *VeryWell Mind,* November 7, 2022, https://www.verywellmind.com/identify-and-cope-with-emotional-abuse-4156673

KATHERIN ELIZABETH

1. Marni Feuerman, "9 Signs that You're Having an Emotional Affair," *Verywell Mind*, April 21, 2021, https://www.verywellmind.com/signs-youre-having-an-emotional-affair-2303079
2. Melody Beattie, The New Codependency: Help and Guidance for Today's Generation (Simon & Schuster, 2009).
3. "Science Shows how a Trip to the Beach Changes Your Brain," The South African College of Applied Psychology, December 20, 2017, https://www.sacap.edu.za/blog/applied-psychology/beach-benefits/

AUNT DIANE

1. Crystal Raypole, "What it Really Means to be Triggered," *Healthline*, April 25, 2019, https://www.healthline.com/health/triggered

KATHY AND BRENT

1. Christopher Ryan, "Are we Designed to be Sexual Omnivores?" TEDTalk, 2013, https://www.ted.com/talks/christopher_ryan_are_we_designed_to_be_sexual_omnivores?language=en
2. Ryan, "Are we Designed to be Sexual Omnivores?"
3. Ryan, "Are we Designed to be Sexual Omnivores?"

BIBLIOGRAPHY

Instead of spending years in therapy, I devoted nine years to reading and learning about trauma, adoption, abandonment, grief, relationships, sex, and sex addiction, applying concepts to my life where appropriate, and then putting into practice how to be a better human being. Here are the books, scholarly articles, videos, and websites that have informed my healing journey and this book.

Adoptions, Lifelong. "Adoption Statistics," n.d. https://www.lifelongadoptions.com/adoption-statistics.

"ADULTERY - JewishEncyclopedia.Com," n.d.https://
www.jewishencyclopedia.com/articles/865-
adultery.

Aron, Elaine N., PhD. *The Highly Sensitive Person: How
to Thrive When the World Overwhelms You.* Harmony,
1997.

Balsam, Rosemary H. "Women Showing Off: Notes
on Female Exhibitionism." *Journal of the American
Psychoanalytic Association* 56, no. 1 (2008): 99-121.

Barbash, Elyssa, PhD. "Different Types of Trauma:
Small 'T' versus Large 'T.'" Psychology Today,
October 18, 2019. https://www.psychologytoday.com/
us/blog/trauma-and-hope/201703/different-
types-trauma-small-t-versus-large-t.

Beattie, Melody. *The New Codependency: Help and
Guidance for Today's Generation.* Simon & Schuster,
2009.

California Healthline. "Addiction Rooted in
Childhood Trauma, Says Prominent Specialist,"
March 4, 2019. https://californiahealthline.org/
news/addiction-rooted-in-childhood-trauma-says-
prominent-specialist/.

Carnes, Patrick. *Don't Call It Love: Recovery from Sexual
Addiction.* Bantam, 2013.—. *Out of the Shadows:
Understanding Sexual Addiction.* Hazelden
Publishing, 2001.

CMI - Chr. Michelsen Institute. "Global Campaign to
Stop Stoning of Women: Off Target in Sudan," n.d.
https://www.cmi.no/publications/6644-global-

campaign-to-stop-stoning-of-women#:~:text=According%20to%20Islamic%20criminal%20law,United%20Arab%20Emirates%2C%20and%20Nigeria.

Conradi, Henk Jan, Sanne Dithe Boertien, Hal Cavus, and Bruno Verschuere. "Examining Psychopathy from an Attachment Perspective: The Role of Fear of Rejection and Abandonment." *The Journal of Forensic Psychiatry & Psychology* 27, no. 1 (2016): 92-109.

Cottone, John G., PhD. "Four Types of Depression." Psychology Today, March 14, 2023. https://www.psychologytoday.com/us/blog/the-cube/202004/four-types-depression.

Ferree, Marnie C. "Females and Sex Addiction: Myths and Diagnostic Implications." *Sexual Addiction &Compulsivity: The Journal of Treatment and Prevention* 8, no. 3-4 (2001): 287-300.

Feuerman, Marni, LMFT, LCSW. "9 Signs You'Re Having an Emotional Affair." Verywell Mind, November 30, 2022. https://www.verywellmind.com/signs-youre-having-an-emotional-affair-2303079.

Gordon, Sherri. "What Is Emotional Abuse?" Verywell Mind, November 7, 2022. https://www.verywellmind.com/identify-and-cope-with-emotional-abuse-4156673.

Gregoire, Carolyn. "Why This Doctor Believes Addictions Start In Childhood." HuffPost, January 27, 2016. https://www.huffpost.com/entry/gabor-

mate-addiction_n_569fd18ae4b0fca5ba76415c?
s284obt9=.

Guzzo, Maria Giulia Amadasi, and Gabriella Gobbi. "Parental Death During Adolescence: A Review of the Literature." *Omega - Journal of Death and Dying*, July 29, 2021, 003022282110336. https://doi.org/10.1177/00302228211033661.

Hay, Louise. *Mirror Work: 21 Days to Heal Your Life.* Hay House, Inc, 2016.

Herbers, Janette E., J. J. Cutuli, Laura M. Supkoff, Angela J. Narayan, and Ann S. Masten. "Parenting and Coregulation: Adaptive Systems for Competence in Children Experiencing Homelessness." *American Journal of Orthopsychiatry* 84, no. 4 (2014): 420.

hooks, bell. *All About Love: New Visions.* Harper Collins, 2018.

Infidelity Recovery Institute. "U.S.A. Laws on Infidelity and Adultery - The Infidelity Recovery Institute." The Infidelity Recovery Institute, October 29, 2020. https://infidelityrecoveryinstitute.com/u-s-a-laws-on-infidelity-and-adultery/#:~:text=In%20Florida%20adultery%20.

Jeanfreau, Michelle M., Angel Herring, and Anthony P. Jurich. "Permission-Giving and Marital Infidelity." *Marriage and Family Review*, February 10, 2016. https://doi.org/10.1080/01494929.2015.1124354.

Kızılok, Gülşah Ezgican. "Sexual Addiction: Definition, Etiology and Treatment." *Psikiyatride Guncel Yaklasimlar* 13, no. 3 (2021): 394-411.

Långström, Niklas. "The DSM Diagnostic Criteria for Exhibitionism, Voyeurism, and Frotteurism." *Archives of Sexual Behavior* 39 (2010): 317-324.

Li, Pamela. "How Co-Regulation with Parents Develops into Self-Regulation in Children." Parenting for Brain, March 2, 2023. https://www.parentingforbrain.com/coregulation/#:~:text=Coregulation%20is%20an%20interpersonal%20process,emotional%20state%20%E2%80%8B1%E2%80%8B.

Mollaioli, Daniele, Andrea Sansone, Giacomo Ciocca, Erika Limoncin, Elena Colonnello, G. Di Lorenzo, and Emmanuele A. Jannini. "Benefits of Sexual Activity on Psychological, Relational, and Sexual Health During the COVID-19 Breakout." *The Journal of Sexual Medicine* 18, no. 1 (January 1, 2021): 35–49. https://doi.org/10.1016/j.jsxm.2020.10.008.

Naftulin, Julia, and Gabby Landsverk. "In Taiwan, Rwanda, and Even North Carolina, Being Unfaithful Can Land You in Jail or with a Hefty Fine. Here Are 19 Cheating Laws around the World." Insider, July 12, 2019. https://www.insider.com/places-you-can-go-to-jail-fined-infidelity-laws-2019-7.

National Kidney Foundation. "What Is Dialysis?," February 27, 2023. https://www.kidney.org/atoz/content/dialysisinfo#how-long-can-you-live-dialysis.

Perry, Nicole B., Jessica M. Dollar, Susan D. Calkins, Susan P. Keane, and Lilly Shanahan. "Maternal

Socialization of Child Emotion and Adolescent Adjustment: Indirect Effects through Emotion Regulation." *Developmental Psychology* 56, no. 3 (2020): 541.

Psycom. "Sex Addiction Test (Self-Assessment)," January 27, 2022. https://www.psycom.net/sex-addiction-test.

Psychology Tools. "Sexual Addiction Screening Test (SAST)," 2023. https://psychology-tools.com/test/sast.

Raypole, Crystal. "What It Really Means to Be Triggered." Healthline, April 25, 2019. https://www.healthline.com/health/triggered.

Ruiz, Don Miguel, and Janet Mills. *The Four Agreements: A Practical Guide to Personal Freedom.* Hay House, Inc, 1997.

Ryan, Christopher. "Are We Designed to Be Sexual Omnivores?" TED Talks, n.d.https://www.ted.com/talks/christopher_ryan_are_we_designed_to_be_sexual_omnivores?language=en.

s2smagazine. "Was Eric Benét Ever a Sex Addict?," September 4, 2008. https://www.youtube.com/watch?v=0CjEjbHEtW4.

Sex And Relationship Healing. "Sex Addiction Test - Sex and Relationship Healing," February 27, 2019.https://sexandrelationshiphealing.com/for-addicts/sex-addiction-test/.

SoberRecovery: Alcoholism Drug Addiction Help and Information. "What Is Psychological Trauma?- SoberRecovery: Alcoholism Drug Addiction Help and Information," n.d. https://www.soberrecovery.com/forums/friends-family-alcoholics/214177-what-psychological-trauma.html.

Today, Psychology. "Comorbidity." Psychology Today, March 16, 2022. https://www.psychologytoday.com/us/basics/comorbidity.

Vanzant, Iyanla. *Get Over It!: Thought Therapy for Healing the Hard Stuff.* Hay House, Inc, 2018.

WebMD Editorial Contributors. "What Is Emotional Dysregulation?" WebMD, April 18, 2021. https://www.webmd.com/mental-health/what-is-emotional-dysregulation.

Wilson, Laura, and Laura Wilson. "Science Shows How a Trip to the Beach Changes Your Brain." SACAP, March 11, 2021. https://www.sacap.edu.za/blog/applied-psychology/beach-benefits/.

Xie, Ivana. "Are You Using Sex to Cope?", December 9, 2022. https://getmegiddy.com/using-sex-to-cope.

CREDITS AND PERMISSIONS

S ome stories in this memoir appeared in the following publications:

∞

The Unhappy Wife (2016)
Daddy: Reflections of Father-Daughter Relationships (2018)
"What it Actually Means to be Pro-Choice" in *PULP Mag* (February 13, 2020)
"Mental Health Matters" series on kwoted.wordpress.com (2020)
"Tough Love" curated in *Love Notes* (2021)
"There's Strength in Softness" in *Raising Mothers* (May 20, 2021)
"There's Some Whores in this House" in *Mamas, Martyrs, and Jezebels* (2023)

9 781735 721989